Alfred Henry Tarleton, Pope Adrian IV

Nicholas Breakspear (Adrian IV.)

Englishman and Pope

Alfred Henry Tarleton, Pope Adrian IV

Nicholas Breakspear (Adrian IV.)
Englishman and Pope

ISBN/EAN: 9783743309975

Manufactured in Europe, USA, Canada, Australia, Japa

Cover: Foto ©ninafisch / pixelio.de

Manufactured and distributed by brebook publishing software (www.brebook.com)

Alfred Henry Tarleton, Pope Adrian IV

Nicholas Breakspear (Adrian IV.)

CONTENTS.

	PAGE
PREFACE	v
LIST OF ILLUSTRATIONS	xv-xvii

CHAPTER I.
1100 TO 1120.

Birth, Parentage, and Early Life—Traditions as to Breakspear's Home—Rejected at S. Albans—Leaves for France . . 1-20

CHAPTER II.

The Condition of England and France in the Twelfth Century—Suger, Abbot of S. Denys—The Pope's Influence in the Church of England 21-34

CHAPTER III.
1120 TO 1151.

Nicholas Breakspear in France—The Abbey of S. Rufus—Prior—Abbot—The Insubordination of the Monks—Eugenius III.—Journey to Rome—Return to S. Rufus—Second Journey to Rome—Breakspear attached to the Pope's Suite—Bishop of Albano—Cardinal—The Second Crusade—Eugenius III. at S. Denys—Breakspear chosen for the Mission to Scandinavia . 35-48

CHAPTER IV.
1151 TO 1154.

Church History in Scandinavia—Breakspear leaves Rome for Norway—Passes through England—His Norwegian Mission—Reform of the Church in Norway—Church Division in Sweden—Breakspear's Diplomacy in Danemark—The War between Danemark and Sweden—Return to Rome—Death of Eugenius III.—Anastasius IV.—His Character—His Death—Breakspear elected Pope 49-67

CHAPTER V.

The Church in the Twelfth Century—The Monastic Movement—The Crusades—Bernard of Clairvaulx—His Teaching—Peter Abelard—The Council of Sens—Arnold of Brescia—His Opinions—Condition of Rome—Effect of the Second Crusade—Frederic Barbarossa crosses the Alps—Adrian's Difficulties 68-92

CHAPTER VI.
1154 TO 1155.

Adrian's Difficulties—Cardinal Boso—Arnold of Brescia in Rome—The Interdict—Adrian's Entry into Rome—Easter, 1155—Advance of Frederic Barbarossa—Negotiations between Pope and Emperor—Capture and Death of Arnold of Brescia—Roman Deputation to Frederic—Adrian proceeds to meet the Emperor at Sutri 93-113

CHAPTER VII.
1155.

Frederic Barbarossa—The Meeting of 9th June—Spiritual Power v. Temporal Power—Adrian's Crisis—Submission of

the Emperor—Entry in Rome of Pope and Emperor—Coronation of Frederic—The Riot in Rome—Frederic leaves Rome—Negotiations with the Emperor Manuel—The German Army recrosses the Alps	114-126

CHAPTER VIII.

English Affairs at Adrian's Succession—The Congratulatory Embassy to the Pope—Adrian's Reception of the Abbot of S. Albans—Henry II.'s Letter to the Pope—John of Salisbury—His Life—His Friendship with Adrian—Conversation with the Pope—His Recollections of Adrian	127-152

CHAPTER IX.

Adrian's grant of Ireland to Henry II.—The Text and Translation of the Bull—Arguments for and against its Genuineness—State of Ireland in the Eleventh and Twelfth Centuries—Historical Evidence—Conclusions	153-181

CHAPTER X.
1155 TO 1156.

Growth and History of the Kingdom of Sicily—William II. of Sicily—Adrian's Letter to him—Attack on Beneventum—Adrian excommunicates William—Roman Defeats in Campania—Negotiations with Manuel I.—Proposed Treaty with William—Divisions among the Cardinals—Failure of Negotiations—William takes Brundisium and Bari—Appears before Beneventum—Terms of Peace with the Pope—Embassy from the Eastern Church—Proposed Reunion—Adrian goes to Orvieto	182-203

CHAPTER XI.
1156 TO 1158.

Frederic's Dissatisfaction at the Pope's Conduct—The Capture of the Archbishop of Lund—Diet at Besançon—Reception of Adrian's Envoys—The Pope's Letter—Cardinal Roland—The Dispute about "Beneficium"—Frederic's Proclamation to the German Church—Preparations for the Second Invasion of Italy—Adrian's Second Letter to the German Bishops—The Answer—Frederic at Augsburg—The Pope sends two Cardinals to the Emperor—Their Misfortunes—Their Reception—Temporary Reconciliation 204-224

CHAPTER XII.
1158 TO 1159.

Causes which led to the Second Invasion of Italy—The Countess Matilda's Possessions—The History of the Guelph Claim—State of Lombardy and Tuscany—Frederic's Army enters Italy—Surrender of Brescia—Siege and Capture of Milan—Diet of Roncaglia—The Case of the Archbishop of Ravenna—Adrian writes again to the Emperor—Frederic's Declaration at Roncaglia—Adrian's Repudiation of the Imperial Claims—Revolt of Milan—Adrian's Courage—Frederic's last Insult—The Embassy of the four Cardinals—Adrian's Ultimatum—Frederic's Vacillation—Adrian Retires to Anagni—War—Preparations for Excommunication of the Emperor—Adrian's Death—His Funeral—His Tomb . . 225-246

CHAPTER XIII.

John of Salisbury on Adrian's Death—Adrian's Character—Boso's Estimate of him—Pictures of Adrian IV.—High Altar Screen at S. Albans—His Literary Works—Improvements in Orvieto and Rome—Concluding Remarks 247-257

APPENDIX I.

Text and Translation of the Facsimile Bull . . . 258-265

APPENDIX II.

Bibliography . . . 266-268

APPENDIX III.

List of Cardinals Living at the Accession of Adrian IV. and of those Created by him—Bulls issued by Adrian IV. . 269-276

INDEX 277-292

LIST OF ILLUSTRATIONS.

		PAGE
The Tomb of Adrian IV.	From a painting by B. Venuti, Rome, 1894. With head of Adrian IV., from a mosaic in the Vatican collection	*Frontispiece*
Seal of Adrian IV. . .	Reproduced from the lead seal attached to the Bull described in Appendix I. .	*Title page*
Initial Letter T to Preface	Date, the twelfth century. From the British Museum Royal MS. I. c. vii. (Shaw's "Alphabets," 1845)	v
Initial Letter N to Chapter I.	From Bail's "Concilia"	1
Breakspears	From a photograph by His Grace the Duke of Newcastle, 1895	16
Initial Letter T to Chapter II.	From Stowe's "Chronicle," 1615	21
Map No. I.	Western Europe in twelfth century . . .	26
Initial Letter W to Chapter III.	From Matthew Paris	35
Pope Eugenius III. (Bernard of Pisa)	From Sacchi, "Historia B. Platinæ de vitis Pontificorum," etc., 1610	41
Initial Letter T to Chapter IV.	From Fuller's "Church History," 1656 . .	49

		PAGE
ADRIAN IV.	From Sacchi, "Historia B. Platinæ de vitis Pontificorum," etc., 1610	65
INITIAL LETTER B TO CHAPTER V.	From the Saxon Chronicle	68
SAINT BERNARD (Abbot of Clairvaulx)	From a print in the British Museum	72
INITIAL LETTER T TO CHAPTER VI.	From Ciaconius, "Vitæ ... Pontificorum Romanorum," 1687	93
MAP No. II.	Showing the movements of Adrian IV. and Frederic Barbarossa at Easter, 1155	104
INITIAL LETTER O TO CHAPTER VII.	From Camden, "Anglica Scripta"	114
THE ENTRY OF ADRIAN IV. AND FREDERIC BARBAROSSA INTO ROME, 1155	From an old panel picture at Breakspears. Date unknown	120
INITIAL LETTER H TO CHAPTER VIII.	From Dugdale, "Monasticon Anglicanum"	127
ADRIAN IV.	From Ciaconius, "Vitæ ... Pontificorum Romanorum," 1687	150
INITIAL LETTER A TO CHAPTER IX.	From Ciaconius, "Vitæ ... Pontificorum Romanorum," 1687	153
HENRY II., KING OF ENGLAND	From a print in the British Museum	156
INITIAL LETTER D TO CHAPTER X.	From Muratori, "Rerum Italicarum Scriptores"	182
ADRIAN IV.	From a print in the British Museum	196

LIST OF ILLUSTRATIONS.

		PAGE
INITIAL LETTER F TO CHAPTER XI.	Date, the twelfth century. From the British Museum Royal MS. I. e. vii. (Shaw's "Alphabets," 1845)	204
FREDERIC I. (Barbarossa)	From a print in the British Museum	204
CARDINAL ROLAND BANDINELLI (Pope Alexander III.)	From Sacchi, "Historia B. Platinæ de vitis Pontificorum," etc., 1610	214
THE PORTICO OF THE CHURCH OF SS. GIOVANNI E PAOLO		222
INITIAL LETTER B TO CHAPTER XII.	From Holinshed's "Chronicles"	225
GENEALOGICAL TABLE		229
MAP No. III.	Italy in the twelfth century	237
INITIAL LETTER I OR J	From Matthew Paris	247
THE HIGH ALTAR SCREEN AT S. ALBAN'S ABBEY	Completed design, from an etching lent by Lord Aldenham	252
FACSIMILE OF A BULL OF ADRIAN IV.		258

NICHOLAS BREAKSPEAR.

CHAPTER I.

1100 TO 1120.

Birth, Parentage, and Early Life—Traditions as to Breakspear's Home—Rejected at S. Albans—Leaves for France.

NICHOLAS BREAKSPEAR or Brekspere,[1] the subject of this memoir, was born somewhere in the neighbourhood of S. Albans. The records of his origin are conflicting and scanty, and if we were tied down to actual authentic proof, we might at once dismiss any conjecture as to when and where was the time and place which has the honour of claiming the earliest evidence of his birth. Before mentioning my conclusions in this matter, it may be well to give verbatim the sources from which we may deduce our information. The narrow jealousy of the monastic orders in the twelfth century caused rumour to be suited to their own particular ends; while early ecclesiastical writers make it difficult for us to sift fact from fancy,

[1] Early French writers speak of him as Briselance; Early Latin as Hastafragus.

owing to their carelessness and their prejudice. But as these are the only original sources on which we have to depend, we must do our best to extract the most probable result from them.

Matthew Paris,[1] "On the Origin of Pope Adrian," says: "About this time, too, a clerk called Nicholas—cognomen Brekespere—a native of some hamlet under the Abbacy, perhaps Langley, came to Abbot Robert and humbly asked if he might be invested with a monk's hood.

"Being a young man of pleasing appearance, fairly well versed in clerical knowledge, the Abbot gave him a trial; but, finding him insufficient in learning, said to him, kindly enough, 'Have patience, my son, and stay at school yet awhile till you are better fitted to the position you desire.' But the young man, shamefaced, and deeming such a postponement tantamount to a denial, withdrew." He then goes on to relate his subsequent history. Now it has always been a moot point among commentators whether Matthew Paris compiled his "Vitæ Abbatum" himself from records and manuscripts in the library of S. Albans, or whether he did not merely edit a compilation by a much older hand. This latter suggestion owes its existence to the fact that the work is very loosely put together, and very often the same incident recurs more than once within a few pages, while frequently the two accounts do not agree.

In his description of Nicholas Brekespere this happens,

[1] "Vitæ Abbatum Sancti Albani." Ed. Mr. Riley, Rolls Series, vol. i., pp. 112-113, Sub annis 1151-65. "De origine Papæ Adriani."

though here the two statements are more or less substantially the same; the second one certainly has the appearance of being copied from some concise history or record now lost to us. A few pages further on, after referring to other matters, he returns to Pope Adrian, and after some description of his later life, he says,[1] "But, as it does not appear to be very foreign to the nature of my material, let us pause here a little to insert in this little history a summary of his life.

"Concerning Pope Adrian.

"This Nicholas, whom we have previously mentioned, was the son of one Robert de Camera, who, after having lived honourably as a layman, and, being to some extent lettered, took the monk's hood at S. Albans. Wishing to bring his son, the memorable Nicholas, into the cloister as clerk and scholar, Robert besought the Abbot in his behalf, praying him to invest the boy also with the monastic hood. The Abbot conceded the request, on condition that Nicholas should prove worthy of it. But when he was tried, the young man was found wanting; thereupon Nicholas fled to Provence, and became a canon in the house of S. Rufus. . . ." Then, at the end of the description, he goes on to say: ". . . His father, as already mentioned, was a monk of S. Albans for fifty years and more, living honourably and dying happily.

[1] "Vitæ Abbatum Sancti Albani," pp. 124-25.

"He was buried in the column of the cloister, this honour falling on him partly on account of his son, the Pope. His tomb was hard by that of Abbot Richard, which was found later, hidden beneath the paving-stones."

I next proceed to take the account handed down to us by William of Newburgh,[1] and it will be seen that he takes a very different line to Matthew Paris. He says as follows:[2] "In the first year of the reign of King Henry II. died Anastatius, the successor of Eugenius, after having been pope one year. He was succeeded by Nicholas, Bishop of Albano, who, changing his name with his fortune, called himself Adrian. Of this man it may be well to relate how he was raised, as it were from the dust, to sit in the midst of princes, and to occupy the throne of apostolic glory. He was born in England, and his father was a clerk of slender means, who, abandoning the world and his stripling boy, became a monk at S. Albans. As he grew older, the lad, having no money to pay for schooling, frequented the monastery daily for his bare subsistence. This so enraged the father that he fell to taunting his son bitterly for his laziness, and at last drove

---

[1] "Guilielmi Neubrigensis, historia sive chronica, rerum Anglicarum, libris quinque, e codice MS. pervetusto, in Bibliotheca prænobilis. Domini Dni Thomas Sebright baronetti uberrimus additionibus completata, longeque emendatius quam antehac edita, studio atque industria Thomæ Hearnii, qui et præter Joannis Picardi Annotationes, suas etiam notas atque spicilegiam subjecit. Oxonii e Theatro Sheldoniano. MDCCXIX."

[2] Lib. ii., cap. 6, pp. 120 et seq.

him indignantly away, destitute of means. So the youth, left to himself and driven to desperation by hard necessity, crossed the Channel into France, being ingenuously ashamed either to dig or to beg in his own country." He also states that Adrian IV. was not forgetful of his early teaching, and chiefly in his father's memory he honoured the Church of the Blessed Martyr Alban with gifts, and distinguished it with lasting privileges.

Muratori,[1] in his "Rerum Italicarum Scriptores," gives three lives of Adrian—two brief summaries and one of greater length, which is ascribed to the pen of the Cardinal of Aragon.[2] Watterich, who studied the question very carefully, came to the conclusion that the latter could only have been written by a contemporary of Adrian; and, in the preface of the book above quoted, has given a number of weighty reasons to prove that it was the work of Cardinal Boso. This Boso was both private secretary and chamberlain to Adrian IV., as well as being an Englishman by birth, so that no man could have been in a better position to write the Pope's biography than he.

It is unnecessary to repeat M. Watterich's reasoning

---

[1] "Pontificum Romanorum qui fuerunt inde ab exeunto sæculo IX. usque ad finem sæculi XIII., vitæ ab æqualibus conscriptæ, quas ex archivi Pontificii, Bibliothecæ Vaticanæ aliarumque codicibus adjectis suis cuique et annalibus et documentis gravioribus edidit I. M. Watterich, philos. et theol. doctor historiæ in lycæo Academico Varmiensi professor publ. ord. In duobus Tomis. Tom. II. (pars IV. to VI.), Paschalis II., Cœlestinus III., 1099-1198. Lipsiæ sumptibus Guilhelmi Engelmanni MDCCCLXII."

[2] Hic Nicholaus Cardinalis Aragoniæ sæculo florebat decimo quarto.

here; but it is very conclusive, and may be read with interest. I have no hesitation in saying that we may safely ascribe the following account to Cardinal Boso:[1] "Adrian IV., of the English nation, from the parish of S. Albans, formerly Nicholas, Bishop of Albano. . . . This man, while still very young, being ambitious of extending his knowledge, left his own country and came to Arles. . . ."

These three principal accounts are the most important sources of information open to us; but it will be well, before I come to the traditions which cluster round his memory, to examine the accounts of later writers.

Ciaconius,[2] who has adopted the narrative of William of Newburgh, adds the allegation that Nicholas was born out of lawful wedlock, and Bale insists that the Abbot rejected him because of his bastardy.[3] "Sed Abbas, homo rigidus ac severus, causatus fortassis quod spurius esset adolescentem quodammodo repulit."

At this stage I must add that not much dependence can be placed on the account of Matthew Paris. To begin with, he attributes the story of Nicholas' rejection to Robert,[4] eighteenth Abbot, which is obviously wrong. And as in all his writings, so in this one, there is a great tendency to dwell upon, even to exaggeration, the magnificence of S. Albans; a magnificence which was so splendid could

---

[1] Vol. ii., p. 323 *et seq.*
[2] Vit. Pont. Rom.
[3] "Illustra. Brit. Centur. II.," N. 90, p. 197 *et seq.*
[4] Robert, eighteenth Abbot, entered office in 1151.

stand clear of flattery at the expense of veracity. In this way he loves to ascribe every virtue to even the meanest official of that house. That a monk of S. Albans should have had a son after obtaining the hood never seems to have crossed Matthew Paris' mind, or rather he was careful not to chronicle the fact. Therefore he does not mention that Nicholas was born previous to Robert's acceptance into the monastery.

This is suspicious in itself. Further, Robert, we are told, dwelt in the monastery for fifty years. In that case he survived his son—a fact which Matthew Paris further attests by remarking that the monk was granted a peculiarly honourable funeral on account of Adrian's magnificence. We naturally ask why, if this man was alive throughout the popeship, did Adrian do nothing for him? And, when the Abbot of S. Albans went to Rome to seek privileges and benediction for his Abbey from the English Pope, did not the Pope's father accompany the mission? Indeed, his name is not even mentioned throughout the account. Surely no flattery or compliments could have pleased his Holiness so much as a message from his own father! Is there not more than slight cause for doubt in this inconsistency?

I shall have cause later to dwell on the invaluable records of John of Salisbury, whose evidence is as a rule unimpeachable; but I cannot but think that in the little he has to say about Adrian's treatment of his relations, he is either repeating hearsay, or speaking without personal knowledge. In the last chapter of "Metalogicus"[1] he records that during the Pope's reign Adrian's mother and brother were both alive. He says nothing about his father. Surely he would have done so had there been one holding office at S. Albans? In the same book, John tells us that Adrian did nothing for his mother, but left her to subsist on charity. Therefore, if Robert Brekespere was living, we must say that in whatever other respect he is to be praised, we can hardly include his callousness in leaving his cast-off wife or mistress to beggary among his "distinguished virtues!" Neither, if this be true, could one applaud Adrian for his rigidity of principle. John affirms that his real motive was to avoid all appearance of avarice or nepotism; if so, he showed great moral cowardice, and at least deserves the censure of history for carrying mistaken zeal to the pitch of unfilial cruelty. Several of his detractors have seized on this incident to prove that the Pope sent his mother no aid because he was unwilling to acknowledge her. A dole of money, sufficient to have kept her in comfort, even luxury, to the end of her days, would have been a very trifling matter to the revenues of S. Peter; but it has been suggested that even the smallest dole would have forced an admission from Adrian that his pride forbade him to make. No. As those who have the patience to follow me through the life of this remarkable man will admit, this suspicion is unworthy, and moreover in distinct opposition

---

[1] See Chap. VIII.

to the weight of evidence against it. When a man has forced his way up from obscurity to high position and worldly power, and his very enemies are obliged to admit that neither selfishness nor sordid avarice ever accompanied him in his upward career, we must do him the justice of assuming his sentiments and motives in private life to have been as pure and lofty as those of his public history. Petty pride never stood in Nicholas Breakspear's path; his life and character stand out clear and pure across the darkness of intervening centuries, and enable us by their silent testimony to scorn the idea of shame which some have endeavoured to affix to the character of this great Englishman.

Now, those who read for themselves the history of William of Newburgh will recognize the trustworthiness of his writings. His work seems entirely free from prejudice, and is characterized by a lofty singleness of purpose far in advance of the age in which he lived. He did not write to please his readers, as Matthew Paris apparently often did; he had no private ends to serve by adopting any one line of argument in preference to any other. He is very careful to authenticate his facts; and where he depends on hearsay, he is equally careful to say so. Above all, like John of Salisbury, he wrote of the times in which he lived, and the occurrences he mentions are those which were taking place around him. His story of Adrian is consistent in every detail, and in the main it agrees with that of Cardinal Boso, who however descends but little to detail, and confines himself to generalities. There is no doubt that the best and most authentic account of how Breakspear worked his way up from very small beginnings to the pontifical chair, is that of William of Newburgh.

We now come to tradition; and here it may be well to remember how large a part the handing down from father to son of local events has added to history. In such a matter as where a great man lived, his birthplace, and his home, these unwritten records command our most serious attention. On a quiet country-side the memory of so great a man would cling and hang round the locality for centuries. Local names, registers, and such like, all offer silent evidence of the truth of the legends associated with them. The rustic brain, dulled by the monotony of agricultural labour, unrelieved by the advantages of the education of the present day, had not in former times the wit or the knowledge to *invent* tales. Exaggeration, in course of time, might grow round the central fact; but I think I may safely say that in nine out of ten cases of local, or folk lore, there is some solid foundation in truth; while in a case where the same tradition can be traced back for centuries from son to father, supported by the evidence of nomenclature, we may almost accept it as historical fact. A tradition of this nature has clung persistently to two parishes which in the twelfth century were under the direct influence of the great Abbey of the Holy Martyr Alban. One, is that of Abbot's Langley in Hertfordshire; the other, Harefield, on the Herts border of Middlesex. In the former, which is a village dating far back into Saxon times, it is said Nicholas Breakspear was born; while in the other is a small country house which has borne the name of Breakspear for certainly since the latter end of the twelfth century, and which is said to have been the place where his family lived, and to have been occupied by their descendants for many years.

I shall presently return to these two places, but first will deal with the accounts of local historians as to Breakspear's connection with this part of the country.

Camden,[1] in his "Britannia," says under the heading of Hertfordshire: ". . . More to the South, lyeth King's Langley, heretofore a Seat of the Kings, where Edmund of Langley, Son to Edward III. and Duke of York, was born, and thence also named. Here was a small cell of Friars Prædicants, in which that unhappy Prince Richard II. was first buried, after he had been barbarously deprived both of the Kingdom and his Life; but not long after, his body was remov'd to Westminster, and had a monument of brass bestowed upon it, to make amends for his Kingdom.

"Almost opposite to this, is another Langley, which (because it belong'd to the Abbots of S. Albans) is call'd Abbot's Langley; the place where Nicholas Breakspeare

---

[1] "Britannia, or a chorographical description of Great Britain and Ireland, together with the adjacent islands, writ in Latin by William Camden, Clarencieux King at Arms. And translated into English with additions by Edmund Gibson, D.D., Rector of Lambeth." 2nd ed., London, 1623; 1st ed., 1586.

was born, who was afterwards Pope by the name of Hadrian the fourth."

Again, in his description of Middlesex, a few pages further on,[1] he again refers to Adrian: ". . . Upon the river Cole,[2] at its first entrance into this County, I met with Breakspear, the ancient seat of a family of that name, of which was descended Pope Hadrian the fourth, mention'd a little before. . . ."

In Fuller's "Worthies,"[3] a book full of interesting and curious facts and legends, further reference is made under the heading of "Hartfordshire." He follows Camden and quotes Bale, in a paragraph about the Pope so quaint and original, that I have reproduced it here in its entirety:

"Pope. Nicholas, son to Robert Breakspear (a lay brother in the Abbey of S. Albans) fetcht his name from Breakspeare, a place in Middlesex, but was born at Abbots Langley, a Town in this County.

"When a Youth, he was put to such servile work in S. Albans Abbey, that his ingenious Soul could not comport therewith. Suing to be admitted into that house, he received the repulse which in fine proved no *miss-hap*, but a *happy-miss*, unto him; for, going over into France, he studied so hard and so happily at Paris, that for his worth he was preferred Abbott of S. Rufus near Valentia, and

---

[1] Vol. i., pp. 365, 366.   [2] Colne.
[3] "The History of the Worthies of England. Endeavoured by Thomas Fuller, D.D., London. Printed by F. G. W. L. and W. G., MDCLXII.," p. 20.

afterward by Pope Eugenius the Third was made Bishop of Alba nigh Rome : Ad natalis soli memoriam, saith my Author, that he, who was refused to be Monachus Albanensis in England, should be Episcopus Albanensis in Italy. He was employed by the Pope for the conversion of the Norwegians, and though Bale saith (he were not Bale if he were not bitter),[1] Anti-Christiano charactere Norwegios signavit; yet his reducing them from Paganisme to Christianity in the Fundamentals was a worthy work and deserves true commendation. He was afterwards chosen Pope of Rome, by the name of Adrian the fourth. There is a mystery more than I can fathome in the changing of his name: Seeing his own font-name was a Papal one; Yet he preferred rather to be Adrian the fourth, than Nicholas the third.

"He held his place[2] four years, eight moneths and eight and twenty days: and Anno 1158[3] as he was drinking was choak't with a fly: Which in the large Territory of S. Peter's patrimony had no place but his throat to get into; But since a flye stopt his breath fear shall stop my Mouth, not to make uncharitable Conclusions from such Casualties."

I have chosen these two historians, as showing the prevalence of the tradition as far back as the sixteenth century.

---

[1] Bale, "De Scrip. Brit. Cent. II.," No. 90, in anno 1159.

[2] Muratori, vol. ii., p. 323 *et seq.*, "Sedit Annis IV., mensibus VIII., diebus VI."

[3] Fuller here makes a mistake; it was 1159.

Quaint old Fuller's expression, "fetcht his name," is probably exactly the truth. In those days it is far more probable that a place should give a name to a man, than that a man should give a name to a place. Now Breakspears, the place, was in all probability in existence before his day. The site is one which would commend itself to any settler in that part of the Colne valley, viz., on the edge of the tableland or plateau on which stands the ancient parish of Harefield, in those days Herefelle,[1] Harvil,[2] or Herefelde,[3] and just sheltered by the brow of the hill sloping down to the fertile valley of the Colne, hidden from the eye of the marauder, or those of wandering bands of soldiers or robbers, by dense woods. Within half a mile is the ancient church of S. Mary the Virgin, which is mentioned in the Domesday Book, and the advowson of which had not then passed to the Knights Hospitallers of S. John of Jerusalem, though it is mentioned as an ancient church[4] when it was given to them by Beatrice de Bollers, widow of Baldwin Fitz Geoffry, in 1180. Down on the banks of the Colne river stood a Camera or Preceptory, which went by the name of Moor Hall, and the remains of it are still visible in the old building standing there at the present day; indeed, the refectory and chapel can easily be traced, and with their walls and blocked-up windows form the sides and ends of a commodious barn!

[1] Domesday Book. [2] J. Norden, "Speculum Britanniæ," 1593.
[3] Breakspear and Moor Hall documents.
[4] Dugdale, "Monast. Ang."

Surely a desecration of ground consecrated for ever to the service of our blessed Lord?

This preceptory or cell was an appanage of the Priory of S. John's, Clerkenwell, and was enriched some time in the twelfth century by a deed of gift of the surrounding manor, by Alice, daughter of Geoffry, son of Baldwin de Clare.[1]

Later on,[2] we find a deed of Sir Roger Bachworth, who was lord of the manor of Harefield in 1284, giving more land to the Holy Brethren at the request of Nicholas Daccombe, "Preceptor domus Hospitalis de Herfeld." I dwell at some length on this little Hospital of S. John, because I think it may account for the name de Camera, in Matthew Paris' history. If Robert Breakspear lived at Breakspears, what more natural than that on moving to Abbot's Langley, and thence to S. Albans, he should mention any connection he may have had with the religious house near his former home?[3] As to the connection of Nicholas Breakspear with the place that bears his name, we have before us the records and papers of a quiet English

[1] "Confirmavi Deo, Beatæ Mariæ et Sancto Johanni Baptistæ, et Sanctæ Domus in territorio de Herfeld."

[2] Moor Hall papers.

[3] Another, and perhaps equally likely source for the name, is the supposition that Nicholas' father was "camerarius" or chamberlain at S. Albans. It is not uncommon for offices to give names to the holders, and Boso, Adrian's nephew, was a "camerarius" at the Vatican. So a chronicler finding Boso de Camera, a nephew of the Pope, and Robert de Camera, the Pope's father, might well be led into thinking de Camera the family name.

country house, the inhabitants of which have from the earliest times lived peacefully, and apparently undisturbed by the upsetting influences of wars, revolutions, and drastic changes.

Deeds, papers, and records have slowly accumulated, and now stand as mute evidence of the life of peaceable country folk, with no startling events to record, beyond the inevitable and monotonous sequence of births, marriages, and deaths, varied only by the household and estate records of management.[1] The family living in the house, at the earliest period I have yet been able to discover, was named Brekespere or Breakspear, and that was in 1317. The records of Moor Hall mention the name at an earlier date still. A deed, dated 1371, now before me, grants a lease of sixty years of some land at Harefield, to William Brekespere of Brekespere, and is signed by one William de Swanland, who was in those days lord of the manor. The house remained in the possession of this family till 1430, and the various Christian names include Adrian, Nicholas, and Robert. In that year, it is said, the last male representative died, leaving an heiress, a daughter Margaret, who married one George Assheby, clerk of the signet to Margaret of Anjou, Queen of Henry VI., and from that date the property passed regularly down in the Ashby family till 1769, when Robert Ashby died, leaving an heiress Elizabeth, from whom the property passed in the female

---

[1] Breakspear papers.

line to the present owner. The above-named Margaret[1] died in 1474, and is buried at Harefield.[2]

The name lingered on, and as late as 1591 we find the marriage of one Anne Breakspear at Harefield.[3] And at the present time it is, with various spellings, a by no means uncommon English surname. There is another tradition which I will allude to, namely, that Nicholas was born at Brill-on-the-Hill, Bucks; but I know of no authority for it. A question on the subject was asked in "Notes and Queries"[4] some years ago; but was apparently never answered. Whether any descendants of the Pope's family remain to this day it would be interesting to discover. At the beginning of the century an English family who spelt the name Brakspear were well known in Paris, and Pope Pius VII. offered the title of Count to a Mr. W. H. Brakspere in 1818, on account of his descent. There is a very interesting correspondence[5] in the same valuable periodical on this subject, in which that gentleman's son takes part; but he does not allude to the Brill tradition. That there were men of that name living at Langley as late as the middle of the fifteenth century, of the Christian name of Adrian, may be proved by a reference to the Cotton MS.[6] In conclusion,

---

[1] Vincent's MSS., Coll. Arms, No. 175, and 1477 Harl. MSS., Brit. Mus.

[2] Brass in Harefield Par. Church.   [3] Harefield Par. Reg.

[4] "Notes and Queries," 2nd Series, vol. i., p. 352, No. 18, May 3rd, 1856.

[5] "Notes and Queries," vol. i., p. 329, 7th Series, No. 17, April 24th, 1886; May 15th, 1886, p. 393; June 19th, 1886, p. 492; July 17th, 1886, vol. ii., p. 58.   [6] Cotton MS., Nero DVII., fol. 116.

then, I think we may be certain that Adrian IV. was the son of Robert Brekespere, and was born at Abbot's Langley somewhere about the year 1100—a few years after the birth of S. Bernard, from whom we shall presently have to trace the cause of much of the stirring part of Adrian's life. His name was Nicholas, and his father either a man of humble means, or from reduced circumstances compelled to leave his home overlooking the little preceptory on the banks of the Colne, and take up his dwelling in Abbot's Langley. If his family were of any importance, Robert was, at any rate, a younger son,[1] and preferred to earn his own living to being dependent on his relations. Here he stayed a few years, and finding his fortunes no better, and losing his wife, he moved again to the neighbouring city of S. Albans, there to be employed at the monastery as an humble serving brother. Let us suppose that there he ended his days peacefully in the oblivion which surrounds his life. Our business is with one of his children, Nicholas, who, even in early life, showed signs of the rare qualities which were in the future to help him to the highest places. We do not know what other children Robert Breakspear had; but Cardinal Boso, the secretary and chancellor of later days, was a nephew of Nicholas, and there must have been others besides his father or mother.

Nicholas tried in vain to gain admittance to the

---

[1] " .... He was an English man, his name was Nicholas Breakespeare .... son to Robert, a younger brother of the house of Breakespeare."—STOWE'S *Chronicles*, p. 150.

monastery—and we have in later days [1] his own authority for this—as a preparatory step to taking the hood and entering the service of Christ; but, whether on account of his poverty or because of his youth, the Abbot Richard rejected him, and he was reduced almost to beggary and well-nigh to despair. But that unconquerable resolve of purpose familiar to all who study the lives of great men, especially those of the Anglo-Saxon race, held him fast to a determination to live his life, and sent him forth, as it has sent thousands and thousands of his countrymen since, to seek his fortune beyond the seas; to add a name of the brightest lustre to the already long list of English worthies; and to leave a high example to succeeding generations. It is pleasant to put on record that the sentiment of love for his country did not leave him in spite of his hard lot in his youth, for in the course of a conversation [2] with John of Salisbury in after years, he expressed a wish that he had never left his native land of England.

After his final failure to enter S. Albans, he worked his way, probably through London and down the high road through Kent—that historic route which has been the main thoroughfare of so many travellers to and from the metropolis—past Rochester and Canterbury, to Dover, from whence he obtained a passage over the narrow seas, possibly in the very same year [3] when the "Blanche Neuf"

[1] "Chronica Monasterii," vol. i., p. 127, sub annis 1151-56.
[2] Joan. Sar., vol. iv., lib. viii., cap. 23, p. 367.
[3] 1120.

was wrecked on the treacherous rocks off Barfleur, and the brilliant company surrounding Prince William, together with that unfortunate son of King Henry, were drowned. Here the career of Nicholas may fairly be said to have commenced, and perhaps it will be not out of place to consider what the condition of England and France was at this period.

CHAPTER II.

The Condition of England and France in the Twelfth Century—Suger, Abbot of S. Denys—The Pope's Influence in the Church of England.

THE England in which Nicholas Breakspear was born had little in common with that of the present day, and it requires a large call on the imagination to picture his surroundings.

If we take the year 1100 as approximately that of his birth, we find ourselves at the beginning of the reign of Henry I. Men just emerging from middle age were living who had fought in defence of Saxon England against the Conqueror, or who had helped in the Norman army to win for him his island kingdom; indeed, the whole campaign was only as far removed from them as the war between the North and South is from the inhabitants of the United States at the time of writing this chapter.[1]

The year 1100 may fairly be taken as marking the time when conquerors and conquered had commenced to settle down together. The rising generation could not

[1] 1894.

remember the catastrophe of Hastings, and mixed unions were beginning to bear fruit in producing the ancestors of the British race of to-day. The harsh cruelties of the reigns of the first two Williams were toning down—cruelties terrible for the people to suffer; a stormy period of trouble and pain; a fierce ordeal which our country went through, but perhaps necessary to the process of welding together those qualities which have produced the strong and powerful characteristics peculiar to the Anglo-Saxon race.

King Henry ascended the throne with a promise of peace; he carried the people with him by his marriage with Matilda, daughter of King Malcolm of Scotland by Margaret, sister of Aedgar the Atheling, the titular boy-king who had surrendered the crown of England to William I. With his reign, and the peace which the land enjoyed during it, and all the stirring history of his time, we have little to do. It is sufficient for our purpose to note that the firmness and statesmanship of this great king found a ready response in the law-abiding instincts which were, even in those turbulent times, beginning to show themselves in our forefathers, and enabled him to establish a constitution and framework of law on so firm a basis as to survive the shock of nearly twenty years of unrest, civil war, and domestic chaos in the reign of Stephen, and to form the foundation for Henry II. to carry on the work of his namesake.

Breakspear, therefore, as a boy lived in a time of quietness, between two stormy periods of history, the one before his time, the other after he had left the country.

The anarchy and disturbance of Stephen's reign made rural life in any part of the island full of danger and alarm. When every night brought with it the fear of attack and pillage, and no man knew but that the morrow would dawn on his imprisonment in some foul dark dungeon, with nothing ahead but torture and starvation, his home in flames, and his women-folk carried off to a worse fate, while no redress from the arbitrary power of the Barons was possible, small wonder that the art of literature did not flourish!

The marvel is that any writing at all should have reached us from those dark days. The Saxon Chronicle itself ends at this time, as if unable to keep the light of history even at a flicker amid so foul an atmosphere. William of Newburgh says: " Wounded and drained of life by civil misery, England lay plague-stricken."

This accounts fully for the meagreness of historical record to help us with any details of the early life of Breakspear. We can, however, to some extent picture to ourselves the aspect of twelfth-century England. In trying to imagine the scenes in which any person of that, or any other part of history took part, it is necessary to make some effort to wipe away modern surroundings from our gaze, and substitute a new background for our objects.

Let us, therefore, in fancy take ourselves back some eight hundred years. Everything is different—language, manners, customs, and even the appearance of the people. One historian has supposed that of all the varied sounds we hear to-day connected with mankind, perhaps the only unchanged one is the sound of the church bells.[1] The vast mass of the people must still have used the Anglo-Saxon tongue, for England, remember, had been Saxon for nigh six hundred years, or as long as from the reign of Edward I. to the present day, though of course the upper and governing classes spoke Norman French, and the two languages intermingling were forming the English of later days. The population has been computed at about 2,000,000, or one-third that of modern London and its suburbs!

London itself was a city of no mean importance, and had since the reign of William I. begun to rival Winchester. It was confined to the north bank of the Thames, and formed a strong strategic position against invaders from the south. There was only one timber bridge, and the walled and fortified city clustered round the Tower, which had been built by the Conqueror in 1079. An immense forest covered all the north part of what is now the centre of the town, and stretched away beyond the modern Islington and Hoxton to the hills of Hampstead and Highgate, and on again with scarce a check to the present Harrow, and so almost to S. Albans. The Lea and other rivers flowed in valleys between these woods; while

[1] Froude.

to the north-east was a large lake, which gave the name Moorfields in later years to that portion of London.

Huge undrained marshes on the east, out of which rose the Isle of Dogs, protected the city in that direction; while it was separated by other marshes from the Abbey of Westminster. On the south side of the river was Lambeth or Lambythe (where the unfortunate Harald is said to have placed the crown on his head[1]), seized by William at the Conquest, and added later to the diocese of Rochester for the maintenance of the monks. London was declared to be the capital of England in the reign of Henry II.

But our interest chiefly centres round the country under the sway of the Abbey of S. Albans, a rich and beautiful domain, which still embraces some of the most lovely of our English country scenery. The abbey lands extended far down the valley of the Colne, and probably included much of the district round the two villages of Abbot's and King's Langley. The population round S. Albans was scanty, but no doubt clustered round the abbey for peace and quietness in those troublesome times. Any man who in those days felt within him the impulse of study and the desire for knowledge would naturally wend his way towards the nearest abbey or monastery, and join the school of the monks, and this opportunity, as we have seen, Nicholas Breakspear probably had. The English kingdom in those days included Normandy, Brittany,

---

[1] Lambarde, "Dictionarium Angliæ Topographicum."

Anjou, Tourraine, Poitou, and Aquitaine, and thus it may be said that the coast line, in addition to the British shores, stretched away from Barfleur all along the north coast of the modern France down to the River Adour, on the frontier line of Spain. So, at the time when the rejected youth reached France, that kingdom consisted merely of the five cities [1] of Paris, Melun, Etampes, Orleans, and Sens, with the country round them, or what is now comprised in the three departments of Seine, Seine et Oise, Seine et Marne, and that of Loiret. Louis VI. (le Gros) was on the throne, and as in the neighbouring country of England it was a turbulent and stormy time, equally so was it in France. This period has been taken by French historians to be the time when the foundation of popular liberties made great progress, and the first steps were taken towards the "Affranchissement des Communes." It was, however, to the traveller a time of almost constant war abroad, and confusion and feudal tyranny at home.

The communications between the great cities were constantly intercepted by armed bands of retainers from the strongly-fortified feudal castles which dotted the country in all directions. Even the churches and monasteries afforded little shelter, as they were often pillaged and burned by the lawless bands, or laid under heavy ransom; poverty seems to have been the only safeguard to the

---

[1] Sismondi, "Hist. des Français." Ordericus Vitalis, lib. ii., cap. 34.

solitary pilgrim or traveller. Nicholas Breakspear, however, managed to reach Paris in safety, and stayed there some time, probably serving and studying under Suger, Abbot of S. Denys, one of the great Catholic churchmen, amongst whose ranks, in a few short years, he himself was destined to take the foremost place.

This great man,[1] who stands on a glorious level with Bernard and a host of other representatives of the Church militant equally with the message of Christian peace, was the prototype of the great ecclesiastical statesmen of France, the forerunner of Richelieu and Mazarin. He was born in 1081 at S. Omer, and was actually received into S. Denys at the early age of fifteen years, and then became the confidential friend of the young Prince Louis, whose minister he afterwards was. Suger was a warrior monk, for in 1112 he headed the royal troops in person, and saved the town of Theury from bands of marauders. He afterwards went on an important embassy to Rome, and became Abbot of S. Denys on his return, from which time on to his death in 1152 he practically ruled, not only the Church in France, but France itself, with wisdom and prudence. He showed to the bishops and clergy of his time the duty of loyalty to their sovereign as well as to their Pope, and he helped Louis VI. to leave behind him a great name, with a larger and better governed kingdom. An instance of how

[1] Milman, "Latin Christianity," vol. iv., cap. 6 ; "Bernardi Opera Epist.," 78, 333 ; Sismondi, "Hist. des Français," cap. v., pp. 7-20 ; "Vie de Louis le Gros," Guizot.

dangerous the state of the country was when Louis came to the throne is afforded by the fact that the high road from Paris to Orleans was laid under a tribute from the castle of a great feudal lord whose territory was traversed by it, and who refused to owe allegiance to the king; this, and many similar acts of insubordination, was removed by the efforts of the powerful Suger.

He rebuilt the basilica of S. Denys and collected the chronicles of the abbey, which he has to some extent embodied in the life of Louis VI.[1]

Whatever may have been the faults of those who guided the Catholic Church during this and subsequent ages, or however disastrous to her future unity the action of her rulers in the example they set of discreditable faction and family differences—of struggles between Pope and Anti-Pope, Cardinals, Abbots, and the great Roman nobles—it must be conceded that the Church, and the Church alone, kept alive the sacred light of study, learning, and literature. In later ages it may be alleged that the Church has at times blocked the way to the advance of science, that bigotry and narrow-mindedness have been responsible for the hindrance of many great inventions and discoveries. I do not dispute this; but at the time of which we write the darkness would have been complete, were it not for the quiet studious monk in his cell, the arguments in the cloister, and the records of the religious houses. Call their ideas mere superstitions,

---

[1] Sugeri, " Vit. Louis Gr."

if you will—their understanding limited—their opinions pedantic and narrow; they at least did their duty according to the amount of light vouchsafed to them, and I believe, in the great majority of cases, with a clear firm faith undimmed by doubt—the faith of simple minds who could see the clear sky where we perhaps can only make out the cloudy mists of superstition, and cannot discern the heavenly vault beyond. The Church was supreme in those days; its authority far beyond anything that we in the present day can realize. The Pope ruled unquestioned, certainly in all spiritual matters; he held the fear of excommunication or interdict over men's heads; he claimed the right to assign territory, to settle disputes between kings, to manage dynastic quarrels and difficulties. In fact, the Church, as the Church of the King of kings, claimed from the kings of the earth that homage which was due to the Saviour as also due to His Vicar on earth, the Pontiff; and literally it may be said that kings bowed down before him. At the Council of Rheims, in 1119, Calixtus II. presided over a brilliant meeting, and in Dean Milman's words—[1] " . . . . never did Pope, in Rome itself, in the time of the world's most prostrate submission, make a more imposing display of power, issue his commands with more undoubting confidence in Christianity, receive like a feudal monarch the appeals of contending kings; and if he condescended to negotiate with the Emperor, maintain a loftier position than

---

[1] Milman, "Latin Christianity," vol. iv., book viii., cap. 3, p. 281.

this great French Pontiff." The Norman chronicler[1] of the day compared this meeting to the day of judgment! Here the Pope listened to a complaint by Louis VI. against Henry I. of England, perhaps the chief case he had to hear. It is worthy of note, that whereas the French monarch appeared attended by his barons in full feudal state, Henry I. was represented only by the Bishop of Rouen. And this leads us to consider the position of the Pope in regard to England, an important question bearing directly on the subject of this book.

While, as I have said before, the Pope was recognized as the universal spiritual head of all Latin Christians, his temporal authority had certain limitations even in France and Italy and the countries of Latin race. Those who recognized and believed fully his power of affecting the spiritual prospects of anyone who, in his opinion, offended him, were nevertheless quite ready to use this, so to speak, spiritual authority in worldly concerns for their own personal advantage and profit, either by intrigue, or conspiracy to obtain the election of a member of their own family to the chair of S. Peter, or by conniving at the " removal " of one who did not respond to their interests. This undermined the whole principle of the Papal authority, and bore fruit in some of the darkest and most disgraceful scenes of degradation through which the Church has passed, thus sullying the sacred cause of handing on the commands of the blessed

---

[1] "Orderic. Vital.," i. 726.

Saviour. Too often, alas! the one whose position on earth was held to be in direct responsibility to the Almighty, lent his aid in furthering these interests and in betraying the holy trust reposed in him. All, of course, were not like this, and the names of those who held the holy banner on high, unmoved and uninfluenced by the various corruptions around them, show clear and bright for our admiration and respect. With these causes working round the centre of the Western Church, it is small wonder that the temporal power should weaken in authority on crossing the Channel to England, and it may be said without contradiction that the temporal power of the Pope was never fully acknowledged in this country. It was not a question of race so much as of geography; for the Teutonic races at this period fully believed in the supremacy of the Pope, and the reader of the history of the Popes will see that many Germans held the chair. In most cases, indeed, the German Popes had done much to preserve the sanctity of the office, and where it was otherwise their compatriots showed their Teutonic blood, not by attempting to shield their shortcomings on the pretext of their having been directly appointed from above, but by holding that their defects might make it necessary for them to be deposed. When William the Conqueror obtained leave from Alexander II., prompted by Hildebrand, to invade England, he did so on the direct understanding that his fealty was to be paid to the Pope for his new kingdom; that all Anglo-Saxon bishops and abbots were to be deprived of their offices and

Normans put in their places, and the payment of Peter's pence was to be made. The two latter conditions were complied with, though the wholesale changes in the Church could not have increased the love of the English people for the Pope; but when the oath of fealty was demanded through the Norman Archbishop of Canterbury, Lanfranc, the Conqueror seems to have learnt something of the temper of English churchmen, for he says: "I have not, nor will I swear fealty, which was never sworn by any of my predecessors to yours."[1]

This spirit has ever animated the English Church, and by degrees, as we all know, the Catholic Christians of England separated entirely from the authority of the Pope.

It is too often taught and insisted that this did not really happen till centuries later, and this is not the place to enter on an account of the Church of England. It is sufficient for our purpose, which is that of describing the life of an English Pope, to point out that even in his day there was a distinct, if small difference, as to the temporal relations of the Pope to that branch of the Holy Catholic Church, which, founded far back in Anglo-Saxon days, on the basis of a still older Church, preserves the continuity of the Catholic religion direct from the Early Fathers to this day.

---

[1] "Fidelitatem facere nolui nec volo quia nec ego promisi, nec antecessores meos antecessoribus tuis id fecisse comperio." See Milman, "Latin Christianity," vol. iv., book viii., cap. 1, p. 35.

But Nicholas Breakspear would of course be brought up strictly at S. Denys to regard the Pope as head of all the world, and his supremacy as quite unquestioned; though no doubt he would know of the state of feeling in England to some considerable extent.

The state of affairs in France during the years he was in that country, from about 1118-20 to 1138, was, as I have already said, troublesome; the principal events happening in the Church will be referred to later.

In political affairs English interest and influence in France was increasing; the war between Louis VI. and Henry I.'s Norman possessions terminated in 1128 by the death of William, son of Robert of Normandy, whose cause Louis was espousing. The Empress Matilda, only daughter of Henry I., married at this time Geoffry Plantagenet, whose father transferred all his dominions to him in 1129. In 1137, however, Louis le Jeune, son of Louis VI., was married to Eleanora, heiress of the Duke of Aquitaine. Before the departure of the Duke for the Holy Land his vast possessions were handed over as a dowry for his daughter, and thus it came to pass that Louis VII. on the death of his father in the same year succeeded to a kingdom largely increased by territory in Guienne and Poitou.[1]

The next scene of action to which we shall follow Nicholas Breakspear is Provence; which, though geo-

---

[1] On the divorce of Eleanora in 1152 these provinces reverted to her, and formed part of her dowry when she married Henry Plantagenet, afterwards Henry II. of England.

graphically a part of France, was at that date politically a portion of the German Empire, being included in the kingdom of Arles, which had been attached to the Emperor's dominions by Conrad II. in 1032.[1] It was the scene of much that is important in the history of the Church, and was at the time of which we write entirely under the influence of the Pope.

[1] Provence was first annexed to France in 1487, by Charles VIII.

CHAPTER III.

1120 TO 1151.

Nicholas Breakspear in France—The Abbey of S. Rufus—Prior—Abbot—The Insubordination of the Monks—Eugenius III.—Journey to Rome—Return to S. Rufus—Second Journey to Rome—Breakspear attached to the Pope's Suite—Bishop of Albano—Cardinal—The Second Crusade—Eugenius III. at S. Denys—Breakspear chosen for the Mission to Scandinavia.

WE have seen how Nicholas worked his way as a young man to France, and I have taken 1119 or 1120 as about the latest date we can assign to this.

I have assumed that the place where he lived the greater part of his time at or near Paris was the Abbey of S. Denys,[1] as this agrees with the accounts of the most trustworthy historians. But wherever it was that he pursued his studies, we now hear no more statements as to his idleness or want of application; we are told on all sides that he became a most painstaking scholar,[2] and betook himself so much in earnest to the acqui-

[1] In the "Memoir of the Life of Adrian IV.," London, 1857, the Rev. E. Trollope, F.S.A., states that he studied in the University of Paris, but I am inclined to think it improbable.

[2] Matt. Paris, "Vit. Abb.," vol. i., p. 113; Muratori, vol. ii., p. 324.

sition of learning, that he excelled all his companions, and proving himself possessed of rare qualities of temper and endowed with a natural gift of eloquence and a sweet voice, received much praise from all his instructors. But, for some reason or other, he decided to leave Paris; whether he was unable to enter the monastic habit, or whether he possessed an inclination to travel, we do not know. William of Newburgh tells us he began to fare badly; perhaps he found his poverty a hindrance, or shall we say with Cardinal Boso[1] that "the Lord called him, and brought it about that he should leave"? At any rate he quitted Paris about the year 1125, adopted a wandering life, and gradually worked and begged his way southwards across the Rhone: little did he know that he was travelling in the direction of his future greatness! Hard indeed must have been his life at this period, learning in the stern school of poverty the lessons of self-denial and privation. No doubt if we only had his record of this year of his life we should find it full of stirring scenes of adventure and peril. He crossed the Rhone and entered Arles, then a town of considerable importance in the large territory of Provence. At this place he frequented the schools for which the town was famous, and we still hear accounts of his diligence and industry. He did not, however, remain very long at Arles, being apparently tired of city life, and having adopted a studious character. It was scarcely possible in those days to carry on the prompt-

---

[1] Muratori; Watterich, "Pont. Rom.," vol. ii., p. 323.

ings of such a nature outside a monastery. His early wish to enter the Abbey of S. Albans returned to him with added force, and he wended his way towards Avignon to see if he could gain entrance into one of the numerous monasteries which in those days were one of the distinguishing features of this beautiful part of France, and the ruins of which may still be seen by many a pleasant stream and on many a commanding hill. There was in the environs of Avignon a large monastery of canons regular, called the Abbey of S. Rufus, the remains of which are still visible,[1] and after some weeks of wandering, Nicholas ended this stage of his life by arriving one evening at its gates and begging for admission. Here he stayed for some years, and found an opportunity of earning his living.[2] William of Newburgh says that "By every means in his power he strove to ingratiate himself with the brothers, and being a man of much personal beauty, cheerful in spirit, cautious of speech, and always obedient to authority, he succeeded in pleasing everyone." In fact, he seems to have won his way with the abbot and brothers as much by his winning personality as by his docility, judgment, and learning. He probably remained in this position for two or three years; at the expiration of which time the canons[3] unanimously agreed to admit him into their order, and thus at last Nicholas took the monk's hood, and vowed his life to the service of Christ.

[1] "Dictionnaire Géographique de la France," etc., par Adolphe Joanne. Deux^me édition. Avignon—Environs—S. Ruf. Paris, 1818.
[2] Guil. Newb., lib. ii., cap. 6, p. 121.
[3] Ibid.

The monastery of S. Rufus was one for "Regular Canons," and as such was guided by the rules ordained by Innocent II. in the Lateran Council of 1139, known as the rule of S. Augustine.[1] Our first acquaintance with the monastery is some ten years or more before this date, and in common with other similar institutions they had somewhat slackened in their discipline and habit, and so required the reformation which Innocent II. administered; indeed, we shall find soon that such measures as were required were actually put into operation by the hand of Nicholas Breakspear. The canons regular of S. Augustine were a kind of middle order between the monks and the clergy, and were formed in the eighth century; their rules in life were supposed to be derived from the epistles of S. Augustine; their dwellings and table were in common, and they assembled for divine service at fixed hours; they kept public schools for the instruction of the young, and compiled records of surrounding events viewed somewhat in the same narrow way as the scenery round the abbey was circumscribed by the cell window. The dress of the friars of the order was a white garment and scapulary, and when in choir or abroad they wore a black cowl with a large hood, and were girt with a black leather thong; while the dress of the canons regular consisted of a long black cassock with a white socket, and over that a black cloak and hood. They

[1] Monastic writers agree in stating that S. Augustine himself instituted no rule, but the so-called "rule" was extracted from his epistles and sermons.

allowed their beards to grow, and wore caps. The difference between friars and canons was that the former went abroad, and passed their time for the most part in travelling, while the latter never left their monasteries. The principal officer of every abbey was of course the abbot, who not only exercised supreme authority over the abbey, but also over all the lesser abbeys or cells which were attached to it; and these again were ruled by priors acting under and owing their position to the abbot. The almoner and pitancer had the oversight of the alms and the distribution of provisions; the chamberlain, or camerarius, the dormitories; and the cellarer had to provide provisions. The infirmarius looked after the sick; and, lastly, the precentor or chantor directed the choir. Besides these there were many minor offices. In addition to these important posts, every ten monks were subject to one called the decanus, or deacon; while every hundred were presided over by a centenarius.

The dean had to keep an exact account of every man's daily task, which eventually came before the abbot every month.

Such was the kind of discipline under which Nicholas Breakspear was passing these years of his life. It appears that although he himself carefully obeyed the rules of the order, the state of rigid observance of routine was growing lax in the abbey, in common with most of the monastic institutions of the age; but he became notwithstanding most popular among his brethren, and so esteemed by the abbot that he was made a prior of the order; and on Abbot William dying in 1137, the brethren unanimously chose him to be their head,[1] and installed him in office with great solemnity. But the man who had passed through the great lesson of learning to obey was now to show them that he had also learnt how to command; if they thought that the modest, unassuming, and compliant brother was going to rule them with a gentle hand, and tolerate any slackness in the hard duties imposed on them by their solemn vows, they were mistaken. Breakspear showed immediately that power of command which comes at once when a man of strong will, rigid principle, and knowledge of mankind is suddenly placed in a position of responsibility. The more heavy that responsibility is, the better do such men rise to it. The easy ways into which the monks had gradually drifted were stopped; the rigid rules of S. Augustine put in force; and by degrees those men who had been unanimous in placing him over their abbey began to murmur among themselves.

In such an institution discontent is easily spread; in the solitude of the cloister, in the absence of any echo from the outer world, the slanderous whisper ever finds a ready ear, and like a snowball gathers bulk as it passes from one to the other. The rule became harder, concealed insubordination helped to magnify seemingly uncalled-for severities; murmurs increased to open discontent, they complained of the foreigner, and almost openly sneered at his origin, while day by day their anger

---

[1] Guil. Newb., lib. iv., cap. 6.

ABBOT BERNARD OF PISA,
EUGENIUS III.

grew more pronounced. At length a combination was formed, and a set of complaints framed to be forwarded to the Pope. By so doing, they unconsciously helped their abbot on in his career, for had he never gone to Rome, he most likely would have lived all his life within the walls of S. Rufus—a life which had great charms for him, as in after years[1] he said that next to the wish that he had never left his native land was the wish that he had at least lived his life quietly in the cloisters of the abbey. The result of the complaints of the brethren was that Nicholas Breakspear went to Rome to defend himself against the calumnies of his flock, rightly judging that it would be better to be present in person, and let his accusers make their charges to his face, rather than that they should have the opportunity, so often used in those times, of by intrigue and corruption influencing the decision of the Pontiff.

Eugenius III.,[2] who occupied the papal chair at that time, was himself a wonderful man, and curiously like Breakspear in character. He had been almost thrust into the glorious office he held by the friends of Bernard of Clairvaulx, who thought him a simple-minded man, easily persuaded, and likely to prove a willing tool in the hands of their party; while Bernard himself remonstrated against the cruelty of dragging him from the peace of the Cistercian Abbey of Pisa, where he had been abbot for many years, as

[1] Joan. Sar., "Polycraticus," lib. viii., cap. 23, p. 266.
[2] Milman, "Latin Christianity," vol. iv., book viii., chap. vi., pp. 287, 288.

leading to a breach of the vows of a man supposed to be dead to the world. But just as the monks of S. Rufus had misunderstood the character of Nicholas Breakspear, so had the followers of Bernard, and even that great prelate, Bernard of Clairvaulx himself, mistaken that of the quiet abbot, Bernard of Pisa. "Is this a man," said he,[1] "to gird on the sword and to execute vengeance on the people, to bind their kings with chains and their nobles with links of iron? How will a man with the innocence and simplicity of a child cope with affairs which require the strength of a giant?" He found that the simple-minded man proved strong in will and firm in character. There was a similarity between the two cases which must have appealed to the sympathies of Eugenius, and the result of the appeal was that the Pope,[2] having listened attentively to the complaints of the rebellious children against their father, and having noticed the prudence and good sense of the latter in his defence, interposed effectually for the restoration of peace, gave much good advice and counsel to either party, advising both to keep the unity of the spirit in the bond of peace, and sent them back to their abbey reconciled, and ready for mutual forbearance and forgiveness. Eugenius III., however, had probably marked out the Abbot of S. Rufus as a man of strong principles and free from corruption; he himself, at least, was this. He has been called the mere tool of S. Bernard. Undoubtedly he was carried away by the wave of

---

[1] Bernard, "Epist.," 236.   [2] Guil. Newb.

enthusiasm for the disastrous second crusade, and he certainly committed some errors of judgment; but his reputation for purity of intention and for real sanctity is unsullied. Though he was responsible for the use of the sword in the cause of Christianity in the war in the Holy Land, his responsibility was in a sense thrust upon him by the wonderful infection of Bernard's eloquence, which carried him away as it did all classes of Christians in Western Europe. His magnificent contempt for earthly wealth gained him the love of the masses and the admiration and respect even of his enemies. For the first time in the history of the Popes treasures and presents sent to a Pontiff from kings and cities by the hands of his returning embassages were sent back to the donors. Dean Milman tells us that no bribes could dazzle, no flattery gain the sturdy spirit of the Cistercian monk. He spent his revenues largely on charity and on church building, and endeavoured to rule his turbulent subjects more in the true spirit of Christianity than, as was then too often the custom, by the sword, the dungeon, and the anathema.

Such was the man who was destined to single out Nicholas Breakspear for honour and preferment. His judgment, as we shall see, proved to be sound; and to his other great qualities must be added the rare and valuable gift of knowing how to select men with regard to their own personal merit rather than to their influence or their position in the world. So the abbot and his monks wended their way back to the quiet seclusion of S. Rufus. The former must have been filled with wonder at the great city of Rome, in those days still the centre of the civilized world as well as the home of the Holy Church; while they, full of the advice of the Pope, remained quiet and submissive under their head for a time. The fire once kindled by the spirit of disaffection was, however, only damped, not extinguished, and after a while, fanned no doubt by the leaders or the agitators of the revolt, broke out again more violently than ever. This time they entered into a conspiracy to procure his deposition, adding a fresh mass of complaints, under which they hoped he might succumb. Again they started for Rome—Nicholas Breakspear the abbot, and the deputation of accusing monks; again they appeared before the same calm, venerable Pontiff who had heard their former complaint.

This time a different result was arrived at. We have from the pen of William of Newburgh a very precise account of what took place. The Pope once more listened to the angry charges of the insubordinate monks, and afterwards to the calm, eloquent defence of the man whose true character had been detected by him at the former interview.

Gazing steadily and earnestly on either side, "I know," said he,[1] "my brothers, where the seat of Satan lies;

---

[1] Guil. Newburg., lib. ii., cap. 6, p. 122. "Scio, inquit, fratres ubi sedes sit Sathanæ; scio quid in vobis suscitet procellam istam. Ite, eligite vobis patrem cum quo pacem habere possitis vel potius velitis; iste enim non erit vobis ulterius oneri."

I know what has aroused this quarrel among you. Depart; choose some superior with whom you can, or rather with whom you shall have the will to be at peace; this one shall not be a further burden to you." With these scathing words he dismissed the brethren; but retained Nicholas in his own service—a result which, probably, was not quite what the brethren expected. This was most undoubtedly for Nicholas the great opportunity in his life—the chosen of the Pope himself he was now almost sure of advancement. Having accompanied him to this point, it will be well to consider the events which were happening at the time, as they must have helped largely in determining his future conduct and opinions. We can fix the date of this event approximately. Nicholas, as we have seen, was made Abbot of S. Rufus in 1137, and allowing seven years before the first outbreak, and two years for the journeys to Rome, we get to 1146, towards the end of which year, moreover, it is certain that he was made Cardinal.

Now Eugenius III. only became Pope in February, 1145, and we know that he received both deputations; so that the spring or summer of 1146 must have been the time when he was taken into the immediate circle of the Pope's suite.

It is somewhat doubtful whether this took place at Rome, the city in that year being in the uncontested possession of Arnold of Brescia. The Pope left Rome at the end of March, and retired to Viterbo and Sienna; in all probability Nicholas Breakspear accompanied him to these places, and was there created by him Bishop of Albano, and a Cardinal.

The Second Crusade was about to commence. The Pope had written his celebrated letter to the King of France, exhorting him and his people to take up arms at once for the defence of the Holy Sepulchre, and a great national council was convoked at Vezelai, in Burgundy. Bernard attended it as the Pope's legate, and the utmost enthusiasm was aroused, King Louis himself holding up the cross, after receiving it in his royal robes on his knees, at the feet of the representative of the Pope. Bernard after this went through Germany, and, emulating the deeds of Peter the Hermit, roused the Emperor Conrad and his nephew Frederick (afterwards Barbarossa) to join the militant host. All preparations were made by the beginning of 1147, and at Easter in that year Eugenius went to Paris and presented Louis with the pilgrim's staff and wallet in the Abbey of S. Denys. We have good reason to believe that Cardinal Breakspear accompanied the Pope to Paris; and if so, what a change in his manner of entering the city to that of some five and twenty years before! I always think that of all the moments of this remarkable man's life —and there were during his career more than fall to the lot of most men—of those which appeal directly to the emotions and rouse into stirring music the silent chords of memory, of all the moments this must have been the most thrilling. Prince, cardinal, bishop, a high and puissant lord of the Holy Church, he rides in, the confidential friend of the

Pope himself, through those abbey gates at which he had begged, a humble suppliant for admission, a few short years before!

What a return, and what a justification of his judgment in choosing the path wherein he intended to tread the stirring pilgrimage of his life! Eugenius returned to Italy accompanied by his retinue soon after this, and took up his residence at Viterbo. The crusade started on its disastrous undertaking, headed by Louis VII. It is not within the scope of this work to trace the steps which led to the utter failure of this, the second Holy War, except in its effect of draining Europe of its manhood. It for a time checked all warlike operations on anything approaching to a large scale, and left a legacy of widespread discontent among the people, showing itself in sullen complaints against Bernard, and calling forth from him one of his most celebrated epistles.[1] Our cardinal advanced in favour not only with his master, but with his brother cardinals, and we hear that he greatly charmed all who came in contact with him by his power of language in the Latin and French, as well as the English tongue. Indeed, he must at this time have advanced rapidly in reputation, for in 1152 he was selected by Eugenius to undertake a mission to Danemark, Norway, and Sweden under circumstances which will be fully related in the next chapter. We have no definite record of his doings during the years which elapsed between his elevation to cardinal

---

[1] "Bernardi Opera," Epist. 333.

and this important appointment, except his signatures to the Bulls of Eugenius III., but he must have taken his full share in the events of Church history during that period.[1]

Suger at this time was regent of France, and served his country well in still further promoting the cause of order and justice, so that on his king's return from the disastrous campaign in the Holy Land he was able partly to recover him from depression at his misfortunes by handing over to him his kingdom in an increased state of efficiency, strength, and order. At and round Rome it was a period of turbulence and war, and Breakspear had ample opportunity of studying the condition of affairs in the imperial city, the action of the Republic, and the career of Arnold of Brescia—a study to bear fruit in after years.

In his native country the civil wars under Stephen were drawing to a close, and the condition of affairs was such that the people, exhausted by oppression and despair, had almost reached the lowest ebb of hope, soon to revive under the beneficent influence of the reign of King Henry II. When this period of Breakspear's life comes to an end we are on the eve of one of his greatest works—the Mission to Scandinavia.

---

[1] From December, 1151, to the middle of February, 1152, nearly all the Bulls of Eugenius III. are signed by Breakspear, the last one being February 20th, 1152.

CHAPTER IV.

1151 TO 1154.

Church History in Scandinavia—Breakspear leaves Rome for Norway—Passes through England—His Norwegian Mission—Reform of the Church in Norway—Church Division in Sweden—Breakspear's Diplomacy in Danemark—The War between Danemark and Sweden—Return to Rome—Death of Eugenius III.—Anastasius IV.—His Character—His Death—Breakspear elected Pope.

THE events which made Eugenius III. decide to send a mission to the Scandinavian kingdoms, arose from the action of Danemark (Denmark) in obtaining from Pope Paschal II., in 1102, an independent metropolitan see, instead of, as previously, being under the Archbishop of Hamburg. The best account of this interesting, but complicated period of Northern Church history is to be found in the pages of Torfæus,[1] who deals most fully with it, and in Munter. But a brief synopsis of events will be necessary to enable us to understand the condition of affairs in

---

[1] Thormodus Torfæus, "Historia Rerum Norwegicarum," tom. iii., lib. ix., cap. 2. Munter, "Kirchengeschichte und Kirchenrecht des Nordens." Herausgegeben, 1792. Buch. I. und II., tom. ii.

the northern churches at the time when Cardinal Breakspear was sent to them, so that the importance of his work and mission may be realized.

The Scandinavian kingdoms consisted of Danemark, Norway, and Sweden—countries closely related by all the ties of geographical proximity, race, and political interests, though they were constantly in a state of bloodshed and warfare. Danemark at this time was the strongest of the three; her national feeling was certainly the most developed. A little over a century before lived the great Knut, the Danish king who ruled over England, and who had brought that country to its knees. He made a pilgrimage to Rome in 1027, and on his return did much to foster the growth of Christianity in his kingdom by founding monastic institutions, endowing churches, and in various other ways encouraging the closer connection between his wild countrymen and the centre of the faith at Rome. After his death, although the country was still powerful, the Danegelt, or tribute, being exacted from England down almost to the reign of Henry II., it decreased much in importance, owing to civil feuds and a succession of bad and incompetent rulers, who by divisions amongst themselves, and neglect of the duties of government, reduced the condition of the country to a worse state possibly than that which I have endeavoured to show obtained in England under Stephen. Sweyn, or Sweno III., was on the throne at the time of the Papal mission, and when he was beheaded as the result of a revolution mentioned hereafter, Knut V.

came to the throne. The state of affairs in Danemark, however, is only of indirect interest to us in this history, the one important fact being that, as I have said, that country was separated from the see of Hamburg, the largest province of the Western Church, in 1102, and obtained a metropolitan see of her own, which was founded at Lund. This concession, which was only won after protracted and continued negotiation, caused the liveliest jealousy in the neighbouring countries of Norway and Sweden. Instead of making the see of Lund an entirely separate province under its Danish archbishop for the control of the Church in Danemark, the Pope, only recognizing the Scandinavian provinces as a whole, and Danemark as the most important of the three, transferred the churches of Norway and Sweden from the province of Hamburg to that of Lund, and so practically placed them under subjection to their near, and, as they considered, objectionable neighbour. Moreover, Danemark did not scruple to make use of this new power, and certainly did not trouble herself, either in the persons of her rulers or her priests, to use this new authority in the direction of that peace and goodwill at which the Christian religion is supposed to aim. The neighbouring country of Norway had been united with Danemark under the rule of Knut the Great, but at his death resumed its independence until the beginning of the fourteenth century, when it was joined to Sweden. During the early part of the twelfth century it enjoyed a period of more or less national greatness, which rapidly declined after the death of King Harald IV., in 1136, by the hand of an assassin, and at the time of which we are writing the country was in a state of anarchy and confusion.

Christianity was introduced into Norway at a very early date, but never made much headway till the reign of Olaf II. (S. Olaf) in 1012.

The introduction of the Christian religion into Sweden is said to have been due to the efforts of English missionaries early in the ninth century. Here, as well as in Norway, the old religion of Scandinavian mythology died hard, and without doubt was firmly rooted in the minds of the people for centuries; even as late as 1168, when the great Waldemar I., King of Danemark, invaded the country, he destroyed many heathen temples. Sweden was more independent than either of the other Scandinavian kingdoms, and probably resented the action of the Pope in making Lund the metropolitan see more even than Norway. Eugenius III., too, had lately supplied these two countries, which had been for some years trying unsuccessfully to obtain metropolitan sees of their own, with a precedent, in granting to Ireland the four archbishoprics of that country. And so now the kingdoms of the Scandinavian peninsula decided to appeal direct to Rome, on the ground that if the barbarian island of Erin was granted a group of metropolitans for the petty kingdoms it contained, it could not be tolerated that Norway, Sweden, and Gothland should remain an appanage, as it were, of the church of a neighbouring state.

Each country prepared a separate argument in support of its application, and a magnificent mission appeared at Rome the year before Breakspear's elevation to the cardinalate—the same year, probably, in which Eugenius first set eyes on the English Abbot of S. Rufus.

The Pope agreed to accede to the request of the ambassadors, and promised to send a legate with full powers to found the sees, start the organization of the church, and, moreover, authority to settle disputes; in fact, the Pope was anxious, as most of those who have occupied the chair of S. Peter have always been, to extend and increase the temporal power of his office, as well as its spiritual authority. But now arose the question of whom to send? The hardy Goths and Norsemen, the grandsons of Vikings and of sea-rovers, looked with contempt on the more civilized, softer race, living under the southern sun. The Goths had been to Rome before, and many of them were quite ready again to pour over the rich lands of cis-Alpine Europe. The stern, hard religion of Odin, Thor, and Woden left its traces deeply cut on the national character, and how was the polished, suave, civilized Italian or Provençal to make his way into the hearts and gain the confidence, much less the obedience, of the uncouth and rugged nations of north-west Europe. But Eugenius had seen his man; a keen judge of character, he saw that the Abbot Nicholas combined all those qualities which were essential to the success of the Papal mission: his choice, moreover, was an Englishman, a native of that sturdy race of islanders who were stirring Europe by the spectacle of a new nation, which, while asserting itself in all the councils of Christendom, dared to question now and again the supreme power of the Pontiff. There was much in common between the England of those days and Scandinavia—the same blood, the same indomitable spirit, and, strongest link of all, the similarity of the languages, noticeable even at the present day. Here, then, was the Pope's opportunity, and here the reason why he did not send the abbot back a second time to enforce salutary discipline over his rebellious flock of S. Rufus.

The Pope then, in 1152, appointed Cardinal Breakspear Papal legate, and sent him with a sufficient revenue to settle the affairs of the Church in Norway and Sweden. His instructions were that he had full powers and was admonished to "preach the Gospel of Life in that province" (Norway), " and to use every endeavour to gain the souls of the natives to the honour of the Almighty God."[1] It is recorded that he passed through England on his way to Norway; he probably passed through London, and embarked from the Norfolk coast, but I do not think he could have visited S. Albans, or some record of his visit would surely be found, for the monkish historians would not have been silent on such a point. It seems probable, however, that in some way he communicated with his family upon the journey. Internal evidence from the

---

[1] Muratori, vol. ii., p. 323.

memoirs of Cardinal Boso points strongly to the conclusion that it was at about this date that he became his uncle's secretary, and consequently we may suppose that he was in communication with his relations in England.

The fact of his nephew rising as he did to be cardinal and chamberlain to the Pope, disposes once for all of the supposition that Breakspear was ashamed of his family. With what feelings must he have revisited his beloved native land, which some years before he had left as a wandering beggar, and now entered as the mighty legate of the Pope, with all the magnificence which in those days accompanied such missions! The doors of abbeys and monasteries now flew open to receive him. People flocked for his blessing and his favour, and to wish him God speed on his way. The awful miseries which our country had been passing through had checked, as I have said before, the cultivation of literature, and we have no records of his progress. Here and there throughout the land are lingering traces of his name and traditions of his doings, which, excepting those round his birthplace and S. Albans, can only refer to this, the only visit he ever paid to his native country after his elevation.

Thus Camden[1] mentions that he was once rector of Tydd, in Norfolk, on the confines of Lincolnshire. Now it is quite impossible that Nicholas Breakspear, the Pope, could ever have been this, as I think the references I have

---

[1] Camden, "Brit.," vol. i., p. 550. Neither Lipscombe or Blomfield mention this tradition.

given will have proved; but it is quite possible that he went to Tydd on this occasion, and perhaps obtained the rectorship for some kinsman or namesake.

There is a Breakspear farm[1] in Hampshire, and I think another in Kent, and many other instances of old name-associations which exist, afford an interesting clue to the tracing of his steps. The Archbishop of Canterbury was Theobald, a man who had been given the legative authority by the Pope in the place of Henry of Winchester, the brother of King Stephen. Theobald had taken the side of Henry of Anjou, who was at that time entering England to endeavour to take the crown from the king, who, by the flight of the Empress Matilda to France in 1147, had been left in sole possession of his ruined kingdom. The Pope was against Stephen and for Henry of Anjou, another instance of his knowledge of men. It is probable then that the legate to Norway met the Archbishop, though on account of the king's quarrel with the bishops, a quarrel which brought his brother Henry to side with Theobald of Canterbury against him, he did not actually meet the king.

Breakspear's spirit must have revolted at the condition of our Church at that time. Coventry Cathedral was a fortress; Ramsey Abbey held as a fortified place by Mandeville; other religious houses sacked and destroyed. Indeed, he must have felt that the strong man was required more in

---

[1] The Breakspear farm near S. Albans probably took its name from one of his family.

his native land than in that to which he was travelling. The cardinal sailed for Norway, and landed there on July 19th, 1152. He found the country in a state of great confusion. The throne was occupied by the three sons of the murdered King Harald, and the inevitable results of ambition and jealousy followed. The eldest was a man of loose and wild character, Sigurd; the other two were named Inge and Eystein. Inge was the most popular of the three, and deservedly so, for he was the opposite to his eldest brother, being indeed a benevolent and virtuous man; but about the time of Breakspear's arrival a serious quarrel was taking place between the brothers, accompanied of course by civil war between their followers and adherents. The quarrel began with a murder committed by a Norwegian nobleman, who killed the brother of a lady who was receiving the compromising attentions of Sigurd; this nobleman was in the service of Inge, who shielded his follower against the efforts of his brother to punish him for his crime. Eystein sided with Sigurd, though we are told he showed more moderation than his brother, and it would appear that there was some justification or excuse for the crime, according to the standard of that age, for the frail lady in question was the cause of intrigue against Inge himself. The Pope's legate intervened; for he insisted on settling the dispute before deigning to listen to any proposals as to the church. The brothers, who would have earned the execration of all classes of their subjects had the legate returned without bringing about the popular desire of the people, bent to his imperious will, and agreed that the matter should be referred to the arbitration of the cardinal. He succeeded in reconciling Sigurd and Inge to each other, while the former and Eystein were made to do severe penance for various crimes of which they were proved guilty.[1] Now came the real work of his visit. In the cathedral of Nidrosia, or Nidaros, the name of the province under the immediate rule of Sigurd, reposed the bones of the holy S. Olaf; and this city was selected for the honour of the archbishopric of Norway. It is the modern Drontheim, and still the seat of the head of the church. Jone, or John (the son of Byrgen), Bishop of Stavanger, was invested with the pallium at an imposing ceremony attended by the three reconciled princes. The see or province of Drontheim, or rather Nidrosia, was made one of great importance. The Shetlands and the Western Islands of Scotland, together with the Isle of Man, were taken from the see of Sodor and Man in the province of York, and added to the new province, under which they remained for 200 years; the Norwegian sees of Apsloe, Bergen, and Stavanger, the Orcades (Orkneys), Hebrides, and Furo (Faroe) Islands, the two divisions of Iceland, and Greenland were also added, as well as a new Norwegian bishopric, that of Hammer, to which he appointed Arnold, Bishop of Greenland. These arrangements necessarily occupied some time, and were not completed till late in the year.

---

[1] Torfæus states this on the authority of Morkinskinna.

The people of Norway having now got all that they had been working for for years, and actually being given a metropolitan see of their own, were ready to throw themselves at the feet of Breakspear. All honour was ascribed to him, and his character and firmness being in such sharp contrast to their own rulers, he became the hero of the whole nation, and was certainly the most powerful man in Norway at that date. He was asked to inaugurate civil reforms of government far beyond the powers which he had been invested with, while all difficulties and complaints, both public and private, were brought to him for settlement.

He thoroughly reformed the church, swept it of abuses, and severely checked the mixture of heathen practices which had been allowed to creep into the Catholic ritual. He also bound the Norwegian Church to the payment of Peter's pence.[1] More than all this, he recommended and caused laws to be introduced for the furtherance of civil peace and the due execution of justice, such as the prohibition of private persons carrying arms in the streets and the regulation of private property. He even limited the bodyguard of the kings. Snorrow, the historian, relates that no foreigner ever came to Norway who was so honoured, or whose memory is so cherished as that of Nicholas Breakspear. To this day his name is mentioned among the greatest in Norwegian history, and is included among the national saints.

[1] Torfæus, "Hist. Rer. Norweg.," pars iii., lib. ix., cap. 12; also Munter.

His departure caused universal lamentation, and he was loaded with presents; in return he promised the Norwegian people that he would never forget them or their interests, and would always do all that lay in his power to help them.

It is satisfactory to be able to record that in those days, as in ours, an Englishman's word was to be relied on; for in after years, when he was Pope, all Norwegians who came to Rome were treated by him with the greatest consideration, and he also sent architects and masons from Italy to Norway to assist in the building of the cathedral for the new see of Hammer. On his death, as already mentioned, the people revered him as a saint.

After leaving Norway, the Papal legate proceeded to Sweden, then under the rule of King Swercus. His fame had preceded him, and he was received with all the honour that the authorities could command. Here he had no civil disputes to settle before beginning the special objects of his mission; on the contrary, the differences lay in the church itself. The church in Sweden of that day consisted of two parts, that of Gothland and that of Sweden, always rivals; and there was here reproduced on a smaller scale, and from the same causes, a state of affairs similar to that existing between Danemark, Sweden, and Norway before the legate came; each section, that is to say, claimed the right to have the archbishopric, the one declining to be in any sense considered the inferior of the other. Here was a difficulty for the cardinal to solve requiring all his power and all his skill. He called a synod in the city of Lingkopin to endeavour to fix on a see which would satisfy all parties; but the clergy would not agree, the Swedish bishops loudly asserting that Upsala was the right place, while the Gothlanders were equally clamorous that Skara should have the honour. By so doing they, as is often the case, found that divided counsels had ruined the hopes of both, for the legate made up his mind not to create a province for Sweden at all. This he was wise enough to keep to himself till he had executed those reforms in the church which he desired, and had regulated the payment of Peter's pence. He then created S. Henry of Upsala bishop of that city, and departed for Danemark. The head of the Danish Church at this time was Eskill, Archbishop of Lund, who naturally was vexed at Breakspear's action in detaching the see of Nidrosia from his province, and in creating it an independent province; though, it must be added, he received him with all the honour and pomp due to his office. Breakspear's diplomacy on the occasion was masterly enough. He handed over to the Archbishop of Lund the pallium which had been intended for the new primate of Sweden, and informed him that when the difficulties in the church of that country were settled, he would still allow the Archbishop of Lund to be styled Primate of all Sweden, and granted him the right of consecrating and investing with the pallium the future archbishops of that kingdom; he further promised to obtain him a grant from the Holy See, adding to the dignity of his archiepiscopal titles "Titulus Legati nati Apostolicæ Sedis" in the three Scandinavian kingdoms.

We now come to another case in which the Papal legate interposed in the civil affairs of a kingdom, and used his influence to affect its councils, though, unfortunately, not with the same success as in the case of Norway. Swercus, King of Sweden, had a son, by name John, who was renowned for his wildness and bad character, caused not only by his own naturally evil disposition, but by a total neglect of education, religious or secular.

This young man, who was quite beyond his father's control, helped by a band of companions as evil as himself, made a raid on the residence of his eldest brother Carlos, and carried off his wife and her widowed sister, two princesses nearly related to the reigning family of Danemark, and dishonoured them. This unheard-of atrocity, made worse by the knowledge of the unsullied fame of the two sisters, naturally caused the deepest indignation, not only in the King of Danemark, Sweno, but in all his subjects, and he decided to raise a fleet and army, and to invade Sweden and Gothland to revenge the outrage. His intention was furthermore strengthened by the remembrance of another unsettled feud between the two nations: Sweno's predecessor on the throne was Nicholas, whose intended bride Swercus himself had carried off by false representation, and had married. Nicholas was unable to go to war with Sweden owing to civil war in his own kingdom, so the insult had been unavenged. Sweno under the second provocation felt doubly resolved to appeal to the arbitration of the sword. All this happened while Nicholas Breakspear was in Danemark, and he sought an audience of King Sweno, and pointed out to him various cogent reasons why the war should not take place, showing how serious an obstacle the sea presented to any expedition, the risk involved in leaving his own country, and the like; but when did considerations of peril deter a brave and strong-willed man? These arguments failing, Breakspear tried to stop him on religious grounds, but with no effect. The king listened respectfully, but would neither be persuaded by the legate or by the ambassadors from Swercus, who came over from Sweden in the cause of peace.

Breakspear is reported to have said: "If the spider by disembowelling herself at least caught the flies she gave chase to, yet the Danes could expect nothing but destruction to themselves in their proposed campaign."[1] The end of it all was that war broke out, and Sweno managed to land a large army on the Swedish coast without much opposition, owing to the fact that the prime cause of the war, Prince John, who had been directed to levy troops to resist the invasion, met his deserts by being killed by the Swedes in a riot on account of his conduct having occasioned the war. Swercus feigned a retreat before the forces of Sweno, and led them far into savage Finland,

---

[1] Joannes Magnus, "Hist. Gott.," lib. xviii., cap. 17.

where his army was surrounded and almost entirely destroyed. Sweno made good his retreat to Danemark; but shortly afterwards was murdered in his bed by two of his nobles who were in secret league with Swercus. During the progress of this disastrous war, the results of which fully justified his foresight, Breakspear left Danemark on his return to Rome, having executed his mission, and gained by his marvellous success the title of "The Apostle of the North." Fagrskinn, Archbishop of Lund *circa* 1250, styles him "The Good."[1] He probably journeyed back to Rome by way of the Low Countries and eastern France. He arrived in Rome early in 1154 to find his friend and patron, Eugenius III., dead, the events of whose closing years are described in the next chapter. The stormy days which marked the last years of the Cistercian monk had given place to a lull, and a peaceful, quiet old man of ninety years of age, Conrad, Bishop of Sabina, by birth a Roman, occupied the Papal chair under the name of Anastasius IV. His benevolence and charity during a famine in Rome earned him the love of the poor; his reign was uneventful; he received Breakspear well, and confirmed all his acts, save that he reserved to Rome the right to appoint the primate of Sweden, thus taking away the privilege which Nicholas had granted to Eskill, Archbishop of Lund. Anastasius sent three bulls confirming the legate's action: one to the Bishop of Sweden, exhorting him to stop

---

[1] Torfæus.

ADRIAN IV.

the quarrelling in his flock, and to bring them into obedience to Rome; another to Swercus and the nobles of Sweden, directing them to obey the laws Nicholas had made for them; and a third confirming the foundation of the church at Trund. The first two are dated November 28th, and the last, November 30th, 1154. Anastasius died on December 3rd, and it is probable that the signing of the bull confirming the church at Trund was the last official act of his life. As the legate would certainly seek to have his acts confirmed at the earliest possible moment, we may assume that Nicholas did not return to Rome until the November of 1154. Anastasius remained in office one year and five months, and died at Rome.

After his death, the conclave of cardinals met in the cathedral of S. Peter to elect his successor. After prayer to the Almighty all the cardinals with one voice elected Nicholas Breakspear to be the successor of S. Peter. All accounts agree in the unanimity of the choice, and his favourite secretary, Boso, relates that he at first refused; but all the clergy and laity alike, taking no heed of his words, shouted, "Pope Adrian, elected by God!"[1] So at last the humble Englishman, the poor student, the modest monk, abbot, bishop, cardinal, and missionary, was called to occupy the position of the greatest and most fearful responsibility upon the earth of those days. What a moment! What a life! Thirty years from poverty to Pope. And

---

[1] "Papam Adrianum a Deo electum." (Muratori.)

what a vista opened out before him! At his age, he might reasonably hope for twenty or thirty years of power, and if he lived as long as his predecessor, forty years.

Mercifully our future lies behind the veil, hidden from our eyes. He could not tell that within five short years he would be called into the presence of the Master whom he had just been chosen to represent on earth; but if he had known this, and had determined to crowd into that short time all the stirring events and great deeds that he could wish for, he could not have made it fuller than it actually proved to be.

By sheer merit and force of character he had risen step by step to the topmost rung of the ladder, never flinching, never losing his head, overcoming every obstacle with indomitable courage, and, above all, with that simple faith and clear character which has ever helped those who, on the thorny path to greatness, have been blessed with these invaluable and divine gifts. And the great example! How many a heart must have thrilled in England as the news slowly reached our island kingdom; how many a lad must have dreamed of similar possibilities for himself; how many a weary worker must have been cheered by the thought of the fellow-countryman who had hewn destiny for himself, making his own friends who had none to help him at the start, gathering his store of learning in the face of apparent hopelessness, and with every drawback winning in the race—chosen unanimously by the proud cardinalate of Rome to rule over the destinies of the Holy Church, to take precedence of emperors, kings, and princes, to stand up before the world unsullied by it in a vicious age, to remain unspoilt and staunch throughout the years he held his glorious charge. And does his life teach nothing to us? Can we see nothing to help us in our march through life? Most assuredly, as his figure rises majestically before our eyes looking across seven centuries, it gives us the message that in all ages and under all changes of the conditions of life, truth and honesty are unchangeable, and honour unsullied is in every age the seal and stamp of our greatest men.

CHAPTER V.

The Church in the Twelfth Century—The Monastic Movement—The Crusades—Bernard of Clairvaulx—His Teaching—Peter Abelard—The Council of Sens—Arnold of Brescia—His Opinions—Condition of Rome—Effect of the Second Crusade—Frederic Barbarossa crosses the Alps—Adrian's Difficulties.

BEFORE relating the events of the pontificate of Adrian IV., it will be as well to consider the condition of affairs not only in Rome itself in the year of his election, but the general state of the Catholic Church at that period.

The movement known to students of Church history as that of Arnold of Brescia had its birth far earlier than the times of which I am writing, and the history of it is so complicated and far-reaching that it will be necessary to give some short account of the causes which led up to the state of things with which the new Pope had to deal. There is not space here for anything more than a sketch of this interesting phase of Christian history; those who care for further information will find it in the authorities from whom I quote. Some study of it is, however, necessary, as the policy of Adrian IV. was entirely moulded and shaped to meet the adverse spirit of which I am about to relate the existence and the growth. The most remarkable features of Church history of the first half of the twelfth century were the increased thirst for what has been termed religious adventure, and the rapidly growing development of the monastic system, which like a meteor flashed across the century, and, to a large extent, died out almost as rapidly as it rose. Monasteries would be founded, and after a few years internal dissension, outside interests, or some other cause would bring about their ruin, perhaps to rise again, but more often to disappear—the buildings to fall into decay, or to be re-born as feudal fortresses or noblemen's castles. This may seem to a modern student inconsistent with the devotional, even superstitious character of the age; but on careful thought it will be found to be the natural result of the restless spirit which everywhere was working in the minds of men. It was the period preceding the birth of the intellectual movement, and these were the thoers which heralding the event shook the mental balance of the world —reason struggling for freedom. The one apparently perfect organization, the only thing firm in an age of cataclysm, was the Church.

The provinces, the bishoprics, the parishes all formed the various links of chains leading up to the highest power on earth, the Pontiff. But this perfect organization was in reality fettered, though mankind could not see it at the time, and everywhere men were chafing with the desire to do something or to go somewhere, to strike a blow for the Holy Church, to win the spurs of chivalry, or in some way find that action which they thought would bring quiet to their troubled minds.

The age was a military one; armies were blessed by the Church—the crusader's sword was wellnigh as sacred as the chalice. Thousands flocked to the Holy Wars; but all could not do this, and so the ever-resourceful intellect of man provided the thought of warring against the powers of evil. The military spirit asserted itself here. Spiritually a man is always at war within himself, his good impulses arrayed against his evil temptations.

This produced the revival of the monasteries; this proved the outlet and opportunity for zeal and enthusiasm; and in the humble cell, cut off from the world, men thought that the severing for ever of all connection with the pomps and ambitions of life—denial of place, rank, and power, surrender of riches, renunciation of lusts and appetites, adoption of celibacy and fasting—would afford them in their meditation the comfort of hope in Christ and satisfy their longing for action in the form of constant battle against the evil one. Besides this, there was the constant individual prayer, the sense of immediate communion with God Himself, and the support of the Cross by the contemplation of the sufferings of His Son. This impulse spread all over England, France, and Italy; even under the calamities of Stephen's reign fresh monasteries were created in our country; and in Germany the extension of monasteries was almost as rapid as in the south and west of Europe. Everywhere men of all ranks flocked to lay down their riches and enter the holy life. One of the central figures of this movement was the great S. Bernard, who was an example of the more consistent among the ranks of the enthusiasts.

He was born in 1091 of noble parents, and educated completely in all that pertained to the religious life by his mother, a lady of noble birth and a model of piety and charity. When she died Bernard stood at the parting of the ways. On the one hand was the world; he was young, high-born, handsome, and rich; all that the court could offer, all the dazzling temptations of a brilliant life were at his command. On the other hand were the prospects of what I may call the "worldly" church if he was so minded; its wealth might turn his way, powerful position be within his grasp, nay, even the chair of S. Peter itself. But Bernard would not so much as look on either of these brilliant prospects; he turned his head away. We are told[1] of the struggle it cost him, of his temptations and of his natural feelings; but he remained firm, and left the glittering scene to seek out the poorest monastery he could find. We cannot pause here to relate how he brought with him by his example more than thirty of his friends; how the humble Cistercian monastery grew too small for his followers; how his brilliant eloquence thrilled the world; nor can we dwell on the founding of his own abbey of Clairvaulx in Champagne, in a valley notorious for its evil deeds. We can only wonder at the irresistible influence of the man, and note the deep impress that he left on his age. His fame and

[1] "The Life of S. Bernard." (William the Abbot.)

his power spread in all directions; Clairvaulx became the metropolis of the whole monastic community; it sent out its branches into all countries; it laid down the rules for all kindred foundations.

Bernard was consulted by all, by kings as well as prelates, and his power extended even to the Pope himself. He steadily refused all ecclesiastical preferment, and lived through his nobly consistent life as simple Abbot of Clairvaulx.

Meanwhile we must watch this sudden rise of monasticism, and try to account for its almost equally sudden decline. This latter may be attributed principally, if not wholly, to the effects of sudden and unexpected accession of riches. The reaction from the poverty which distinguished the religious orders before this time, and which assimilated them close to the practical lesson of our Lord's life, to the worldly prosperity consequent on the wave of enthusiasm among the noble and wealthy classes, proved too great a strain for human self-denial and self-control. In an eloquent passage Dean Milman tells us of the result[1]: "Most of the old monasteries which held the rule either of S. Benedict or of Cassian had become wealthy, and suffered the usual effects of wealth. Some had altogether relaxed their discipline, had renounced poverty; and the constant dissensions, the appeals to the bishop, to the metropolitan, or where, as

[1] I would recommend all interested in this wonderful movement to read closely the whole of chapter iv. of book viii., vol. vi., Milman, "Latin Christianity," from which this quotation is taken.

SAINT BERNARD,
ABBOT OF CLAIRVAULX.

they all strove to do, they had obtained exemption from episcopal jurisdiction, to the Pope, showed how entirely the other great vow, obedience to the abbot or prior, had become obsolete. . . . Even where the discipline was still severe, it was monotonous, to some extent absolute; its sanctity was exacted, habitual, unawakening. All old establishments are impatient of innovation. . . . Monasticism had been and ever was tracing the same cycle. Now the wilderness, the utter solitude, the utmost poverty, the contest with the stubborn forest and unwholesome morass, the most exalted piety, the devotion which had not hours enough during the day and night for its exercise, the rule which could not be enforced too strictly . . . the inventive self-discipline, . . . the boastful servility of obedience; then the fame for piety, the lavish offerings of the faithful, the grants of the repentant lord, the endowments of the remorseful king—the opulence, the power, the magnificence.

"The wattled hut, the rock-hewn hermitage, is now the stately cloister; the lowly church of wood the lofty and gorgeous abbey; the wild forest or heath the pleasant and umbrageous grove; the marsh a domain of intermingling meadow and cornfields; the brawling stream or mountain torrent a succession of quiet tanks or pools fattening innumerable fish. The superior, once a man bowed to the earth with humility, careworn, pale, emaciated, with a coarse habit bound with a cord, with naked feet, is become an abbot on his curvetting palfrey, in rich attire, with his silver cross borne before him, travelling to take his place amid the lordliest of the realm." It was at this time, when the rigid asceticism of the monastic orders was giving way under the temptation of opulence and luxury, that the majestic form of the Abbot of Clairvaulx appeared on the scene and showed to the astonished world the effect of strong example and courage. He from his strictly disciplined abbey in the lonely valley of Wormwood in Champagne literally ruled the world. At his word sovereigns gave way, and even popes bowed before his authority. When the Catholic Church was torn asunder by the disputes of Pope and Anti-pope, all Europe looked to Bernard with hope as the one man who remained firm and unaffected by the contagion of corruption.

Bernard was of the Church, for the Church, with the Church. His whole life was spent in the endeavour to strengthen her power and to render her authority final and absolute. His belief was that unless and until the world was brought—each nation subject in all things, temporal as well as spiritual—to the sway of S. Peter, there would be no hope of salvation. Rigidly he fixed his gaze on this one goal; no room would he allow for difference or divergence. Strong himself, he expected all to bend before his inflexible will; he was ever on the watch to detect heresy or schism either in his own country, or wherever it was found to be showing a head. Bernard was the prototype of those stern good men who are hard on themselves and equally hard on others. I cannot but add that much as we may admire his consistency and his character, it must not be forgotten that such hardness is scarcely consistent with the gentleness of the teaching of Christ, and in all ages has had its evil as well as its beneficial effect on public and private life. This spirit shows itself when at its worst in bigotry and intolerance, and has led many an earnest man to condone murder at the stake. It shows itself at each extreme, in Puritan narrow-mindedness as much as in Roman bigotry or Calvinistic pride of self. Only now and again can the dangerous doctrine of unyielding dogma be really beneficial, and then only in the mind of the right man. Having said so much, we may well believe that Bernard was that man, and that he literally saved the Church at a most critical period of her history.

We have to trace his influence on one particular set of events, and must leave out all the wonderful and interesting acts of the saint's life which do not bear directly on our subject, such as his treatment of Innocent II., the Councils of Rheims and of Liége, and the Pope's visit to Clairvaulx. We must, in fact, confine ourselves to his action in regard to the lives of the other two men, Abelard, and Arnold of Brescia, who helped to create the difficulties which Adrian IV. had to solve. Peter Abelard was the pioneer in the campaign of intellect against superstition, full of faults perhaps, but still in one sense a martyr and a victim. He was born in 1079 at Nantes in Brittany, and was endowed with talents of a very brilliant order; he was educated in the schools of Paris, where he soon distinguished himself as a keen reasoner and clever professor of dialectics, eventually founding a school of thought of his own.

The romantic story of his love and passion for Heloïse is well known, and need only be mentioned here as being the keynote of his character in after years. It is one of the instances of human love overriding the first considerations of prudence, as well as of honour. While there is nothing but condemnation for the action of Abelard in his base seduction of a girl some twenty years his junior, and his pupil, we cannot but admire, though reason forbids us to accept, the beautiful unselfishness of the woman whose love was so great that she declined to save her honour by marriage rather than be a hindrance to the worldly advance of Abelard. We cannot enter into the story at length; it is well known that she took the veil in the convent of Argenteuil at the advice of Abelard; and that her uncle, whose house had given the opportunity to the master for the meetings with his pupil, was so enraged against the man who had ruined his niece, that he hired some ruffians, who, attacking Abelard, inflicted on him a terrible mutilation, no doubt embittering his whole life, and encouraging the pessimism with which he ever after viewed all human passion. He retired humiliated to the Abbey of S. Denys, and there first encountered the theological difficulties which, combined with vigorous persecution, caused him to found the Paraclete. But we have to deal with Abelard, not in his personal character, but in that of the brilliant thinker, the author of " Sic et non." While Bernard was issuing his edicts from Clairvaulx, Abelard was leading a brilliant school of thought in Paris. These two men were widely different in nature, and it is impossible to conceive either giving way in the smallest point to the other, though, like all earnest men, we can now see that there was much in the aims of each which was actually common to both, though they worked to attain their desired end on entirely different lines. Bernard, as we have seen, believed in and worked for the absolute supremacy of the Church, for blind unreasoning obedience on the part of her children, and for sharp punishment on all who dared to leave the beaten track of the narrow road pointed out by her fathers. Abelard, on the other hand, as a calm logician and reasoner, was, like all great thinkers, not only far in advance of his times, but completely misunderstood. He posed as the champion of the emancipation of intellect, of the right of reasoning, and as we have pointed out the danger which besets characters such as Bernard, so we may easily see that if pure reason is carried to its conclusion without faith, it must end in scepticism or unbelief. It was impossible that two such men should live in the same age and not come in conflict; especially when, as in Bernard's case, one of them was always watching for the first signs of any unorthodox movement. All the forces at the powerful abbot's command were brought to bear in a stern persecution of Abelard, and needless to say the strong power of Bernard completely crushed the weak, unhappy, mutilated being in whom, nevertheless, he recognized a foe worthy of his mettle. But as well try to stop the rising tide, as attempt to check any great intellectual movement when once the pioneer thought has given it birth; Bernard could crush Abelard, but it was beyond his power to stop the effect of his teaching.

For five hundred years the world of intellect had slept, except at the rare intervals when a lambent ray of light flashed out, only to contrast more strongly with the darkness, which soon enveloped it again.

Abelard appeared and roused it; his arguments may have been sound or unsound, his philosophy logical or the reverse—that is not the point. The point is that he taught men once more to reason for themselves. Reflect for a moment on the import of the following words at a time such as the beginning of the twelfth century:

"So it happened[1] that I was the first to apply myself to the study of the foundations of belief,[2] bringing to bear thereon analogies drawn from human understanding; and I wrote a theological tract on the Divine Unity and Trinity, which I gave to my pupils, who insisted on having physical and philosophical reasons for everything, reasons such as they could really comprehend, and not merely repeat. They contended that the mere utterance of words, unless the intellect grasped their import, was valueless, and nothing could be believed which was not first understood. They added that it was obviously absurd for any man to attempt to preach to others about what he neither under-

[1] "Petri Abælardi Opera, Hist. Calam.," cap. 9, *ab init.*
[2] ". . . . fidei nostræ fundamentum . . . ."

stood himself nor had the power to make them understand. . . ."

Nothing could be believed unless it was first understood. With what a shock must these words have fallen on a world which had been taught for generation after generation that individual reasoning was sinful, that the message of the Church was to be accepted and believed in silence!

The result therefore is not surprising, and we cannot wonder at his enemies demanding his instant punishment.

The whole body of Catholics denounced him as a heretic; but Abelard had the most marvellous moral courage in this instance at least. He stood with his back against the wall, and dared his formidable foes to make good their charges of heresy — a challenge which was taken up.[1] A great council had been convened at Sens for the translation of the body of the national saint; all the splendour of the Church was there, together with Louis VII. and his court. It was decided that this council was also to hear the arguments of Abelard, and decide the case.

A great testimony to Abelard's skill as an orator and logician is that Bernard rather shrank from appearing. He says in a letter to the Pope: "How shall an unpractised stripling like myself, unversed in logic, meet the giant who is practised in every kind of debate?"[2] But he decided after all to appear; and what an unequal tournament!

[1] June 2nd and 3rd, 1140.   [2] "Epist. ad Innocent Papam."

Bernard, the practical head of the Church, who could depose popes and overawe kings, the man on whose words the whole world waited, backed up by all the powers, spiritual and secular, against the discredited philosopher, friendless, persecuted, his moral character stained. We are told by one of Abelard's disciples that what little he said was sarcastic, cutting, and incisive—" we know that on your will depends the mercy of heaven," " the very devils are thought to roar at thy behest,"—two examples of language which must have made Bernard writhe. The world waited for the result; when Abelard took everyone by surprise, refused to plead, and appealed to Rome. He was sentenced by the Council to be condemned to silence, and his disciples to excommunication. It is not clear why Abelard took this step; it was a fatal one, for what little chance he had of justice was from the combined opinion of the assembled ecclesiastics at Sens. He had no prospect of even a fair hearing at Rome, for Innocent II. was completely in the power of Bernard, and allowed himself always to be guided by him. But we are near the end of his life; he set out for his journey, and on his way stopped at the Abbey of Clugny. Whether he suddenly altered his mind and determined on flight is not known, but he never proceeded any further. After a brief stay within the hospitable shelter of the abbey, he was taken with a mortal illness, and soon the wearied, chafing spirit was at rest.

It is pleasant to record that the venerable and gentle

Abbot, Peter of Clugny was more truly Christian in this case than his hard brother of Clairvaulx, and made the last moments of the so-called heretic as peaceful and as happy as it was possible for a faithful priest of God to do. So Bernard won; his adversary was routed even to death; the authority of the Church was vindicated; surely now she might rest again undisturbed. And Bernard never saw it really disturbed again; but though he knew it not, the seed that Abelard sowed was to bear fruit. Then if ever the Church of Rome had an opportunity of leading the intellectual thought of the age. The opportunity was missed, with the unfortunate result that the followers of Abelard were obliged to carry on the development of their principles in secret, a course which history teaches us invariably leads to revolution and violence. It is only where a strong ruler or government has the forethought to anticipate popular feeling that reforms can be carried out peaceably and according to law. S. Bernard undoubtedly felt that a great issue was at stake, and his summing up of Abelard's arguments is tersely expressed in his letter to the Pope, which, owing to Abelard's death, Innocent never had to act upon. He says: "Inasmuch as Abelard is prepared to explain everything by means of reason, he combats faith and reason too; for what is so contrary to reason as to wish to go beyond the limits of reason, by means of reason? And what more contrary to faith, than to be unwilling to believe that which one is unable to reach by means of reason?"

And now we see the effects of the teaching of the ascetic of the Paraclete. He had led an attack on the spiritual ascendency of the Church, as a kind of intellectual insurrection against her doctrines. But he did not live to take part in the attack on her temporal power which followed. She defeated and discomfited his followers at Sens, and now they turned their forces against her weakest side. I cannot enter into the complicated events which led to the rivalry of Pope and Anti-pope; but it was this rivalry which fostered, if it did not produce, the growing spirit of independence in Italy. The Emperors, whose title of authority was certainly admitted, very seldom appeared on the southern side of the Alps. The result of this absence and of the divisions at the Vatican was that the Lombard cities formed themselves into separate and independent republics, which repudiated the authority of Rome or the Emperor. The repudiation brought them into conflict with the representatives of the Church; much discontent, helped by the reforming party, was engendered; and as in these days, when an agitator is wanted, he is generally to be found, so then the country soon swarmed with demagogues who found it easy, and no doubt often lucrative, to tickle the public ear by denouncing the laxity and corruption of the ecclesiastical body, and even by inveighing against the whole influence of the Church. It must not be supposed that Arnold of Brescia, on whose career I am about to dwell, was by any means the first to utter such denunciations. As early as 1119, when Calixtus II. was Pope, one Peter de

Bruis tried to bring about a revolution against several of the doctrines of the Church. Again, Arnulf, in 1125, managed actually to get into Rome itself, but the people would not hear him, and he was seized and thrown bound into the Tiber. In 1134, Henry the Hermit obtained a considerable following. The corruption which, as we have seen, had begun to spread in the monasteries, and the preaching of Abelard combined to open the public mind, and at the right moment appears the dramatic figure of Arnold of Brescia. Of the youth and early life of Arnold we know little except that he was born in the city from which he has taken the name, probably about 1105. He was both ambitious and clever, but had a larger stock of enthusiasm than of judgment. Like Nicholas Breakspear he travelled into France to pursue his studies, and found his way to Paris, where he became an enthusiastic pupil of Abelard—"Goliath's armour-bearer," as Bernard scornfully described him at the Council of Sens, and he afterwards proved that the title was a true one. But while he imbibed much of his master's spirit and learning, he gained none of that deep desire to inquire into the mysteries of religion which was so marked in Abelard. In him the ruling passion was to act the liberator; he devoured the pages of Livy and other classic writers, and dwelt with ardour on the principles of heathen philosophy, republicanism, and the ancient grandeur of the Senate of Rome. On the other hand he had learnt in the Paraclete to view the doctrines of the Church with faith and devotion, and recognizing that no questioning about the mysteries of faith could bring one nearer to the great truth, it never occurred to him to indulge in such speculation. His genius was practical, and there was work lying nearer to the hand—work in which success meant some tangible result achieved.

Around him he saw a wealthy clerical body, living in splendour, in luxury, and often, it must be confessed, in open sin. Simony and concubinage were the too common vices of a demoralized clergy. How was all this reconcilable with the teaching of the New Testament, and of Him whose life was moulded on so different a pattern? If to follow Christ meant to bear His Cross, to suffer His crown of thorns, what need had the abbot of his gorgeously caparisoned palfrey or the bishop of his costly retinue of servants. The contention of Bernard that it was the office, not the individual, which was glorified by such magnificence, appealed not at all to the glowing mind of the young reformer.

Following the lessons of his master and devoting himself to a still closer study of the classics, he soon arrived at the conviction that he was born to remedy the religious and political abuses of his age. We have described above his view of the state of the actual Church; his ideal church was a purely spiritual one, working for spiritual ends only, whose ministers would be humble, but earnest followers of the Master. He would take from the Church all its privileges, all its wealth, its land, its money, its dues, and force the clergy to support themselves on the freewill offerings of the people. He could conceive of no other use for property than that it should be held by the sovereign for the common good. A great Christian commonwealth with laws modelled on the best of the ancient philosophy; Rome the centre of the world in all her old time grandeur; everyone working for the good of all, and no one for the transitory purposes of his own immediate gain. "A beautiful Utopia indeed!" one is almost tempted to exclaim, but one which, like all other theories based on an equality which does not exist, will, as long as human nature shall endure, be realized in the imagination only. If, at the close of the nineteenth century, amid all the potent forces of our boasted civilization, we regard the Socialist and the Liberator as dreamers, what name can we apply to the man who attempted to promulgate such doctrines among the untutored intellects and savage natures of the early mediæval times? And it is only just to point out that, like all dreamers, Arnold was one-sided in his judgment; his enthusiasm only enabled him to see the abuse of riches in the Church, and failed to show him that she must, if she was to live, have the means necessary to carry out her mission, to keep up her dignity, to relieve her poorer members, and to maintain the worship of God; not to mention the training of her sons and the mission work of bringing fresh sheep to the fold.

We must now revert to the Council of Sens, and trace Arnold's subsequent career. Bernard, in ordering the condemnation of Abelard, decreed also that Arnold should be incarcerated in a convent; but he managed to evade the authorities and fled to Zurich, then, owing to its freedom and its proximity to the republics of Lombardy, as well as to its trade with both Germany and Italy, the most flourishing town in Switzerland, and from that place, where he was enthusiastically received, he preached and spread his new doctrine. The tide of public opinion was in his favour, and everywhere events were quickening to help on his career of reform.

In the city of Brescia a conflict between bishop, as representing the imperial interests, and people had resulted in the defeat of the former. Innocent II., a somewhat weak man, hesitated, and at length, perhaps hoping to quiet things by concessions, or because he regarded the Emperor as a more serious foe than Arnold, leant towards the populace. This strengthened the hands of Arnold enormously, and his preaching became more and more socialistic. Whether his ideas were properly understood by the people is doubtful, but matters little; they at least comprehended that the immediate result of his teaching would be to take the wealth from the clerical party and to place it in their own hands. Arnold was proclaimed a liberator; his name was honoured, and his praises were in everyone's mouth. The man who preaches a doctrine of spoliation, which, however disinterested or noble in conception, tends to weaken the distinction between " meum " and " tuum," is always assured of a considerable following.

In Rome itself the spirit of independence was growing

rapidly. Tivoli, Palestrina, Tusculum, and Albano had all tried to throw off the Roman yoke and secure their independence, and in 1143 the Romans themselves, on Innocent II. concluding a treaty with the first-named city against their wishes, burst out into open rebellion, defied the Church's authority, and set up a senate which declared the papal government at an end and the ancient republic restored. Innocent tried hard to make head against this movement, invoked a synod at the Lateran, and made a protest; but he had neither the spirit nor the power to check the insubordination of the republicans, who emboldened to further effort saw in their imagination Rome restored to her former high place among the nations— Rome the secular no less than the spiritual head of the world. In the intoxication of their ambition they called on the Emperor Conrad to return and take his place as their king. Conrad, either doubting the fickle nature of a mob, or because he feared the papal authority, refused, and though all preparations were made for his coming, did not appear, and perhaps lost thereby the chance of altering the history of Rome. The same year saw the death of Innocent, broken-hearted and full of grief. Celestine II., who succeeded, had been himself a pupil of Abelard, and moreover had, as Cardinal of Castello, befriended Arnold, who took advantage of this to appear in Rome. Celestine died only six months after his accession, and was succeeded by Lucius II., a Bolognese by birth. The republic, strengthened by the peace of the short pontificate of his predecessor, was more bold than ever, and announced to the Pope their intention to acknowledge his spiritual authority and nothing beyond. Lucius was a man of firm character, but found it impossible to stem the rising tide, which eventually assailed even his spiritual powers by electing a brother of the Anti-pope Analectus to be "Patrician," and to usurp the power of the papal prefect. The populace were delighted at this encroachment on the power of the Church, and in the riots which ensued destroyed many of the buildings in Rome, including some of the palaces of the cardinals. Finally, in the year 1145, Lucius II., going in person at the head of the pontifical troops to expostulate with the rioters, in one of these outbreaks was struck by a stone and killed.

It was at this moment that Bernard of Clairvaulx thought it necessary to step into the breach, and, as we have seen, also thought that in electing Eugenius III., the Cistercian abbot, he had a tool ready made to his hands.

I have already dwelt on the character of Eugenius; he dealt with affairs as he found them with some firmness. The Roman mob burst in upon his election, and angrily demanded him to recognize the authority of the senate. He made no answer, but left the city, and the election was completed at the Convent of Forsa. He then retired to Viterbo, and from there commenced to launch anathemas at his persecutors. At length a reconciliation was effected, the Pope agreeing to recognize the senate on condition that those only whom he approved should be elected, and that the patrician should give way to the papal legate. He triumphantly entered the Eternal City, and celebrated Christmas, 1145. But the peace was short-lived, and fresh riots taking place, he was compelled to flee from Rome.

It may now be asked why Bernard did not come himself, and with his strong personality redress the evil state into which the government had fallen. I think the answer to this is to be found in the second crusade, to which I have already alluded. He hoped by this to re-establish the weakened power of the Church, and to a very considerable extent he succeeded.

Bernard had a very low opinion of the Romans. He says:[1] "What is so well known to the world as their licence and pride . . . ." "They are ever given to sedition." "They strive after the appearance of being feared by all, while in fact they fear everybody." And again, "They cannot endure submission, but yet know not how to rule." No doubt he expected the second crusade to right the wrong at home as well as abroad. We know how disastrously it failed in the Holy Land; but it produced consequences of some moment. The Pope, being brought into close contact with the most powerful sovereigns of Europe, had taken advantage of the opportunity to make alliances and to strengthen his authority. The Romans, who had at first laughed at the papal displeasure, were gradually beginning to regret their hasty action, when they saw

---

[1] "De Consideratione," lib. iv., cap. 2.

that it led to the glories of Rome as the centre of the religious world being transferred to other places and to other countries, and many of those who had been foremost in the revolution began to have doubts as to whether they had not paid too great a price for civil liberty. Eugenius, whose firm nature was combined with generosity and mildness, was until his death in 1153 becoming more and more popular. Bernard of Clairvaulx and his Cistercian namesake died in the same year, the former never recovering from the shock of the failure of his efforts to free the Holy Land; he leaves behind him the foremost name in the history of the Church of the twelfth century.

Anastasius IV., as we have seen, enjoyed a reign free from internal troubles, and we may now look round on the aspect of affairs which the new Pope had to face.

Arnold of Brescia had found his power much undermined during the reign of Eugenius; but Rome was still governed by the senate, and as their mouthpiece Arnold had, on the death of the Emperor Conrad, invited his successor, Frederic Barbarossa, nephew of Conrad, to come and receive the imperial crown from the senate. The great Emperor refused, owing to the insolent terms in which the letter was worded, whereupon the republic determined by the advice of Arnold to choose an emperor for themselves.

No additional incentive was required to induce Frederic to cross the Alps and reassert the power of the emperor over Italy. Frederic Barbarossa is another of the brilliant cluster of commanding men who lived at this period. He was a prince of the most unbounded ambition, proud, assertive, and powerful; unquestionably the most striking figure among those who have ever worn the iron crown. His strong will was well suited to overcome every obstacle, and now his intention was to assert his absolute supremacy in Italy as in Germany, and, above all, to be crowned in Rome by the Pope.

Just before Adrian's election by the cardinals, namely, in November, 1154, Barbarossa crossed the Alps at the head of a large and imposing army, accompanied by all the rough knighthood of his Teutonic subjects, and on the plains of Roncaglia summoned all the feudatories of the Empire to do homage. City after city, petty republics, domains and territories passed one by one nto his hands. What would he do when he arrived before Rome?

No wonder, then, that on the death of the peaceful old Pope Anastasius IV. the cardinals looked round for a strong man to meet the critical state of affairs in and outside of Rome. Nicholas Breakspear was the man of all others for the position. They wanted a statesman and diplomatist, as well as a ruler of firmness and unquestioned integrity to steer the Holy Church and her fortunes through this crisis in her history; and such a man was he whom they had chosen. Of quite a different stamp from the venerable father who had just passed away; a man of singular courage, who could take occasion by the horns, who had always boldly kept to a high idea of duty, and who had just returned from a most successful mission to the barbaric North, he was not a man likely to truckle to a Roman mob, or even to lower his head before the mighty Barbarossa. In the next chapter we shall see how Adrian IV. rose to his position, and how he dealt with those problems in the condition of Rome, the growth of which I have endeavoured to describe.

CHAPTER VI.

1154 TO 1155.

Adrian's Difficulties—Cardinal Boso—Arnold of Brescia in Rome—The Interdict—Adrian's Entry into Rome—Easter, 1155—Advance of Frederic Barbarossa—Negotiations between Pope and Emperor—Capture and Death of Arnold of Brescia—Roman Deputation to Frederic—Adrian proceeds to meet the Emperor at Sutri.

HE first difficulty Adrian IV. had to meet on his succession was that of the peremptory demand of the senate, prompted by Arnold of Brescia, that the Pope should recognize the temporal authority of the republic. Thus the problem was at once presented to him, was he to rule, or were the people ? As might be expected from what we know of Breakspear's previous action, he rose to the occasion ; stern and unyielding, he hurled back at the deputation his defiance of their pretensions, and announcing that no compromise was possible, and that he and he only would lead the Roman people and be their head, he dismissed them haughtily from his presence. The idea of bargaining with those whom he regarded merely as disaffected subjects never entered his mind.

Arnold of Brescia on this returned to Rome, and once

more began to inflame the popular mind with his revolutionary doctrines, and to preach resistance against the Pope's decree. Adrian had conceived the loftiest notions of his power, and like Bernard was determined that the Church should be supreme. After his meeting with the envoys of the senate, he retired to Anagni and prepared for war. Here we cannot do better than read the description of his triumph over the followers of Arnold which has come down to us from the pen of his secretary, Cardinal Boso, an actual eye-witness of the scenes which he records. As I have said before, this Boso was a nephew of Adrian, and had been his secretary for some time. Perhaps some details of his life may be of interest, and fortunately in Ciaconius[1] there is a very good account, which, in a list of Adrian's first creation of cardinals, runs as follows: "Boso (English), a nephew of Adrian IV., Pope, and, according to Ughell and John Pits, 'de scriptoribus ecclesiasticis Angliæ,' his clerk. He was formerly a Benedictine monk at S. Albans. Raised by Adrian IV. to be cardinal deacon of S. Côme et S. Damien, and a chancellor of the church.

"Further created cardinal presbyter with the title of San Pudenziana by Alexander III.[2] He was held in warm esteem by the first-named Pope, who, when he had reason to suspect the Emperor and Roman people of playing him false, entrusted to him the custody of his stronghold in S. Peter's.

[1] Prima creatio cardinalium Hadriani Quarti Papæ. Anno 1155. Ciaconius, tom. i., p. 1064.
[2] Adrian IV.'s successor, 1158.

"After Adrian's death he was a principal agent in securing the election of Alexander III., whose claims against the Anti-pope Octavian he warmly advocated. On Octavian's pseudo-election, he took under his protection all those cardinals who refused to recognize the schismatist, and gave them shelter from the popular anger in the castle of S. Angelo, which—as we have already said—had been entrusted to him by Adrian.

"Here he kept them until the fury of the mob had subsided, when he released them, upon which they promptly declared Alexander III. to have been duly elected Pope by them. He attended Alexander III. constantly, especially at Venice, and directed all his efforts towards the attainment of peace. Pope Innocent III. mentions in the first volume of his register that Boso was sent as a legate to Portugal; while Alexander IV. also mentions that he performed a legation in Alexander III.'s pontificate. He died towards the end of Alexander III.'s reign, or, if we accept John Pit's version, in the time of Lucius III., that is to say, about 1181.

"He was buried at Rome. As a clerk of the Church he wrote a diploma which Eugenius III. gave to the canons of S. Peter; afterwards, in his capacity of cardinal, he subscribed many papal letters, both of Adrian IV. and Alexander III. He was a pious man and a learned, and contemporary English writers may well rank him among the foremost ecclesiastics of his time."

I have mentioned before that Adrian probably met

him on his way through England to Norway; he was, in all probability, sent by him to Rome with letters to Eugenius III., and was one of those who greeted the "Apostle of the North" on his return.

The account of Boso runs as follows:[1] "About this time the famous heretic, Arnold of Brescia, boldly entered the city, and began to sow the poisonous seeds of his heresy among the ignorant, whose minds he sought to seduce from the true way of life. This man had caused incessant trouble to Eugenius and Anastasius, both of whom had tried hard to expel him; but so cunningly had he ingratiated himself with the citizens, and more particularly with the senators—who at this time were elected by popular vote—that all efforts to dislodge him were vain; and now, in the face of Adrian's strict prohibition, he insolently tarried in the city"—Adrian had issued a peremptory command for him to leave—"laying his plots and openly declaring his hostility to the Pope. But the culminating point was reached when the venerable Cardinal Guido, Presbyter of S. Potentienne, was openly attacked on the Via Sacra while on his way to the papal presence, and dangerously wounded by some impious follower of Arnold. The Pope immediately laid Rome under an interdict, and forbade the observance of any holy office until the Wednesday of Holy Week. Then were the senators impelled by the voice of clergy and laity alike to prostrate themselves before his Holiness, who made

---

[1] Hadriani IV., Vita, apud Card. Boso, ed. Migne.

them swear a solemn oath that they would drive forth the heretic of whom we have been speaking, together with all his followers, and chase them from the confines of Rome, unless they, the heretics, undertook to return immediately in obedience to the jurisdiction of the Holy Father. This was done. The heretics were cast forth, and the ban of interdiction removed from the city. Immediately a great joy came upon the people, who fell to praising the Lord and blessing Him with one voice. And on the following day, the anniversary of our Lord's supper, while on all sides men flocked to receive the annual absolution of their sins as they were wont, the venerable Pontiff, attended by an immense suite of bishops, cardinals, and nobles, and followed by thousands of the laity, came forth in state from the Leonine city, in which he had held his court ever since the day of his ordination, and took up his abode amid expressions of universal joy in the Lateran of his predecessors. Here he remained six days—Good Friday, Saturday, Easter Day, and Monday, Tuesday, and Wednesday in Easter week—celebrating the holy rites of the Church, and eating the passover with his clergy in the Lateran Palace, according to the time-honoured custom of the Church. And when at last the period of glad festivity had drawn to a close, each one returned home with gladness in his heart."

Adrian had shown his power indeed! Let us recapitulate. The haughty decree for Arnold to leave the city had produced the usual riots, but without frightening the man who sat in the papal chair. He is sterner than ever, and as unyielding. Then came the assault on old Cardinal Guido at the hands of the mob, precipitating the crisis, and causing the storm to break. A cardinal is dead; but remember, some years before the Roman rioters had slain the Pope himself. And now Adrian brings up all the forces of the Church—" Ready to smite once and smite no more." The rising feeling against the Church must be crushed, the whole might of the spiritual authority must be used, the force employed so colossal as to pulverize the body of discontent arising from heretical teaching and prevent it from ever again being revived; and so he came to use the last great weapon in his power, the interdict, never used in Rome before. Adrian was not a man to be bound by precedents; he laid down his own course, and kept to it; consulted no man, bent to no ancient custom which would prevent his free exercise of power.

No calamity which could befall a city in those times —and they were days when calamity had full meaning, days of the storm and sack, of the plague and the famine—could be more dreaded than that of an interdict.

Religious fervour might be failing; but the awe which was inspired by the searching spiritual power of the Church was as firmly rooted as ever it was in the minds of the people, and an interdict brought all the terrors of the loss of heavenly future, of prolongation of years in purgatory, and the absence of the comforting rites of the Church. Adrian IV. chose his time well by commencing on Palm Sunday, for all Europe flocked to Rome as a devout pilgrimage at

Easter time, and he thus struck a blow at the trade brought by them to the city—smote their earthly as well as their spiritual interests. A Roman Catholic writer[1] has well described the condition of the city under the interdict, a description which I am tempted to repeat. He tells us that it commenced at midnight by the funereal and muffled tolling of the church bells; whereupon the entire clergy might presently be seen issuing forth, in silent procession, by torchlight, to put up a last prayer of deprecation before the altars for the guilty community. Then the consecrated bread, that remained over, was burnt; the crucifixes and other sacred images were veiled up; the relics of the saints carried down into the crypts. Every memento of holy cheerfulness and peace was withdrawn from view. Lastly, a papal legate ascended the steps of the high altar arrayed in penitential vestments, and formally proclaimed the interdict. From that moment divine service ceased in all the churches; their doors were locked up; and only in the bare porch might the priest, dressed in mourning, exhort his flock to repentance. Rites, in their nature joyful, which could not be dispensed with, were invested with sorrowful attributes; so that baptism could only be administered in secret, and marriage celebrated before a tomb instead of an altar. The administration of confession and communion was forbidden. To the dying man alone might the viaticum, which the priest had first consecrated in the gloom and solitude of the morning dawn, be given; but extreme unction and burial

[1] R. Raby, 1849.

in holy ground were denied him. Moreover, the interdict seriously affected the worldly as well as the religious cares of society. Such, then, was the state to which Adrian boldly reduced the proud city of Rome. At first the interdict was received with an assumption of bravado, which, however, as the gloomy days passed on, soon subsided into a deep feeling of terror and horror. Men had time to reflect on the error of their ways. Easter always heralded joy and forgiveness of sins; but this year it seemed as if the weight of fresh sins and their accompanying penalties were being added to the whole community, and as Holy Week drew near, and the people realized the awful idea that there would be no services in the churches, the mob veered round and completely surrendered all they had demanded, and more. As Boso has told us, they greeted the triumphal entry of the Pope with joy and enthusiasm. The heretic at last had met his match, and the world learnt something of the character of the man who was guiding the destinies of the Holy Church. Firmness and prompt decision had conquered, as so long as the earth shall endure they always will, the changeable passions of a mob.

Adrian's terms before he would remove the interdict were absolute and exacting, and he gained all that he demanded. Meeting the envoys of the populace-driven senate at Viterbo, he declined to listen to anything but a complete abrogation of the republic, the banishment of Arnold and his lieutenants, and the return of the citizens to absolute submission to the Pope. The Church had conquered in the most complete manner.

Arnold fled to the country, a disappointed and beaten man, and at Otricoli was taken prisoner by the Cardinal Gerhard of S. Nicolas, but was rescued by one of the viscounts of the Campagna, who had obtained some estates by a grant from the republic properly belonging to the Pope, and under his protection, combined with that of other wild noblemen of that part of the Campagna, continued in a fitful way to try to stir up dissension in Rome. Adrian was now approaching the central crisis of his life; ever since the autumn of 1154 had been heard the news of the slow but sure advance of the mighty Emperor Barbarossa through the rich plains of Lombardy. A few short weeks after the triumph of Easter at Rome he had received the iron crown in the church of S. Michael at Pavia;[1] some resistance had been made, but it was useless against the inflexible will of the advancing potentate. Lombardy was at his feet; Tortona the last city to fall after a brave and gallant resistance; and at length the Germanic hordes entered the northern marches of the Campagna. Adrian viewed this advance with apprehension, and took all the measures he could, sending troops to fortify Viterbo, Orvieto, and Civita Castellana; but he knew that resistance would easily be overcome if the Emperor was really hostile, and he determined to act in accordance with the principles he had so recently declared with such effect; he put the spiritual side of his position foremost, and in this decision

---

[1] Easter Day in 1155 was March 27th. Frederic received the iron crown at Pavia on April 10th in that year.

showed not mere clever diplomacy, but the true spirit of statesmanship. He carried out this by despatching a deputation consisting of three cardinals, S. John and S. Paul, S. Pudenziana, and S. Maria in Portico, to meet Frederic at S. Quirico, to endeavour to open negotiations with the Emperor, and to discover his intentions; also, if possible, to obtain his aid in capturing Arnold of Brescia out of the hands of the rebellious nobles of the Campagna. The embassy started on its errand, and Adrian waited quietly in Rome till he should hear the result.

He must have been anxious indeed; for if an enemy, here was a far more formidable one than the excitable, injudicious Arnold, a warrior flushed with success, who was accustomed to dictate his own terms, backed up by all the power of Germany. What would be the conditions demanded if Rome became a beaten foe? But Adrian continued to carry on his pontifical duties calmly and quietly, ready for whatever action he felt would be justified in upholding the high dignity of the Church. It was in the meantime Frederic's intention to receive the imperial crown at the hands of the Pope; so he was, in a sense, coming in peace, and was prepared to treat, though he had no intention of giving up any right or dignity which he conceived that he possessed in his worldly title. At the same time, as Adrian IV. had despatched his cardinals, Frederic had sent two envoys to treat with the Pope in the persons of the Archbishops of Cologne and of Ravenna, who were to ascertain whether the Pope was ready to receive their master in state and invest him with the imperial crown at S. Peter's.

These two important embassies crossed each other without knowing it, and thus it came about that when Frederic's messengers to Rome arrived in the presence of Adrian IV., they were unable to tell him the result of his message to the Emperor. Before their arrival Adrian IV. had gone to Civita Castellana[1] in case of another outbreak in the city, or so as to be in a fortified place under his own absolute power if the crisis ripened into difficulties with the Emperor. Here the archbishops came; the Pope took at once the firm, bold stand consistent with his character, and having made himself sure that no answer had been sent in return to his messages, absolutely refused to consider any of the proposals of the Emperor until he should have heard definitely the view Frederic was going to take about Arnold and the report of the cardinals he had sent; also he told the envoys that a preliminary to any negotiations must be a declaration from the Emperor that no hostility was intended.

We must now follow the fortunes of our northward journeying cardinals. They found Frederic Barbarossa strongly encamped with his powerful army at S. Quirico in Tuscany, and were received, much to their relief, with every honour. Like the Pope, however, Frederic declined to treat until he had heard of the reception his own ambassadors had met with at the hands of the Pontiff.

[1] On the borders of the Campagna, about midway between Viterbo and Rome.

They, however, learnt one important thing, and that was that the Emperor considered Arnold of Brescia as an enemy to the imperial interests as well as to the papal authority, and in no way countenanced either his acts or those of the senate of Rome. This cleared the air considerably, for it showed that whatever Frederic's ultimate intentions might be, he at any rate regarded the Pope as supreme in Roman territory.

This encouraged the Cardinals to again urge that part of their instructions which related to Arnold, and as the Emperor was still much incensed by that demagogue's letter to him on his accession, which he regarded as impertinent and fanatical, they were able to play on his outraged feelings, and induced Frederic to promise to put his words into force and make Arnold a prisoner. With the power at his hand this was easy, as the nobles of the Campagna dared not resist the conqueror of Lombardy, Piedmont, and Tuscany; so despatching a force sufficient to overawe his protectors, Arnold fell a prey into his hands and was brought in chains to the camp.

Arnold had played his game boldly, but dangerously; he had disputed the power of the Pope and also had dared to dictate to the proudest monarch in Christendom, and had thereby brought the irresistible force of both potentates to unite against himself. He had staked all and lost, and in losing had destroyed his cause. Frederic handed him over to the Romans, and released the Campagnian nobles he had seized as hostages for his safe delivery.

II.

Map shewing
ADRIAN IV. AND
THE EMPEROR'S MOVEMENTS
1155.

.... Frederic's advance on Rome
— — —   "   Route leaving Italy
— · — · — Adrian's advance to Frederic
          "   movements after the coronation

English Miles.

Arnold's thoughts must indeed have been bitter as he travelled with his escort to Rome,—the liberator in chains!

In the meantime Frederic had advanced to Viterbo, and so was now within a few miles of the Pope, who was still at Civita Castellana. The two embassies in returning to their respective sovereigns met, and, holding a council together, determined to return to Frederic and endeavour to arrange terms of meeting between the two. Arnold of Brescia on arrival at Rome was imprisoned in the Castle of S. Angelo, in the custody of Cardinal Boso, whom Adrian had left in charge of his stronghold in Rome. The most important post of honour, he had chosen him as his most trusted adherent, and relied on him to keep the ever-rebellious senate in check, who were, even after their sharp lesson in Lent, again conspiring and watching for another opportunity of riot and revolution amongst the easily-inflamed citizens of Rome.

We now come to a dark and awful episode in our history. The presence of Arnold as a prisoner was the greatest danger to peace which could be imagined. Most of the papal troops were in garrison in the fortified posts in the Campagna; some to the north; others in the south, on account of the advance of the armies of the King of Sicily, which I shall soon have to relate. Two dangers presented themselves to those left in charge of Adrian's interests. The one, that of a successful revolt in favour of Arnold, in which case, what excuse might not Frederic make of it to assume absolute power in Rome? With the great ceremonials of coronation looming in the near future, a fresh interdict of course was out of the question. On the other hand, if, as Frederic intended, Arnold was kept a prisoner till the arrival of the Emperor, might he not by his eloquence induce him to consider himself a useful check on the power of the Pope, and so destroy the firm basis of power and majesty which Adrian was beginning to build? It must be remembered that those left in this post of double danger could not know of Frederic's animosity against Arnold; to them all was still uncertain, and the only way to ensure peace, and strike fear into the hearts of the people, was the removal of their leader. The Church took the law into its own hands; and, early one morning in June, the wretched man was led out and secretly put to death. There are various accounts of this; but it seems generally agreed that he was fastened to a cross and burnt alive; his ashes were flung into the Tiber to prevent their being collected and made into a national relic; the execution was carried out with haste for fear of the people. So ended the life of the fiery, obstinate reformer.

In judging the act of execution we must be careful not to measure the sentiments of those days by the moral standard of our own, and Arnold's death seems to have been the only course left to those responsible to the Pope for the order of the city. On the other hand, we must apply some moral standard to acts like this, and not allow the consideration of difference in custom and thought to weigh against the sentiment of justice. Rarely, if ever, in history, is there an occasion when the execution of a man without trial can be excused. And I regret to say that in describing the horrors of Arnold's death as related by Sismondi,[1] a Roman Catholic writer, whose history is in other respects admirable and impartial,[2] attempts to excuse the cruelties which were committed by saying that, however shocking it may seem to enlightened benevolence, yet from the Church point of view, viz., that the visible punishment of a crime should be commensurate with, and symbolize its moral enormity, the culprit received no more than he deserved. I do not attempt to minimize the crimes of Arnold of Brescia, but I cannot help mentioning this as illustrating the tendency of the Roman Church to regard all new theories as heretical, and to preserve that attitude towards improvement and progress which has lost the whole body of the Holy Catholic Church so much, lying as it does at the root, not only of our many unhappy divisions, but of much of the scepticism of the present day. This sentiment strained to its logical conclusion may be used to justify all the horrors of the Inquisition, many of the so-called religious wars, and also

[1] Sismondi gives a dramatic account of the slow burning of Arnold fastened to a cross at the Porta del Popolo, which is not verified by early authors, and is characterized by Dean Milman as "pure fiction" (Milman, "Latin Christianity," vol. iv., book viii., chap. vii., pp. 412, 413, etc.).
[2] R. Raby, "Life of Adrian IV.," p. 41.

such movements as the fanatical destruction of so much that was beautiful, sacred, and holy in our Anglican Church. For we must take the conclusion as applying generally, and not only to any one age or to any one church or country. Arnold was before his time. We cannot doubt but that much of his teaching was sincere and honest, but he was obstinate, impatient, rash, and, above all, intolerant. Like many ardent so-called liberators, he would wipe away tyranny with one hand, and set up intolerance with the other. Because the Church had its corruptions, the Church was corrupt; because society was full of abuses, it should therefore be swept away. Sudden changes of the hand of power bring fresh abuses with them, and no doubt he sowed much mischief and did a very great deal of harm; but we may admire his courage and respect his strength of mind. He expiated his crimes with his blood; and if one who gives his life for his cause is a martyr, Arnold of Brescia was one. In later times, under different conditions, he might have been a great and useful man; but it must not be forgotten, before we leave the subject, that if the Church had been pure and incorruptible, there had been no need for Arnold of Brescia.

Adrian IV. was now waiting for the return of his ambassadors, and, as he was still uncertain of Frederic's movements southward, he withdrew to Nepi, in order to wait still further the result of a deputation which the Roman republic, in defiance of Boso, had sent to meet Barbarossa. This deputation assumed a haughty and overbearing air little suited to the man whom they had come to propitiate. They met Barbarossa a little to the south of Sutri, and were ushered into his presence. What they expected him to say or to do is hard to imagine; but their want of wisdom, of tact, and of prudence, contrasts strangely with the firmness and decision of the Pope's course, and shows how ill fitted they were to take upon themselves the responsibilities attaching to diplomacy and foreign relations. Perhaps in their inflated conceit they thought the mighty Barbarossa would condescend to fill the place of the slaughtered demagogue; perhaps that they would be able to extort concessions through him from the Pope; but whatever their hopes, they were doomed to disappointment.

They began by reading a lofty and arrogant harangue of great length, well calculated to provoke the impatience of the Emperor. In this production they congratulated him on his arrival before the gates of Rome, and welcomed him in the name of the senate and people; they hailed him as their future liberator from the oppressions and yoke of the Church; they inferred that he would take the side of the people against the Pope. Passing on from one flight of rhetoric to another, they went on to recapitulate the ancient glory and grandeur of their city, and pointed out with rare insolence that they were the inheritors of the ancient republic to whom all these glories were due, arguing therefrom that they were entitled to dictate to the world, and even that it was great condescension on their part to dream of bestowing the imperial crown on an emperor who came from Swabia, and was not Roman by birth or nationality.

After this preamble,[1] in itself superbly injudicious and tactless, they proceeded to formulate their demands, in which they commanded him to respect all their ancient institutions and laws, to protect them against neighbouring powers, to take their part in disputes with the Pope, and to pay a sum of 5,000 pounds of silver as an indemnity.

They wound up by demanding a solemn oath from Frederic to maintain the republic, if necessary, with the help of the sword, and to seal this agreement as a perpetual treaty. The great Barbarossa seems to have contained his rage at first, even amid the angry mutterings of his knights and suite, and, after a pause, he began a calm, dignified reply. He quietly corrected their view of the history of Rome by relating at equal length the rise of Charlemagne and the transfer of the imperial power to him and his successors. Then, waiting to let his words sink in, he loosed his tongue, and, amid thunders of applause from his nobles, roared out at the frightened envoys, while pointing to the circle behind him: "Here are my Teutonic nobles, my banded chivalry; your only laws are those I choose to enact, your only liberty is allegiance to me, your sovereign."[2]

---

[1] Gunther, iii., p. 450, *et seq.*

[2] For the text of this address, and the Emperor's reply, see Gibbon's "Decline and Fall of the Roman Empire," edition of 1855, in eight vols., with notes by Milman and Guizot, vol. viii., cap. lxix., pp. 206, 207, 209.

This was the haughty and humiliating reply to the forwardness of the Roman senate. The deputation withdrew amid the jeers and taunts of the Germans, and wended their crestfallen way back to Rome, with the news that these rough soldiers, who called themselves nobles, were styled by Frederic the perpetual senate of Rome! Now came the turn of the ambassadors of the Pope who returned with Frederic's own envoys. They had a favourable interview with the Emperor, and were able to take back to Adrian the Emperor's solemn promise that he had no hostile intentions whatever against the Pope, that he was ready to pay all honour to the Holy Church and the see of Rome, and asked if Adrian would publicly and with all solemnity crown him in S. Peter's.

Adrian was cautious; and just as in Norway he laid down his conditions before granting the favour asked, so now did he determine to extract a solemn oath from the Emperor first,[1] and to obtain all the guarantees that were possible for keeping him to his word. He sent word to Frederic, who was encamped at Sutri, that if he swore on the gospels and on the cross before the papal ambassadors that he would protect the Pope and all his cardinals against aggression, and would uphold the dignity of the papal office, nor usurp any of its functions, he would ride out to meet him, and would not only crown him as he wished, but would accompany him in state into Rome. Adrian's

---

[1] Muratori, vol. vii., p. 135.

demands were complied with.[1] In solemn state, bareheaded, and with uplifted sword, the Emperor solemnly gave his oath to the cardinals and kissed the sacred volume handed to him; then, on his knees, surrounded by his court, he reverently saluted the cross also.

With joy the cardinals departed, and Adrian promised to ride out and meet the Emperor. Thus had he obtained the interview he required without any loss of the dignity which he considered due to his high office. He was well aware, however, that the crisis was only approaching; it was not sufficient that the Emperor should merely declare his allegiance to the Church, backed though the declaration might be by any number of solemn oaths; it was necessary that in his own person, in the presence of his own people, the mighty conqueror should do homage before the Vicar of Christ for his kingdom.

This claim to such homage may seem mere haughtiness on the part of the Church, the homage itself a degradation to the Emperor; but it must be remembered that the Pope represented literally to the minds of all devout Christians our Blessed Lord Himself; and, however great the earthly potentate, he lost none of his dignity in the eyes of the faithful by doing homage to the Holy Father, as he was thereby regarded as actually prostrating himself at the feet of the Saviour's own person.

How Adrian IV. gained this most important point

---

[1] 8th June, 1155.

and at the same time the respect and the friendship of Frederic Barbarossa, I shall now proceed to relate. Before doing so, it is as well to point out the fact that in all these negotiations the strong will of Adrian, served by his unerring judgment, was not merely dealing with the delicate situation created by the appearance of Frederic on the southern side of the Alps, but was shaping the whole future policy of the Church for centuries to come.

CHAPTER VII.

1155.

Frederic Barbarossa—The Meeting of 9th June, 1155—Spiritual Power *v.* Temporal Power—Adrian's Crisis—Submission of the Emperor—Entry into Rome of Pope and Emperor—Coronation of Frederic—The Riot in Rome—Frederic leaves Rome—Negotiations with the Emperor Manuel—The German Army recrosses the Alps.

OF all the heroes who can be claimed by German history, there is no one around whose memory has clustered so many legends, or who has more claim to the title of national hero than Frederic of Hohenstauffen. His memory lingers in Germany as does that of King Arthur in our country; like our hero of the Round Table, Fritz Redbeard is to return again and wield his sword in defence of the Fatherland. He is buried at Untasburg, near Salzburg, on the Kyffhausen, in Thuringia; his great red beard, the legend says, is still growing, and has grown through the table where he sits with his favourite warriors, waiting for the time when he is to return.

And he was a great man; born of the noble house of Hohenstauffen of Swabia, he succeeded his uncle Conrad in

1152 as Emperor. He was one of the few princes who obtained any glory out of the second crusade, and when by universal consent he ascended the throne, he had already the reputation of being a great soldier. With his history, except so far as it concerns the few years of Adrian's pontificate, we have little to do, but a study of his character is necessary to appreciate the struggle for supremacy as it arose between these two great men. When Adrian IV. came to the chair of S. Peter, Frederic was by far the most powerful of the monarchs of Europe. Louis VII. of France was still smarting under the disgrace of the crusade, and moreover had lost not only the flower of his army, but his trusted friend and minister Suger, who had died in 1152. Henry II. had but just ascended the throne of England, and had not yet become the powerful monarch of later days; moreover, he was occupied at home in settling the disordered state of his country, and in a war with Wales. So Frederic was without rival, and free to execute his cherished idea of crossing the Alps and being crowned in state at Rome. He was a man of boundless ambition, combined with great personal strength and courage—in physique he was an ideal hero; but he was unscrupulous, masterful, and imperious. He combined many rough, savage qualities with a high sort of gallantry or chivalry, a rude though real sense of honour. His one object was to rule a united Germany combined with Italy, to be supreme on the Tiber as well as on the Rhine and Danube. He proclaimed the loftiest notions of the absolute supremacy of the Emperor, and carried with him the enthusiastic support of all the great princes of Germany. He had asserted that he derived his power from God alone, and not through the intermediary of the successor of S. Peter. It was this sentiment, echoed to the full by the rough Teutons who accompanied him to Rome, which made matters doubtful for the papal interests in the city, and which was the main cause of Adrian's careful action in binding him by his solemn promise.

This, then, was the man whom Adrian was to meet, the representative of temporal power and earthly might; what would be the result was the question which was in the mouths of everyone in both camps? Adrian advanced from the picturesque castle of Nepi with his following of cardinals, and came towards Frederic's camp at Sutri—the ancient Sutrium, a small stronghold called the "Key of Etruria," which occupies the crest of one of the numerous rocky hills in that part of the country.

What a scene must it have been on that morning of a beautiful Italian June day, as the sentries of Frederic's camp saw the papal procession wending its way along the road from Nepi! How brilliant everything must have looked: the gorgeous robes of the cardinals; the canopy over the Pope's mule, to protect him from the midsummer sun; the accessories of banners and crosses; the sounding trumpets of the Vatican guard—a noble sight, this small force advancing to demand the homage due to the King of kings! As they neared the numerous tents of Frederic's camp, a brilliant group of German nobles, their armour flashing in the sunlight, their flaxen hair streaming under their headgear, galloped out to meet him, and, dismounting, prostrated themselves at his feet; then joining the procession they escorted the Pope amid the shouts of the soldiers and the blare of trumpets up to the space in front of the imperial tent; the supreme moment had come. The highest temporal potentate is about to greet the first spiritual power in Christendom; it was a moment symbolical of the condition of the Church in those days. Nearer drew the Pope, leaving his attendants at a little distance in the rear. Frederic Barbarossa emerged from his tent, a majestic figure, with white armour, and long red beard, his great sword girt by his side; behind him and around him stood the rough chivalry of Germany, great fair-haired, blue-eyed men, the descendants of the hordes who in earlier days had sacked the same city they were now almost in sight of; some of them half scornful, half believing, but all full of contempt for what they considered an inferior race, and each one ready to shout to any sentiment their Emperor chose to utter; the coarse jest only half suppressed; the swords loose in their scabbards. The Emperor advanced to meet Adrian, and, bowing low, offered to assist him to dismount; but the Pope waited—part of that homage which he intended to exact to the utmost consisted in the ancient custom of holding the papal stirrup as its owner dismounted. This Adrian waited for, and Frederic evidently did not intend to grant; his pride forbade him, after all his lofty speeches, to humble himself before any power on earth. The soldiers began to grumble;

the early mutterings which herald a disturbance were heard. Adrian's suite could not live up to the cool, calm courage of their lord; they turned and fled, nor drew rein till they reached Castellana, leaving the Pope alone in his critical position. But Adrian did not for a moment hesitate; the scale was trembling in the balance, the moment of danger had come, quickening his senses, and, true to his temperament, making his determination firmer than ever. His faith held him in good stead here,—one man, except for a few servants, against Frederic Barbarossa and his host!

He quickly decided on his action, and knowing that to wait longer would provoke the nobles, and possibly also to avoid any semblance of the ridiculous, he dismounted without insisting for the moment on the desired homage, and allowed the Emperor to lead him to the chair or throne prepared for him, on which he seated himself with dignity and allowed Frederic to kneel and kiss his feet. After this ceremony the Emperor rose and approached for the kiss of peace. It was now Adrian's turn. In dignified words he refused to grant it, and told the Emperor that until his homage had been paid in full he would withhold his blessing and would refuse to crown him. The magnificent courage of the man fills us with admiration; the cardinals had indeed chosen a worthy representative of the lofty claims of the Church.

The Emperor urged by all the arguments he could that the homage was not customary, that he could not condescend to so menial an act; but it was of no avail, he might as well have argued with the rocks of Sutri. The dispute lasted all that day; but no threats or entreaties would move the steady resolution of the Pope, who at last quitted the camp and returned to Nepi.

The situation had developed into a deadlock; the two most strong-minded men in Europe were pitted one against the other, and who could foretell the result? But Frederic was as equally determined to receive his crown as Adrian was to maintain his rights. The Emperor had in fact two considerations to weigh against each other: he had declared that he would be crowned by the Pope as the finishing touch of his triumphant progress through Italy, and he had also declared that he would not pay the necessary act of homage. Which was he to give up? He could not carry out both. The Pope, on the other hand, had but one determination, and that he meant to adhere to, come what might. Doubtless the astute mind of Adrian had foreseen the dilemma, and with his knowledge of human nature felt more easy than his frightened cardinals. At last the Emperor made up his mind to the lesser of the two evils, and on June 11th set out for Nepi.

He approached the place where Adrian had taken up his residence, and, as he drew near, again the Pope rode out to meet him. The Emperor dismounted, advanced on foot, and kneeling down held the Pope's stirrup and assisted him to dismount. This done, Adrian enfolded him in his arms and gave him the kiss of peace amid the ringing cheers of both parties of followers and spectators. Adrian IV. had won. He had triumphantly gained his point, and at the most trying crisis of his life his splendid firmness had gained him a wonderful success. No deed of Adrian's is more celebrated than this; and this alone would stamp the greatness of the man, the son of a plain English countryman, who had now succeeded in humbling the proudest noble in Christendom.

All this minute detail of ceremonial may seem, at first glance, to be trivial and petty; one may be tempted to accuse the Pope of making too much of one very small detail of the homage due to him. It may be argued that Frederic had practically rendered all that could be expected from one in his position, and that to insist on so exact a punctilio was arrogant and uncalled-for. But again we must put ourselves far back into the Middle Ages, and remember that, inasmuch as the Pontiff was held to represent our Lord Himself, the same reverence was expected from all who came in official contact with him. If the Saviour Himself had appeared on earth, what potentate was there who would have failed to render the most humble and reverent worship? and it is in this light that we must look at the action of Adrian.

The two magnates now had become friends, and proceeded to make arrangements for their triumphal entry into Rome. The Pope feared the condition of Rome after Arnold's death, and on his advice their entry was preceded by a force of 1,000 men under Cardinal Octavian, who entered the city in the night, and, welcomed by Cardinal Boso, occupied

that portion which contained S. Peter's, and so ensured the peaceable entry of the Pope and the Emperor. When they got within a short distance of Rome, Adrian went on and preceded Frederic, in order to be ready to receive him, and, on the early morning of June 18th,[1] Frederic triumphantly entered the city between the lines of his troops, and, attended by his nobles, knights, and followers, ascended the steps of the Basilica of S. Peter, where he was received by the Pope with all the cardinals in full ceremonial. The whole company went in; Adrian celebrated high mass, and then at a splendid gathering Frederic was crowned and blessed by the Pope, and took the solemn oaths prescribed by ancient custom, and received the sceptre of his mighty kingdom, while all the people burst out into loud shouts and acclamations. Nothing was omitted to add to the magnificence of the ceremony, and it must have been a splendid and picturesque sight such as those present would remember for the rest of their lives.

We must now return to the discomfited envoys of the republic, who, returning to the city, had so inflamed the people on the farther side of the Tiber, that they determined to rise, cross the river, and attack the forces of the Emperor and Pope. Something of the spirit of Arnold of Brescia must have been in them to induce them to attempt so forlorn a hope.

Frederic's generals had posted a guard at the bridge

[1] "Geschichte der Hohenstauffen." Von Raumer. Vol. ii. This book gives an interesting and full account of these negotiations and events.

near the Castle of S. Angelo, and across this bridge rushed the now infuriated populace, who felt that they had been duped both by Pope and Emperor. They overcame the German guard almost in the presence of Adrian himself, who was then retiring to his palace to rest after the fatigues of the day. The Emperor and the rest of his troops, accompanied by his staff, had repaired to their camp in the Neronian fields, and, not expecting any danger, were celebrating the successful termination of their long campaign by carousals and feasting, Adrian having distributed largess amongst the soldiers.

They soon, however, heard of the disturbance. Veterans, as they were, were not to be caught unawares. They advanced under Frederic himself, and attacked the Roman troops; the latter, exasperated by their fancied wrongs and wrought to a high pitch of enthusiasm, fought well. Two or three times they were driven back across the Tiber, only to return again in spite of the efforts of the skilled troops of the empire.

Fighting lasted all through the hot summer's day and far on into the evening, but at last discipline told its usual tale. The last time the desperate city forces were driven over the bridge they were routed completely, and fled into the streets of the city. Over 200 fell as prisoners into Frederic's hands, including most of the leaders, and more than 1,000 were killed by the imperial troops or were drowned in the Tiber. The Emperor lost very few of his men, and is said to have exclaimed, doubtless remembering the haughty terms of the republican envoys when he received them at Sutri, "Such, O Romans! is the price your Emperor pays for the imperial crown. This is the way in which we Germans treat for our empire!"[1]

Frederic handed over all his prisoners to the papal authorities on the following day; but, though one or two of the ringleaders were executed, Adrian IV. felt strong enough to be merciful, and, being naturally of a gentle disposition, released them on condition that they would accept the inevitable and endeavour to keep the peace among their turbulent fellow-citizens—an act of clemency which deserves praise when we consider the provocation which the Pope had received on the very day of his triumph. It is a pity to have to record that they had not even then the good sense to keep quiet and orderly; for shortly after, as the Pope was riding through one of the streets with the Emperor, their lives were endangered by a turbulent mob, who so threatened them with stones and other weapons that they had to make a long detour to avoid them. It is said that on this occasion the Emperor's life was saved by Henry the Lion, Duke of Bavaria.

Two causes were now operating to make it necessary for the Emperor to leave the city: one, the difficulty of providing provisions for his troops, a difficulty principally caused by the hostility of the Roman peasantry, and the other, the increasing heat of the summer, for it was now

---

[1] Otto Frisingensis, lib. i., cap. 23; Von Raumer, vol. ii.

getting well on to the hottest period of the year, and the Germans, mostly coming from the North, were beginning to suffer from the effects of the climate. So at the end of June the army left Rome, and the Pope accompanied Frederic to Ponte Lugano, where they solemnly celebrated the feast of S. Peter, on the 29th June; and, after high mass had been celebrated, the Pope absolved all the troops from the guilt of bloodshed in the slaughter of the Romans on the 18th June. Whilst the two monarchs were here, a deputation arrived from the citizens of Tivoli, placing their city at the disposal of the Emperor and his troops, and delivering up the keys of the gates. Here arose a point at which Barbarossa, had he not intended to be loyal to his solemn oaths, might easily have raised a fresh difficulty with the Pope. Tivoli was a town owing feudal duty and allegiance to the papal see, and as such the city authorities had no right to treat with any foreign sovereign except through the Pope. Frederic might here have insisted on the ever-thorny question of the temporal power. He had been crowned Emperor by the Pope; here was an opportunity to test his authority.

But it is satisfactory to relate that, whatever we shall have to recount as to the Emperor's good faith later on, he on this occasion at least was staunch to his vows, and refused to accept the honours the citizens sought to pay him. He wrote a letter, which he gave to the envoys to take back, recommending the people of Tivoli to obey their lord and father the Pope in all things, though he somewhat inconsistently added the words, "saving the imperial right." No doubt the envoys did not expect to find the Pope with Frederic, and their underhand intentions were thus frustrated—a result, however, for which Adrian publicly thanked the Emperor. Here the two, Adrian IV. and Frederic Barbarossa, separated, so far at any rate on terms of equal respect and regard; two strong men, they had honourably agreed, and had acquitted themselves nobly towards each other. We shall see something in this history of Frederic's second and more important invasion of Italy, which happened two years later, and lasted into the reign of another Pope. In this one, at least, both sides had successfully held their own, and for a short time the temporal and spiritual authorities were on amicable terms.

Frederic pursued his course northward with all despatch, stopping on the way to take Spoleto by storm—a city which had refused to submit to him. He allowed his soldiers to sack it, and razed it to the ground. From that place he marched to Ancona, where he met the ambassadors of the Greek or Byzantine Emperor of the East, who offered him heavy considerations and a large sum of money if he would enter into an alliance and advance against William, King of Sicily, who had lately succeeded his father Roger. But sickness and desertion were decimating the splendid army which had marched right down to Rome, while the enervating Italian climate was proving a worse foe than any of their enemies. So Frederic wisely determined to continue his progress home across the Alps, and not spoil his successes by any risk of failure in a campaign in the still hotter climate of South Italy. Thus terminated the expedition which had been fraught with such important consequences to the new Pope. But now Adrian had to face a new foe, this time from the south, not perhaps so formidable, or involving so many important considerations, but still sufficient to stop him from resting in satisfaction on the greatest success of his career. Before I relate his difficulties with William of Sicily I will attempt to describe his relations with his own country, surely not the least important part to us of the life of the only English Pope.

CHAPTER VIII.

English Affairs at Adrian's Succession—The Congratulatory Embassy to the Pope—Adrian's Reception of the Abbot of S. Albans—Henry II.'s Letter to the Pope—John of Salisbury: his Life: his Friendship with Adrian—Conversation with the Pope—His Recollections of Adrian.

HENRY OF ANJOU, the second of his name, came to the thrones of England, Normandy, and the French possessions, together with his earldom of Anjou, on the 25th October, 1154.

He proved one of our greatest kings. He came at a moment when the anarchical state of the kingdom required a strong ruler, and he took a very strong position in regard to the Church, based on much the same principles as those of Frederic Barbarossa.

One of his first acts was, as was natural, to send an embassy to the new Pope, to congratulate him on his accession; and, besides the question of Ireland, which I have fully dealt with later on, he had a concession to ask from the Church which was to him of the most vital personal importance.

Geoffry Plantagenet,[1] his father, Earl of Anjou, had,

[1] "Gul. Newbrig. de Reb. Angl.," lib. ii., cap. 7.

by the Empress Maud, three sons, Henry, Geoffry, and William. Knowing that his own dominions would of course descend to his eldest son Henry, and that the kingdom of England, with the duchy of Normandy, would also fall to him in the right of his mother, he left by his will the earldom of Anjou to his second son, Geoffry; and to render this more secure, he exacted an oath of the bishops and nobility not to suffer his corpse to be buried till Henry had sworn to fulfil every part of his will.

When Henry came to attend his father's funeral[1] the oath was tendered to him, but for some time he refused to swear to observe the provisions of a writing with the contents of which he was unacquainted.

However, being reproached with the scandal of letting his father lie unburied, he at last took the oath with great reluctance. On his accession to the throne Henry felt that he ought to be absolved from his oath, and determined to petition the Pope for a release from its terms. I have not been able to find whether any correspondence took place either between Eugenius III. or Anastasius IV. and Henry about his marriage with the divorced Queen Eleanor of Louis VII.; but I think one of these Popes must have been asked for the necessary dispensation, as it would have been mentioned in the letter which Adrian wrote to Henry had any such request been preferred to him. The deputation selected by Henry to go to Rome consisted of

---

[1] 1151.

the Abbot of S. Albans, Robert of Gorham,[1] and three bishops. Robert was the eighteenth abbot, and the third since the Abbot Richard, the one who rejected Adrian in his early days; he was one of the most excellent rulers of the monastery of that period, and nephew to the celebrated Geoffry of Gorham, sixteenth abbot.

The account of this expedition is given in the chronicles of S. Alban's Abbey, and I cannot do better than give a translation from the original.[2] After a brief description of the life of Nicholas, from the time when he was rejected by the Abbot of S. Albans, where his father lived, to his final triumph in 1154, the chronicler proceeds to describe how Robert, the eighteenth abbot, conceived the idea of making a journey to Rome, to plead with the Pope and pray him to restore the monastery to the high position it had held before the civil war and tumult of the previous reign; also for certain special privileges on the ground of the nationality of the newly-elected Pope, and on that of the proximity of his birthplace to S. Albans. The old chronicle goes on as follows:[3]

"*The Abbot goes to the Pope.*" "So when the news of his lordship Pope Adrian's succession reached us, Robert the Abbot got himself ready for a journey across the Alps,

[1] "History of the Abbey of S. Albans." Newcome, 1795. Richard, fifteenth abbot, 1097-1119.

[2] "Chronica Monasterii S. Albani, Gesta Abbatum S. Albani a Thomas Walsingham, A.D. 790-1290." Rolls Series. "Chronicles and Memorials of Great Britain and Ireland," 1867, vol. i., p. 124, 1151-1156, Robert, eighteenth abbot. [3] *Ibid.*, p. 126.

hoping thereby to restore the erstwhile dignity of this church; he collected horses, requisitioned his expenses, and furnished himself with presents to the estimated value of 140 marks (besides fine pieces of plate, three costly mitres, sandals, and other pleasing offerings). On S. Dionysius's day,[1] he accordingly started for Rome, and with him as escort went three bishops, of the sees of Mans, Evreux, and Luxeuil or Luxen"—the old diocese of Besançon. "And King Henry II., who had recently been anointed, gave orders to these bishops and to Robert the Abbot concerning the despatch of certain intricate royal business at Rome (about which it would be out of place to say more here). And the King specially constituted Robert the Abbot his chief and foremost procurator, and gave into his charge letters signed with the royal seal, addressed to the Pope, in which he begged his Holiness in humble and dutiful spirit to consider the business of the church of S. Albans of as much importance, and to treat it as kindly as if it were personal to himself, since from its proximity to his native place it had peculiar claims on his protection."

The story continues that no sooner had they embarked on the sea than the winds rose and the waves grew rough, so that they were in imminent peril of their lives. But the abbot made pious supplication, invoking the aid of S. Margaret and the Blessed Virgin, which, to the "surprise of the others on board was promptly regarded." (This

[1] October 9th.

naïve remark does not seem to prove a very strong belief in the efficacy of prayer to the saints, at any rate in those whose life was passed on the sea!) At length, after running many risks from storms and robbers by sea and land, they reach their journey's end in safety, finding the Pope at Beneventum.

His Holiness received them with every expression of goodwill, and showed them signal honour. So they see to the King's business and make ready to depart once more. But the Pope will not hear of the abbot going so soon; he says there are many subjects he particularly wishes to talk over with him, and finally prevails on him to stay, letting the other bishops go back to Henry to explain his absence and make good his excuses. The abbot being now in a position to talk freely to the Pope, displays considerable ingenuity in attaining his ends, as will be seen in the following account.

"*The Abbot's conversation with the Pope.*"[1] "Then the abbot offered his Holiness the Pope the gold and silver (of no mean weight) and the other costly presents, even the three mitres and the sandals of exquisite workmanship, which Christina, Prioress of Markgate, had so diligently made. And his lordship accepted everything with a pleasant smile, but would keep nothing, save only the mitres and the sandals, for the beauty of their fashioning. But he praised greatly the devotion and courtesy of the abbot, adding pleasantly: 'I refuse to accept your gifts, since when I

[1] "Chron. Mon. S. Albani," vol. i., p. 127.

once fled to the shelter of your religious house, and begged to be invested with the monk's hood, you refused to accept me.' 'My lord,' replied the abbot, 'we could never have taken you in, for God, in His all-seeing wisdom, willed it otherwise, since He had set apart your life for a higher position.'

"'An elegant and a courteous reply,' responded the Pope, highly pleased with his words. 'But, my dearest abbot,' he added, 'pray ask out boldly for what you want; you know that the Bishop of Albano could never refuse anything to S. Albans.'"

This flattering reception doubtless caused Robert's hopes to run high; but he allowed it in no wise to turn him from the cautiousness he invariably exercised in his dealings. Before proceeding, he requested the Pope's permission, granted easily enough, to distribute among the cardinals and papal suite the costly presents he had brought with him to Rome.

"This he did,"[1] says the chronicler, "knowing full well that the Romans are insatiable as leeches, and ever thirsty for money." And he adds rather quaintly: "Need I say more? His name was extolled to the heavens, and he found favour with all Romans."

Having thus paved his way, Robert proceeds with his own especial business.

"*Pope Adrian's privilege.*" "Now one day when Pope and abbot were alone together, conversing familiarly, the

[1] "Chron. Mon. S. Albani," vol. i., p. 128.

latter, his voice broken, with tears and sighs, told his Holiness of the cruel oppression of the Bishop of Lincoln,[1] and how the episcopal servants, even the meanest, conducted themselves with intolerable pride, how they laid traps for others, abused their position, made lordly prayers, and cared not what injustice they might inflict.

"Whereupon the Pope, full of wrath and pity, granted to the church of S. Albans the well-known privilege by which we, both monks of the cloister and followers living outside the monastery in the village, are made free of all episcopal authority, save only that of Rome, to all time. And further, his Holiness granted us other such special privileges, that there is no monastery in all England which can compare with S. Albans for liberty."

After a little more parleying, Robert, elated with his success, concludes his master's business, receives the apostolic blessing, and sets out on his homeward journey, bearing important letters from the Pope to King Henry and the English legate. Some modern historians have stated that John of Salisbury accompanied this mission to Rome; but, as we shall see presently, this is a mistake, founded on a confusion of the fact that John had many interviews with the Pope at Beneventum, where much of the first year or two of the pontificate found Adrian.

Throughout the whole of the chronicle above quoted it is evident that the writer is doing his utmost to extol and magnify the share undertaken by Robert the Abbot in the

[1] S. Alban's Abbey was then in the see of Lincoln.

mission. No doubt he does this for politic reasons. But it is hardly likely, however jealous he might be for the honour of his own monastery, in which respect all monkish writers are alike, that he would deliberately suppress the name of John of Salisbury. The mistake may have had its rise in the fact that the King, hearing John intended to visit the Pope, sent messages and letters through him to his Holiness, in addition to employing a regular messenger, in the person of Robert the Abbot. The fact that both thus occupied a quasi-official position will easily account for a confusion of the missions having arisen.

The letter written by Henry II. to the Pope, whether the bearer was John, Robert, or one of the bishops, has fortunately been preserved in the works of Peter de Blois, the celebrated Archdeacon of Bath, from which fact some writers have assumed that Peter was the author. This, however, is pure conjecture. The letter is couched in such pure, vigorous language that I have ventured to translate it in full, though of course it loses much of its beauty in the process.[1]

"*Ad N. Pontificum Romanum.*

" Sweet indeed are the tidings that have reached our ears; for we have learnt the news of your exaltation, which

---

[1] "Peter Blesensis, Bathoniensis Archidiaconi, opera omnia," ed. J. A. Giles, LL.D. Oxon., MDCCCXLVIII., vol. ii., Epis. clxviii., p. 116. (This book is incorporated in the series, "Patres Ecclesiæ Anglicanæ," edited by the same author.)

has dispelled the sombre gloom of the Roman Church, as some brilliant aurora rising in a desert place.

"The apostolic chair rejoices safe in the knowledge of its well-being. The world rejoices, seeing a new light rising in the Church, and hails the time when the glad morn shall have grown into the perfect day. But our occident rejoices above all, seeing that it has deserved the honour of producing the future light of the universe, that it has brought fresh glory to the sun of Christianity,[1] which so lately set in the East. In our own heart, holy father, we rejoice exceedingly at the honour which has fallen on you, and, believing that the power of the Divine Majesty has truly descended to your Holiness, we shall confide in you with filial devotion and tell you the more openly the vows we have made in your behalf. For if a son of the flesh freely opens his heart to his father concerning his mundane ambitions, how much more freely ought a spiritual son to tell his father of his spiritual aspirations. Amongst our many good wishes for you, then, not the least is that, since the hand of God has transplanted your reverend person from our land into His own orchard, as it were, like a tree of life, which He takes from this earth and causes to grow in Paradise, you may ever strive so to nourish all the churches by your good works and doctrines, that the nations of the earth shall say, 'Blessed is the land of his beatitude!' And we devoutly trust that the spirit of strife, which so often falls most heavily on the highest dignity,

[1] Alluding to the second crusade.

may never for a moment tear you from your love of sanctity; lest, which God forbid, the pinnacle of dignity be the prelude to the abyss of degradation.

"The ordinance of the entire Church rests in your hands, and we therefore earnestly desire that you will without delay elect cardinals willing and able to share your burden with you, taking no thought of a man's nationality, nor his birth, nor wealth, but choosing such men as fear God and hate avarice, such as will see justice done, and are zealous after men's souls.

"The unworthiness of the clergy is the greatest evil to the Church; we therefore pray you to exercise great care in the disposal of ecclesiastical preferments, lest haply one unworthy should enter into the patrimony of the Cross. And when, above all things, the Holy Land, thrice blessed in the birth, the life, and the death of our Saviour—that land which all Christian nations must surely hold in special veneration—is, alas! as you know, overrun and polluted by the incursion of infidels, we do fervently exhort you to use your whole strength by mediation and prayer to liberate and set it free. As for the Empire of Constantinople, erstwhile so illustrious, now in such grievous plight, who is there who does not long for the day when you, by taking careful thought, will raise it again to its former high station.

"For your own honour's sake and our common weal, we do pray that you, being raised by God's own hand to rule over the universal Church, may jealously guard the good discipline and stability of all the churches. Now we confide you into God's good keeping. As you have striven ever to be a light to those in need, and so have been extolled from virtue to virtue and from honour to honour, until at length you have reached the highest place of all, even to the apostolic chair, we do make prayer that you may ever so go on lightening and encouraging the Church, that none shall hide himself from the radiant warmth of your presence; and that when, lastly, death takes you away, you may leave such proofs of your sanctity behind as shall make the happy land of your nativity thrice happier in singing praise to the Lord.

"Finally, we do most confidently seek your fatherly protection, begging you always to bear us kindly in thought and mention us in prayer—ourselves, our dear ones, and our kingly staff."

And now we must relate the conversations and opinions of John of Salisbury, which may be described as the most valuable personal records we have of Adrian. John of Salisbury—Joannes di Saresbria,[1]—was born at Sarum, or Salisbury, between 1115 and 1120. Being a youth of decent birth, he was sent to Paris for his education, where he became a pupil of Abelard. He had a devout nature, but was, for his time, singularly open-minded, and imbibed the best of the knowledge which his master had to impart, but with little or none of his peculiar tenets. He was not long under that great philosopher. After remaining in Paris some time he attracted the attention of Peter,

[1] "Dict. of Nat. Biog.," 1894.

Abbot of Moutier la Celles, near Troyes, whose secretary he became for a while. He was present at the Council of Rheims, in the time of Eugenius III., and was then presented by the great Bernard to Theobald, Archbishop of Canterbury. From there he went to Rome, but, though he passed much of the next five years in that city, he came more than once to England, and afterwards lived at Canterbury till 1164. He died about the year 1181, and has left numerous records of the things he saw and heard. He was a close and intimate friend of Adrian, and was always admitted to his full confidence.

In all probability he was employed on various secret missions by his friend, and no doubt knew more of the secret history of the times he lived in than he has chosen to put on record.

John of Salisbury was better known, perhaps, under his later title of Parvus, Bishop of Chartres. He was a great favourite with King Henry II., who constantly employed him on diplomatic service where delicacy of management and extreme tact were required in order to bring the various schemes of the statesman-king to a successful issue; and it is saying a great deal for his ability that he was selected by so keen a judge of men as we know Henry to have been.

In those remote days, when news travelled slowly and printing had not been invented, the personal element weighed heavier in the balance, and discretion and calm judgment were gifts which, when added to scholarly knowledge, rendered such a man as John invaluable to his sovereign.

One of our highest authorities[1] on this period says of him: "He was without doubt superior to all his contemporaries, and his works are by far the most valuable compositions which have come down to us from the twelfth and thirteenth centuries."

There can be little doubt but that John of Salisbury enjoyed the full confidence of his sovereign for a considerable period. This adds great weight to his accounts of such matters as were entrusted to him in the relations between Henry II. and Adrian IV. Unfortunately, however, for his worldly prospects, he ultimately warmly espoused the cause of Thomas à Beket, and was one of the first to share his exile, being afterwards present at his murder.

John of Salisbury compiled a discursive treatise on many subjects, treated chiefly from a literary and philosophical point of view; but here and there throughout this invaluable work are to be found precious records of personal experiences, which throw a gleam of bright light across the dark perspective of the twelfth century, and enable us to gather a little of the daily life and thought of his time. Some of these introduce us into the immediate presence of Nicholas Breakspear, enabling us to picture to ourselves the open frankness of the Englishman showing itself in spite of the traditions and customs of the office which he held.

---

[1] The Rev. J. A. Giles. "Joannis Saresberiensis postea Episcopi Carnotensis opera omnia nunc primum in unum collegit et cum codicibus manuscriptis contulit." J. A. Giles, Jur. Civ. Doc. et collegii Corporis Christi Oxon. olim Socius. In 5 vols. 1848. Vol. i., p. vii, preface.

This work was called "Polycraticus, or Court Life and the Footsteps of Philosophers," and is a wonderful compilation, being somewhat of the nature of an encyclopædia of miscellanies; he published it in 1159, shortly before his other celebrated work, the "Metalogicus," which was a reply to some unknown critic, and consists of four books of equally valuable material.

In the sixth book of "Polycraticus,"[1] John, mingling philosophy with brief descriptions of men and places he has become acquainted with in his many travels, according to his wont launches out into a discussion on military topics; and in order to emphasize the need of discipline in an army, records the following account of a conversation with the Pope. His argument is enunciated in the heading of the chapter, which runs as follows: "The evils attendant on authority must be borne, for in them lies the germ of the public well-being, and they disseminate health, just as the stomach of an animal distributes nourishment; and this is the opinion of his lordship, Pope Adrian." Then, after a few introductory remarks, in which he quotes passages from Scripture, "I recollect," he remarks, "a journey I once made into Apulia, for the purpose of visiting his Holiness, Pope Adrian IV., who had admitted me into his closest friendship; and I stayed with him at Beneventum for nearly three months. And when in the course of frequent conversations on divers subjects, such as are wont to arise

[1] "Polycraticus; sive De Nugis Curialium et Vestigiis Philosophorum," vol. iv., lib. vi., cap. 24, pp. 58 *et seq.*

between friends, he would ask me freely and earnestly what men were thinking about himself, and indeed about the whole Roman Church,[1] I spoke to him quite openly and laid before him without reserve the ill criticisms I had heard in many provinces. 'It is commonly said,' I told him, 'that the Church of Rome, which is the mother of all the churches, behaves to the others more like a stepmother than a mother.

"'In the first place it is filled with Scribes and Pharisees, who impose grievous burdens on the shoulders of the laity—burdens which they themselves do not so much as touch with their finger-tips. They lord it in things spiritual, but never think of setting an example to their congregations, who naturally enough continue to live as they please; they hoard up valuables; they load their tables with gold and silver; at times they will even stint themselves in their greed. They never admit a beggar, or very rarely, and then it is not in Christ's name, but for the purpose of vainglorification. They ruin churches; stir up quarrels; bring priests and people into collision; take no pity on the struggles and miseries of the people in distress; grab eagerly at church moneys; and then reckon all this mongering as so much piety!

"'They mete out justice, not because they ought, but for the sake of gain. Indeed, everything has its price nowadays, and you can get no justice unless you buy it.

---

[1] "Romana Ecclesia."

"'They do more harm than good; so I say they are very little better than devils, for the moment they stop injuring people, they immediately think they are conferring a benefit. No doubt there are a few exceptions, and one or two could be found who discharge the functions of the priest in deed, as well as in name. But the very Pope himself is an almost intolerable burden on mankind.

"'The whole world is crying out against him, that, while the churches are going to rack and ruin—those churches built by our pious forefathers—and the altars lie uncared for, my lord builds himself palaces, and struts about in purple clothing, aye, and in golden for the matter of that! The houses of the clergy are resplendent, but the house of God falls into squalor. They wrangle over the loot of provinces, as if they wished to acquire the wealth of Crœsus himself.

"'But the Almighty deals justly with them, for as a rule they fall into the clutches of others—not infrequently of the lowest of the low. And it seems to me that while they thus pursue the path of iniquity, the punishment of the Lord is never far from them. For verily hath the Lord said that in what manner they have judged, so shall they be judged, and in his own measure it shall be meted out to each man.

"'These things, Holy Father,' I said, 'are what the people are saying, since you desire me to tell you the truth.'"

John certainly does not seem to have been afraid of the Pope, and it is to be questioned whether Adrian had a single friend, excepting perhaps Boso, who would have said so much, and the latter, from the nature of his office and his relationship to his master, would not be in the way of hearing any unfavourable reports of a personal nature, as people would have been afraid of the consequences of indiscreet candour. It is probable, nay certain, that little of John's remarks as to the degradation of the clergy was new to the experience of Adrian.

John goes on with his narrative. "'And for your own part,' he asked quietly, 'what think you?' 'Your question,' I replied, 'places me in a quandary; for if I put myself in opposition to the verdict of the people, I fear me I shall get the name of liar and flatterer. And if, again, I take their view, I fear I shall be impeached of treason against the divine majesty. But since Guido Clement, Cardinal of S. Potentienne, upholds the opinion of the people, I shall not take it on me to contradict him. He asserts that deceit and avarice are at the very foundation of the Church of Rome, and that these two things are the cause of the evil, root and branch; nor does he say this in any hole or corner, but affirmed it openly at a meeting of the cardinals, over which S. Eugene[1] presided, when the anger of the Ferentines was kindled against me, innocent as I am. One thing, however, I will make bold to say, and I can say it conscientiously, that nowhere have I met priests more upright or less tolerant of greed than some in the Church of Rome. Does not everyone praise Bernard de Rennes, Cardinal-deacon of S. Como and S. Damien, for

[1] Eugenius III.

his strict abstention from the acquirement of wealth? The man has yet to be born from whom he would deign to accept a gift! Yet I doubt not even he is sometimes persuaded to take his share of church money, when it unquestionably belongs to the cardinals for division.

"'And does not everyone admire the scrupulousness of the Bishop of Præneste, who, for conscience' sake, takes no share of ecclesiastical emoluments. The majority doubtless are unassuming, earnest men, who may be favourably compared to Fabricius; indeed, who surpass him in much, seeing they have found the true path of life. One thing is sure, I must not tell a lie to the Holy Spirit; and, seeing you earnestly request, and even expect me to speak out, I will say this: though I think you must be obeyed in all that you say, I do not think a man need copy you in all that you do. The man that dissents from you in doctrine is a heretic or a seceder; and yet, praise be to God, there are some who do not copy the works of you clergy. It is the backsliding of a few men, then, which causes a blot on the righteous, and covers the whole Church with infamy. I think it is on this account that these die more frequently, so that they may not corrupt the Church throughout. But even the good ones are taken away from time to time, doubtless for fear they might be corrupted themselves by the contamination of evil. And it would not be worthy if Rome were corrupt in the eyes of the Lord. Do you, therefore, Holy Father, find men humble of heart, who care not for empty glory nor riches, and place them in the priesthood. But I am afraid that while you are pursuing your search for what you do want, some thoughtless friend will tell you of what you do not want. Why, father, do you so keenly criticise the lives of others and hardly give a thought to your own? The whole world flatters you; you are called father of all men and lord of all men; and over your head every sinner pours his oil. Now, if you are father, why do you look for presents and offerings from your children? Or, if you are lord, why do you not strike terror into your Roman subjects, crush their independent spirit, and lead them back to the true faith. But you are trying to keep Rome in the Church by bribery! Think you it was by like bribery that S. Sylvester won her over in the beginning? You are walking the crooked path, and not treading the true way, my father.

"'Rome must be kept in the Church by the same gifts with which she was induced to enter it. Give as freely as you accept. Justice is the queen of all virtues, and she blushes with shame at the mention of a bribe. If she treats you kindly in the future, let it be without reward. Never attempt to prostitute her by bribery, for she is incorruptible. Her integrity is unassailable, and remember that, as you deal hardly with others, so surely shall you be more hardly dealt with yourself.'

"His Holiness laughed, congratulated me on my boldness in speaking so to him, and exhorted me to come straight to him whenever I heard any ill reports about the Church.

"Then he discussed the matter at length, sometimes

exonerating himself, sometimes admitting himself to be at fault. And finally he summed up as follows. 'Once upon a time all the members of the body,' he said, 'conspired against the stomach, complaining that he, in his greed, consumed the labour of all. The eye had no rest from seeing, nor the ear from hearing; the hands persevered continuously with their labours; the skin of the feet had grown quite hard from much walking; the very tongue was constantly exercising its discretion as to whether it should talk or be silent. In fine, every member was on the alert for the common weal; and while all helped each other by careful and combined labour, the stomach alone lay there idle. And when everything had been got ready by co-operation, the stomach alone enjoyed the result. Need I say more? The members agreed that they would do no more work, but would crush this lazy fellow, this public nuisance, by starving him out. So the first day dragged wearily by; the second became worse. By the third, the evil had grown to such proportions that nearly all broke down. So, forced by necessity, the members came together again to consider their own position and that of the public enemy. But when they were met together, the eye was dull, the feet could not support the weight of the body, the arms hung listless, and the tongue lolled so helpless against a sickly palate that it could not be got to give voice to the common cause. So the matter was referred for arbitration to the heart, who, after due deliberation, explained the cause to them. The stomach, which they had begun by denouncing as the common enemy, was in truth waging war upon them. For when they refused to pay tribute to him, he, as public paymaster, retorted by refusing aliment to each of them. So, since no one can fight without the sinews of war, the army becomes crippled and disbanded if the money is not forthcoming. Nor can the blame be cast upon the paymaster, for if he receives nothing himself, he surely cannot make distribution to others. Is it not far safer to give to one that he may make distribution all round, than that all should go hungry to spite the one? Reason prevailed, and the matter was arranged. The members received their nourishment as usual, and peace was restored on all sides. So I think the stomach is not to blame after all, and its greed even for the fruit of other men's work is pardonable enough, seeing it seeks not its own but the advantage of others, and of others which could not manage to sustain themselves if it were to die. Exactly the same thing,' continued his Holiness, 'occurs in a corporate state, if you examine the matter. The chief absorbs more, of right, so that he may sustain others rather than himself. If he is starved, what is there to distribute to the others? The moral, of course, is that the stomach holds the same office in the body as the prince does in the state. What does Q. Severus say?'[1]

---

[1] "Polycraticus," vol. iv., lib. vi., cap. 24, p. 64 :

    "Qui stomachum regem totius corporis esse,
    Contendunt viva niti ratione videntur.
    Hujus enim validus firmat tenor omnia membra,

"'Man's seat of power in his stomach lies,
And he who owns its sway, is surely wise.
Grant it it's due, it does it's part, nor fails;
Neglect it's wants, and straight each member ails.
Swift to revenge, now cheated of it's toll,
It spreads the ill, and vitiates the whole.'

"'Wherefore, my friend, don't trouble yourself to measure our severity or that of the secular powers, but simply look to the common good.'"

The recitation of this familiar fable from Æsop appears to have removed the lingering doubts in John of Salisbury's mind, for he declares himself to be thoroughly satisfied.

"Thereupon," he adds, at the close of the Pope's lecture,[1] "I gratefully put my shoulder to the wheel, . . . nor did I find the task anything but agreeable when I knew that I was working for God's sake and at His command."

The passage above quoted is the one on which those who assume that John accompanied the mission of Robert the Abbot rely. But it will be noticed that the author himself says nothing about being sent by the King; indeed, he mentions "causâ visitandi," and not "causâ congratulandi," as the object of his journey. In the "Annales

At contra ejusdem fraguntus cuncta dolore
Quin etiam, nisi cura juvet, vitiare cerebrum
Fertur et integros, illinc avertere sensus."

This was cleverly translated for me by Mr. S. Lamert, 1895.

[1] "Polycraticus," vol. iv., lib. vi., cap. 25, *ab initio*.

Ecclesiastici,"[1] Baronius expressly states that the interview in question took place in 1156. And Henry certainly did not wait for two years after his succession before sending his congratulations to the prelate. It may also well be argued from internal evidence that John would hardly have taken upon himself to complain of the Pope's avarice and laziness, which in substance he does, had the latter only just been appointed to his high position. Nor is it likely that men would be murmuring in many provinces that the Pope was building himself palaces and allowing churches to fall into decay, within the first few months of his pontificate; also, John meeting the Pope alone would in all probability have referred in some way to the report he should make to the King.

These considerations—in addition to the fact that in the extract I have given from Thomas of Walsingham he is not mentioned—confirm, I venture to think, the opinion that he was not one of the congratulatory mission.

But of the most important mission on which he was sent by the King, John of Salisbury unfortunately says nothing more than the mention of it as a fact without further comment. Henry II., wishing to invade Ireland, and either deeming it necessary to obtain the Pope's permission, which would be an admission of the temporal power of Rome, or else desiring the blessing of Providence on his undertaking, sent John to the prelate to obtain a bull to this end. This historic bull may be found in the

[1] "Bar. Ann. Eccl.," tom. xix., p. 103, col. 2.

epistles of Peter de Blois,[1] and there is another version preserved by Baronius.

This bull is so important, and has given rise to so much warm discussion, that I have dealt with it fully by itself in the next chapter.

A second most interesting passage in the "Polycraticus" is well worth quoting as throwing a valuable sidelight on Adrian's private thoughts and the feelings with which he regarded the pontificate.[2] "The highest position," says John, " brings with it the least liberty ; and there is none so high as to be above keeping God's laws. Surely the man who is subject to no one is thereby only bound the closer to abstain from what is wrong. The Pope of Rome, who, as a man, has most freedom, is in reality the most tied down of all men. The privilege of the Apostle descends on his successors, and this is clearly part of it. . . . Above all, the Pope must be ready to serve others of God's servants for the sake of the Church: and that, not, as some hold, nominally for the glory of the thing; but actually, in practice, however unwilling he may be. Everyone serves the Lord. . . . Angels and men serve Him; righteous and sinners alike. The very devil, prince of this world, serves Him most of all. Even a Roman tyrant serves the Lord, seeing he serves the Pope. Indeed, a man must either be a heretic or a seceder who does not serve God.[3]

---

[1] *Vide* vol. ii., ep. ccxxxi., p. 199.
[2] "Polycraticus," vol. iv., lib. viii., cap. 23.
[3] *Ibid.*, lib. viii., cap. 23, p. 366.

ADRIAN IV.

And I call his lordship Pope Adrian, whose lot in life the Lord hath blessed, to be a witness of all I have said; for there is no man more wretched than the Roman Primate, nor one who holds a more arduous position than his.

"If ever it happens that he is free for a space from external worries, the very weight of his own work is sufficient to weigh him down. Why, he told me that his seat involved such hardships on him, that taking the present for all in all, he would reckon his previous sorrows little short of happiness and an easy life. 'The office of Pope,' he assured me, 'was a thorny one, and beset on all sides by sharp pricks; indeed, the burden of it would weigh down the strongest man, and grind him to the earth.'

"'Rightly did people speak of his crown and gold vestments as glittering, for they burned like fire.' He wished, indeed, that he had never left his native land of England, or at least had lived his life quietly in the cloister of S. Rufus, rather than have entered on such a narrow path; but he dared not refuse, since it was the Lord's bidding. Ask him yourself while he is still with us, and believe one who has tried. He impressed this fact on me frequently, that, after rising grade by grade, from an humble position in a cloister to the highest place in the world, the chair of S. Peter, he had gained nothing by his elevation—no happiness, no peace, no rest. I will quote his own words to you (and remember that in my presence he wished no detail of his life to be hidden). 'It seemed once,' he said, 'as if God was constantly beating me and stretching me out, as with a hammer on an anvil; now I pray Him to aid me with this burden He has placed on my shoulders, for I find it unbearable. Surely the man who strives to gain such a burthen deserves to have it to carry. He may be the wealthiest of men when he is chosen, but the next day he will be a beggar, and responsible to the meanest creditor. And what does a man deserve who is never called to this position by election, but allows himself to be thrust forward by blind and ruthless ambition, careless of shedding his brother's blood? Such a man, I say, aims at succeeding Romulus in fratricide, rather than Peter in managing the affairs of the United Church of Christ.'"

The next reference John makes to Adrian is his sorrowful account of his death, and will be found in its proper place. It will now be seen how vitally important and precious is this almost the only trustworthy record we have of his personal character.

Adrian ever remembered his native land, and we are told always spoke of it with pride. He undoubtedly did all he could for its welfare, and had he lived longer would probably have done more. I must now examine the arguments concerning the grant to Henry II. of the island of Ireland.

CHAPTER IX.

Adrian's Bull granting Ireland to Henry II.—The Text and Translation of the Bull—Arguments for and against its Genuineness—State of Ireland in the Eleventh and Twelfth Centuries—Historical Evidence—Conclusions.

ADRIAN'S bull granting Ireland to Henry II. has been the subject of so much dispute that it may be well to examine the question at some length.

The editor[1] of Giraldus Cambrensis' works in the "Rolls" series speaks thus of this bull which Adrian IV. is reputed to have granted to Henry II.: "It is most indisputably genuine; and so now allowed by all Irish scholars." In face of this emphatic opinion of so able a commentator and so learned a scholar,[2] further discussion would appear to be unnecessary and impertinent; but the grave importance of the question involved in this assumption of pontifical right—an importance, indeed, which it would be wellnigh impossible to over-estimate while discussing Henry's claim to invade Ireland—and the nature of this work will, I trust, be suffi

---

[1] The Rev. J. Dimock.
[2] The Right Rev. Dr. Creighton, Bishop of Peterborough, also considers this bull to be undoubtedly genuine.

cient excuse for entering at some length into a discussion regarded by Mr. Dimock as at an end.

The overwhelming preponderance of evidence is directly in favour of the genuineness of the bull. A great many arguments have been brought up on the other side, but they are all founded on purely negative facts, and have no shadow of claim to be regarded as proof. By English law a man is either innocent or guilty, and he is assumed to be the former until he is proved to be the latter. Scots law is more subtle; a jury of North-countrymen, without wishing to commit themselves entirely, may record their suspicions by a verdict of "not proven." The charge against Adrian's bull may certainly be regarded as not proven.

It would, undoubtedly, save a great deal of trouble, and clear up a very dark period in Irish history, if we could prove that Adrian's bull was spurious. Several ingenious theories have been mooted from time to time to meet the case; one in particular, of which I shall have more to say later, is so plausible, and so thoroughly in consonance with facts, that, were we to adopt it, many rough ways would be made smooth. But how often in history might not the same thing be said? Adrian's bull has held the field now for more than seven centuries, and until we have very strong proof to the contrary—proof as yet not forthcoming —we must regard it as genuine.

Before proceeding, it will be necessary to take a cursory glance at the affairs of Ireland during the eleventh and twelfth centuries.

The comparative proximity of Ireland to the shores of England had suggested the idea of invasion to more than one English monarch. William the Conqueror would, we know, have carried out this project had he been able to find time for it, and the first Henry only abandoned the idea when he found that the whole of his energies were required towards directing those internal reforms of his kingdom upon which he had set his heart. It was but natural that the project should recur with increasing force to the son of the Empress Matilda. A young prince, ambitious, crafty and courageous, it would indeed have been strange had so palpable a scheme escaped his notice. The fact that he enjoyed wider dominion and owned more land than any of his predecessors would merely serve to whet the appetite of a man of the second Henry's character.

Henry II. mounted the throne in December, 1154. Before he had held the reins of power for more than half-a-dozen months the half-formed wish to add the island of Hibernia to that of England and the vast territories in France over which he ruled grew into a fixed resolve. But on what ground to justify this unprovoked attack on a free and unoffending people?[1] He had no quarrel with any of

---

[1] A writer in the "Dublin Review," July, 1883, thus disposes of the difficulty: "The slave trade against which the Conqueror and Bishop St. Wulstan had striven, and which they had for a time succeeded in suppressing at Bristol, was again carried on during the disturbed times of Rufus and his brother, the first Henry. . . . Thus it came to pass that Ireland on the accession of Henry was full of Englishmen who had been kidnapped and sold into slavery. This would have furnished a pretext sufficient for

the princes of Ireland; there was no historic feud to rake up as a pretext for his rapacity. To have descended upon the island as a simple matter of conquest would have been a fatal error in the eyes of the world. A solution of the difficulty at length presented itself.

About the same time that Henry II. had succeeded to the throne of England, Nicholas Breakspear had been elected to the chair of S. Peter. Now though, as I have said before, the claim of the Popes to temporal power had never been recognized in this country—and, indeed, Henry himself would have been the first to repudiate any such claim—the head of the Holy Catholic Church was admittedly spiritual lord of all the world. Why not make a tool of his countryman, and conceal treachery under the cloak of religion? It immediately occurred to Henry's facile mind that if he were to enter Ireland as the avowed ally of the Church, and with the declared intention of extending the Christian faith, so far from execrating his design all the faithful must applaud and extol him. What more natural than that an English Pope should entrust the task of converting a rude and ignorant people to an English king? The scheme pleased Henry vastly, for it enabled him to

---

war." But it is by no means certain that Ireland was "full" of kidnapped Englishmen at this time. Many able critics are agreed that Giraldus Cambrensis, on whose testimony the writer presumably depends, grossly exaggerated an evil which, though undoubtedly existing, was by no means so widespread as has been thought. It is at least significant that no mention of this "trade" appears in any contemporaneous writer in this connection.

HENRY II., KING OF ENGLAND.

kill two birds with one stone: he could satisfy his own ambition and ingratiate himself with the Pope at a stroke. In the spring of 1155 John of Salisbury set out for Rome, bearing letters from Henry praying the Pope to authorize the projected invasion of Ireland.

These letters have unfortunately not been preserved, though Rohrbacher, in his "Histoire Universelle de l'Église Catholique," by the simple expedient of deducing what the King said to the Pope from what the Pope replied to the King, arrives in a general way at their contents. He says: "Le roi Henri II. fit donc entendre au Pape Adrien, par Jean de Salisbury, qu'il songeait à conquérir l'Irlande afin d'y fortifier l'action de l'Église, de pourvoir à l'instruc- d'un peuple ignorant, d'en extirper les vices, et d'étendre à ce pays le payement annuel du denier de Saint Pierre; mais que, comme toutes les îles chrétiennes étaient la propriété de l'Église romaine, il ne se permettrait pas d'entreprendre cette expédition sans l'avis et le consentement du successeur de Saint Pierre."

There are several different versions of the bull extant, but substantially all agree. The text here given is taken from Migne,[1] and is identical with that preserved in Mansi.[2]

"*Adrianus episcopus, servus servorum Dei, charissimo in Christo filio illustri Anglorum regi, salutem et Apostolicam benedictionem.*

"Laudabiliter et satis fructuose de glorioso nomine pro-

---

[1] "Patrologiæ Cursus," tom. 188, p. 1441.
[2] "Concil.," xxi., 788.

pagando in terris, et æternæ felicitatis præmio cumulando
in cœlis, tua magnificentia cogitat, dum ad dilatandos ecclesiæ terminos, ac declarandam indoctis et rudibus populis
Christianæ fidei veritatem, et vitiorum plantaria de agro
Dominico exstirpanda, sicut Catholicus Princeps, intendis,
et ad id convenientius exsequendum, consilium Apostolicæ
sedis exigis et favorem. In quo facto, quanto altiori con-
silio et majori discretione procedis; tanto in eo feliciorem
progressum te præstante Domino, confidimus habiturum;
eo quod ad bonum exitum semper et finem soleant attin-
gere, quæ de ardore fidei et de religionis amore principium
acceperunt. Sane Hiberniam, et omnes insulas, quibus sol
justitiæ Christus illuxit, et quæ documenta fidei Christianæ
ceperunt, ad jus Beati Petri et sacrosanctæ Romanæ Ecclesiæ
(quod et tua et nobilitas recognoscit) non est dubium
pertinere. Unde tanto in eis libentius plantationem fidelem
et germen gratum Deo inserimus, quanto id a nobis interno
examine districtius prospicimus exigendum. Significasti
siquidem nobis, fili in Christo charissime, te Hiberniæ insulam, ad subdendum illum populum legibus et vitiorum
plantaria inde exstirpanda, velle intrare, et de singulis
domibus annuam unius denarii Beato Petro velle solvere
pensionem, et jura ecclesiarum illius terræ illibata et
integra conservare, nos itaque pium et laudabile desiderium
tuum cum favore congruo prosequentes, et petitioni tuæ
benignum impendentes assensum: gratum et acceptum
habemus, ut pro dilatandis Ecclesiæ terminis, pro vitiorum
restringendo decursu, pro corrigendis moribus, et virtutibus

inserendis, pro Christianæ religionis augmento, insulam illam ingrediaris, et quod ad honorem Dei et salutem illius terræ spectaverit, exsequaris; et illius terræ populus honorifice te recipiat, et sicut Dominum veneretur: jure nimirum ecclesiastico illibato et integro permanente, et salva Beato Petro et sacrosanctæ Romanæ Ecclesiæ, de singulis domibus, annua unius denarii pensione. Si ergo quod concepisti animo, effectu duxeris complendum: stude gentem illam bonis moribus informare, et agas tam per te quam per illos quos adhibes, quos fide verbo et vita idoneos esse perspexeris, ut decoretur ibi Ecclesia, plantetur et crescat fidei Christianæ religio, et quæ ad honorem Dei, et salutem pertinent animarum, per te taliter ordinentur, ut a Deo sempiternæ mercedis cumulum consequi merearis, et in terris gloriosum nomen valeas in sæculis obtinere." [1]

---

[1] "*Adrian, Bishop, servant of the servants of God, to his dear son in Christ, the illustrious King of England, sends greeting and Apostolic benediction.*

"Your Highness is filled with a laudable and fruitful desire to extend your glorious name in this world, and to increase your reward of immortal happiness in heaven, whilst, as a good Catholic prince, you set yourself to extend the bounds of the Church, to declare the Christian Faith to ignorant and barbarous peoples, and to extirpate the nurseries of immorality from the estate of the Lord; and the more effectively to put this design in execution, you have come for advice and assistance to the Holy See. And in this undertaking we are confident that the shrewder the judgment and the greater the discretion with which you proceed, the happier the success you will with God's help have; because those things always come to a good issue and end which have taken their origin from enthusiasm for the faith and love of religion. Surely there is no doubt—what your Highness also admits— that Ireland, and all other islands o'er which Christ the sun of righteous-

There is some little confusion as to the date of this bull and the place where it was granted. On this subject I shall have more to say in another place; meanwhile, we are following the best authorities in assigning it to the spring of the year 1155.

At Michaelmas in 1155—so Robert de Monte relates

ness has shined, and which have accepted the lessons of the Christian faith, do of right belong to the Blessed Peter and the Holy Church of Rome. And the more clearly our own examination shows us the need, the more readily do we introduce among them the planting of faith, a seed so pleasing to God.

"Since you have advised us, dearest son in Christ, of your intended expedition into Ireland, to subject the island to just laws and to root out thence the hotbeds of vice, and you promise to make from every house a yearly payment to S. Peter of one penny, and to maintain the rights of the Church without the least detriment or diminution, we, therefore, being willing to assist you in this pious and laudable desire with fitting favour, and benignantly consenting to your petition, hold it a pleasing and acceptable thing that you make a descent on that island, to enlarge the bounds of the Church, to check the career of profligacy, to reform morality, and to promote virtue with a view to the increase of the Christian religion; and that you carry out what shall have regard to the honour of God and the salvation of that land, and that the people of that land receive you honourably and respect you as their sovereign lord—provided always that the rights of the Church are preserved undiminished and entire, and one penny be duly paid out of every house to the Blessed Peter and the Holy Roman Church. If therefore you put your design in execution, be careful to reform the manners of the people, and so act, both in your own person and in the persons of those whom you employ, having seen them to be worthy in faith and language and life, that the Church of God may be beautified there and the Christian religion may be planted and grow, and that all things tending to the honour of God and the salvation of souls may be ordered in such manner by your efforts as may entitle you to obtain a large eternal reward in heaven and enable you to win a glorious name on earth for all ages."

in his "Norman Chronicle"[1]—the King, sitting in council at Windsor with his barons, mooted the projected invasion of Ireland. But the Empress Matilda was so strongly opposed to the scheme—an opinion in which she was backed up by several of the barons—that the King reluctantly abandoned his pet idea. The bull was temporarily laid in the archives of Winchester, together with a papal ring—"annulum aureum, smaragdo optimo decoratum"[2]—which Adrian appears to have sent to Henry as an investiture of right, much in the same way as Alexander had granted William the Conqueror a holy standard to be used against Harold. Both John of Salisbury and Girald of Wales go out of their way to make special mention of this ring as "investituræ signum," the former adding somewhat quaintly that the beauty of the emerald was so great that he could write a whole volume singing its many noble qualities.

So it came to pass that the bull, which Henry had been at such pains to obtain, was quietly laid to rest at Winchester, where, but for extraneous circumstances, it might have remained for centuries, unknown and harmless. By an apparent irony of fate, the conquest, abandoned by the King as untimely and presumptuous, was at length forced on him by the very people he had sought to conquer. What he—most powerful of sovereigns—had not cared to attempt, a handful of English adventurers brought to pass in the course of a few months!

---

[1] "Chron. Norm.," 691.   [2] Joan. Sar., "Metalogicus."

Ireland, it must be borne in mind, was at this time still divided up into the five ancient provinces or kingdoms, viz., Leinster, Desmond or South Munster, Tuamond or North Munster, Connaught, and Ulster. Each of these provinces owned its own petty king, the most powerful of whom claimed the dignity of monarch of the whole island. This honour had rested for some time with the family of O'Neal, but had recently been usurped by the O'Connors, kings of Connaught. With so many varying and antagonistic interests in the island, it is easy to see that the whole country could never hope to be at peace for long.

So far back as 1152, according to Giraldus Cambrensis,[1] Dermot MacMurrough, King of Leinster, had eloped with the wife of a neighbouring sovereign, one Tiernan O'Rourke, King of Breifny. The lady appears to have been not altogether averse to this proceeding—"quia et rapi voluit"—a fact further attested by Regan; but the husband, unable to brook such an insult, called upon Roderick O'Connor, monarch of the island, to aid him in chastising the adulterer. At first Dermot weathered the storm he had raised bravely enough; but gradually, as his tyranny alienated the support of his own subjects, he found the tide becoming too strong for him, and at length, in 1166, was obliged to fly the kingdom. "Multis itaque patet," adds Girald, naïvely enough, " rerum eventibus, tutius esse volentibus, quam invitis imperare. Sensit hoc Nero, sensit Domitianus. . . . Expedit a subditis prin-

---

[1] "Expugnatio Hibernica," *ab init.*

cipi milibet potius amari quam timeri." The words have a strange significance when one thinks of Henry's own end.

Passing through England, Dermot sought out Henry, who was at that time in Aquitaine, plotting deep vengeance on Thomas à Beket. The English monarch received the fugitive with vast affability, accepted his homage, and granted him letters patent empowering him to engage such help as he could in his (Henry's) dominions. The letter concludes thus: "Unde et quisquis ei, de amplitudinis nostræ finibus, tanquam homini et fideli nostro, restitutionis auxilium impendere voluerit, se nostram ad hoc tam gratiam noverit quam licentiam obtinere." This extension of aid to an avowed adulterer, fleeing from justice, comes rather oddly from a king whose sole anxiety a few years previously had been to enter Ireland for the purpose of inculcating morality among the people.

I must run over the next few years very hurriedly. Dermot's offers attracted the cupidity of Richard, Earl of Striguil (the famous Strongbow), at this time an out-at-elbows, needy adventurer, ready for any quest which might present itself, with nothing to lose in defeat and everything to gain in victory. But for some reason or other Strongbow, though pledging himself to the undertaking, could not be induced to start at once; and Dermot, impatient and headstrong, returned to Ireland to do battle for his kingdom, having no greater force to his hand than two Welsh knights with their retinues. His success far exceeded his most sanguine expectations. After a short but brilliant campaign the erstwhile fugitive found himself strong enough to aspire to the monarchy of all Ireland. With this end in view he despatched a letter[1] to Strongbow, reminding him of his former promise of aid.

Meantime Henry had changed, or at least modified, his policy of partisanship; and now we find him absolutely prohibiting Strongbow from setting out for Ireland. That nobleman, however, had gone too far to retract. Pretending never to have received the king's prohibition, he crossed the channel with a body of twelve thousand archers and many knights. In a very short space of time Waterford fell before him; even Dublin did not long withstand the now overwhelming force of the invaders. But the victors had hardly installed themselves in the capital of the island ere death intervened, and Dermot, in the midst of planning fresh victories, was struck down by fever.

Henry's contemptuous indifference had gradually been giving way to a feeling of jealousy at the success of the English adventurers, and when Strongbow, having married Eva, daughter of Dermot, assumed the royal power, his anger kindled into a flame. He determined to go to Ireland himself, and forthwith set about collecting an army. Strongbow, realizing the hopelessness of his position, hastened to throw himself at the King's feet, offering homage for his kingdom. At first Henry treated his advances with marked coldness, but eventually—conciliated by his abject submission—granted him leave to accompany the expe-

[1] This extraordinary missive is preserved by Girald.

dition, which accordingly set sail from Milford towards the close of the year 1171.

Though taking with him a very considerable force of troops, it was Henry's wish rather to receive the voluntary submission of the kings than to force obedience at the point of the sword. To this end not a single blow was struck on the triumphal march to Dublin. Encouraged by the apparent kindness and affability of the great monarch, and overawed no doubt by an exaggerated sense of his magnificence, the princes one after another proceeded to swear allegiance. Of the whole island, the chiefs of Ulster alone refused to submit to the foreign yoke; while O'Connor, King of Connaught, a man of haughty pride, purposely delayed coming in person to own his superior. But even he gave a nominal oath of submission to Henry's messengers on the banks of the Shannon. The clergy, meeting in synod, agreed to recognize the claims of the English king; and the opportunity was seized to effect various pressing reforms in the Church.

Now, it may be thought, would have been the time to produce Adrian's bull of authorization. The clergy, whose power over the people was by no means nominal, must have recognized the papal letter, the more so as the Roman legate had presided over their synod. The princes, on the other hand, would have had less cause for wounded pride had they been made to recognize the authority of their spiritual lord. But this palpable course apparently never occurred to Henry. He was content to let his claim rest on the benignity of his character and the salutary effects of his supremacy. Christmas was spent in feasting, and when, in the spring, more urgent affairs recalled the King to England, he returned thoroughly satisfied with the success of his enterprise.

But peace, established on such a basis, could not last. In a very few months the storm had burst forth again with renewed vigour. Strongbow was not powerful enough to hold such antagonistic elements in check, and Henry, deeply occupied with his own affairs, could find no time to recross the channel. The power of the English in Ireland dwindled rapidly.

At this juncture it apparently occurred to Henry, for the first time, to make use of the papal authority with which he had been invested. But the bull was now twenty years old, and Pope Adrian, who had granted it, had been in his grave for more than a decade and a half. Fresh privileges were accordingly obtained from Alexander III., Adrian's successor,[1] the document granting which, together with the original bull, was sent to the Irish clergy. Girald states that a synod was summoned at Waterford,[2] in which John of Salisbury played a leading part; but it is

---

[1] These privileges are preserved in the "Liber Niger Scaccarii," Hearne's edition.

[2] "Hiberniæ Expugnatæ," lib. ii., cap. 6: "In Hiberniam itaque privilegio transmisso per Nicolaum Wallingfordensem tunc priorem . . . nec non et Guillelmum Adelmi filium: convocato statim apud Guaterfordiam episcoporum synodo, in publica audientia, ejusdem privilegii cum universitatis assensu, solemnis recitatio facta fuit per Joannem Saresberiensem. . . ."

doubtful whether John (afterwards Bishop of Chartres) could have been present on that occasion. At any rate, Adrian's bull does not seem to have attracted much notice one way or another.

In the following year (1176) a nominal treaty was formed between Roderick, King of Connaught, and Henry, by which the former undertook to hold his crown directly under the English sovereign, to whom he agreed to pay tribute. This treaty was never formally rescinded, but in a very short space of time it had lapsed. The Irish, chafing under the foreign yoke, lost no opportunity of harassing their invaders. Strongbow's death, in 1177, brought matters to a head. As a last resource, Prince John, Henry's younger son, was sent into Ireland. He stayed for nine ignominious months, powerless to effect anything, after which he was summarily recalled. Henry, preoccupied with his own schemes, and beset by the arduous difficulties of civil dissension, never found opportunity to recross the channel; and Ireland, rent asunder by the disintegrating forces of the invasion, gradually lapsed into a worse state than it had previously known.

Now, even from this brief outline of the first Irish invasion, it will be seen that Adrian's bull, whether genuine or not, played an utterly insignificant part in Henry's policy. For some twenty years it lay unknown at Winchester. When an opportunity to produce it really arrived, it was overlooked; and only as a last resource, when all else had failed, it was routed out of its hiding-place and sent to the Irish clergy—a sort of gratuitous spiritual admonition. But the fact that Henry neglected to use the bull in no way proves that he did not obtain it, nor must the contemptuous use he made of it blind our eyes to the important principle of which it was the outcome.

Let us now consider the claims on which the authenticity of the bull rests.

(1.) In the last chapter of the "Metalogicus"—the philosophical treatise already referred to, and which was dedicated by the author to Thomas à Beket—John of Salisbury himself,[1] as I have related, records the fact that he obtained a privilege from Adrian IV. granting leave to Henry to enter Ireland.

(2.) Giraldus Cambrensis, the historian of the Irish invasion, speaks of the bull incessantly, and never throws doubt on its authenticity.[2]

(3.) Ralph de Diceto[3] gives a copy of the bull, as also, in effect, does Roger de Wendover.[4] The latter prefaces

[1] "Metalogicus," lib. iv., cap. 42: "Ad preces meas illustri regi Anglorum, Henrico Secundo, concessit et dedit Hiberniam jure hæreditario possidendam, sicut literæ ipsius testantur in hodiernum diem. Nam omnes insulæ de jure antiquo, e donatione Constantini, qui eam fundavit et dotavit, dicuntur ad Romanam Ecclesiam pertinere. . . ." This is a most important passage, and deserving of close attention.

[2] Girald gives the bull in his works no fewer than three times: "Expug. Hib.," lib. ii., cap. 5; "De rebus a se gestis," cap. 10; and "De Instructione Principis." The texts do not always agree *verbatim*, but the inequality of the readings may possibly be put down to the blundering of amanuenses. In the main they are identical.

[3] "Hist.," *sub anno* 1155.   [4] "Flores Historiarum," *sub anno* 1155.

his statement with the following words: " Per idem tempus, rex Anglorum Henricus *nuntios sollemnes*, Romam mittens, rogavit Papam Adrianum ut sibi liceret," etc. Several later chroniclers—*e.g.*, Matthew of Westminster—adopted this idea of a solemn embassy, presumably as adding dignity to the mission.

(4.) The Norman Chronicles testify to the fact that the bull and the ring were deposited at Winchester.

(5.) The privileges granted by Alexander III. to Henry, about the year 1175, support the bull of his predecessor, Adrian IV.

(6.) The Princes of Ireland in addressing a remonstrance to Pope John XXII. against the English, after the battle of Bannockburn, make constant and repeated reference to Adrian's bull, assuming throughout its authenticity.

(7.) Cardinal Baronius, in his "Annales Ecclesiastici," prints the bull *in extenso*, as he says, " ex codice Vaticano, diploma datum ad Henricum, Anglorum regem."

(8.) The bull is printed in the " Bullarium," published at Rome in 1739.

These, then, are the chief reasons for supposing the bull to be genuine, and it is clear that, before the contrary can be proved, each of the authorities above quoted will have to be separately refuted. It were obviously idle to say that Girald started the forgery, and that all his contemporaries promptly adopted it. Neither can the primary blame be summarily cast upon John of Salisbury. And, to begin with the latter writer, no one, I think, will dare to impugn his scrupulous integrity. At a time when honest men were not to be found under every hedge, he lived a life of spotless purity, and through all his writings the consciousness of a noble singleness of purpose is invariably present. The editor of the "Analecta,"[1] at any rate, does not relish the task; he adopts another method. This is simply to dispute the whole passage in the "Metalogicus" as spurious. Many things, it may be at once said, combine to lend colour to this theory. The words that John of Salisbury is supposed to have written are contained in a chapter carelessly tacked on at the end of the work. The "Metalogicus" proper ends with the forty-first chapter. The thread of the narrative up to that point is more or less in sequence. Suddenly deserting his subject, the author breaks off to interpolate an exceedingly strange tale about his friendship for the dead prelate, and to anathematize the aspiring anti-Pope. Such an aposiopesis is rare in literature, but by no means unknown. It may be regarded as condemnatory evidence, but certainly not as proof. Might not John, while sorrowfully penning the last lines of a long labour of love, hearing of Adrian's sudden demise, and careless of relevance or continuity, in a sudden paroxysm of grief, hasten to unbosom himself to his trusted friend?[2]

[1] "Analecta Juris Pontificii." Mai-Juin, Paris, 1882. Victor Palmé, ed.

[2] A writer, Mr. Sylvester Malone, in this connection instances the case of Chevalier Artaud, who, "while finishing the life of Pope Innocent III., was quoting the testimony of Gregory XVI. . . . in praise of Innocent,

We may at once concede that the whole chapter is strangely out of place and alien to the context. But would not a forger have been at some pains to make his interpolation agree with the rest of the work? Would he, for instance, have hazarded the statement that Theobald, Archbishop of Canterbury, had made over his power to John of Salisbury, when, from all apparent circumstances, the latter knew the English prelate only very slightly? And would he have been so severe on the anti-Pope in face of the King's admitted personal support of Octavian?

Had the authenticity of the bull rested on the unsupported word of Giraldus Cambrensis, I should have been very slow to accept it. Girald's editors, in the "Rolls" series, refuse him credence on the ground that "truth was not his main object; he says he compiled the work for the purpose of sounding the praise of Henry II." When an author has the effrontery to make such an admission as this, a reader must be pardoned if he takes him strictly at his word.

The character and writings of Girald were first hotly assailed by Dr. Lynch, who, in an exhaustive treatise entitled "Cambrensis Eversus," attempts to vindicate the character of the Irish people from the foul charges made

when news came of the former's death. He breaks off the life of Innocent, and gives a sketch of the pontiff of whose death he has just heard, and thus blended the twelfth with the nineteenth centuries." There is also another instance in the "Dublin Review," April, 1884.

against them by the author of the "Expugnatio." It is a regrettable circumstance that this commentator should have allowed zeal so completely to outrun discretion, and to have turned criticism into personal abuse. The rancour he displays throughout the work precludes us from placing more faith in his historical deductions than in those of his unfortunate victim; though, on the simple principle of setting a thief to catch a thief, we may perhaps be allowed to accept his proofs of Girald's mendacity without accepting his conclusions therefrom. In a word, Dr. Lynch justifies his assertion that nothing in Girald's history must be accepted without hesitation unless supported by extraneous proof.

Ralph de Diceto, like Girald, "received his honours" (in the words of Dr. Moran) "at the hands of Henry II." He is extremely inaccurate in places, and actually states that the Synod of Cashel was held in Lismore in 1172. Roger de Wendover, on the other hand, admittedly compiled his "Flores Historiarum" from the MSS. lying at his hand. It would, therefore, be best for us to leave these authors out of court altogether, and to refuse their testimony as affecting the question one way or other.

Leaving for the moment the Norman chronicle of Robert de Monte—to which I shall refer presently—we come next to the papal bulls of Alexander III., which, it is claimed, support the authenticity of Adrian's grant to Henry. There are four of these altogether. Three, written in 1172, are preserved in the "Liber Niger Scaccarii," whence the learned Hearne edited them. So far from confirming a grant made by Adrian, these three would appear to furnish the most cogent argument yet produced for setting it aside as groundless and unauthentic. "They are entirely devoted to the circumstances of the invasion of our island and its results, and yet the only title that they recognize is 'that monarch's power and the submission of the Irish chieftains.' They simply ignore any bull of Adrian, and any investiture of the Holy See." The words are Dr. Moran's.

The fourth bull is not preserved in the "Black Book," and, indeed, depends solely on the testimony of Girald, who alone gives its text. It amply confirms the authenticity of Adrian's bull; indeed, it has a suspicious suggestion about it of having been written solely for the purpose of bolstering up the former papal brief. Once more criticism is forced to fall back on the somewhat crude method of disputing a passage *in toto*, though this time, as must be admitted by everyone, the sceptics are able to make out a strong case.

"The question at once suggests itself," says Dr. Moran, "is this bull of Alexander III. to be itself admitted as genuine and authentic? If its own authority be doubtful, surely it cannot suffice to prop up the tottering cause of Adrian's bull. Now, its style is entirely different from that of the three authentic letters of which we have just spoken. Quite in opposition to these letters, 'the only authority alleged in it for Henry's right to Ireland is the bull of

Adrian,' as Dr. Lanigan allows.¹ The genuine letters are dated from Tusculum, where, as we know from other sources, Alexander actually resided in 1172. On the other hand, this confirmatory bull, though supposed to have been obtained in 1172, is dated from Rome, thus clearly betraying the hand of the impostor. Such was the disturbed condition of Rome at that period, that it was impossible for his Holiness to reside there; . . . it was only . . . in 1178 . . . that Alexander III. was able to return in triumph to his capital."

But the strongest piece of evidence is yet to come.

There is another reason why we must doubt the authority of this confirmatory bull. The researches of the Rev. Mr. Dimock have proved what Ussher long ago remarked, that this bull of Alexander originally formed part of the work of Giraldus Cambrensis, although later copyists and the first editors, including the learned Camden, recognizing its spuriousness, excluded it from Giraldus' text. The matter is now set at rest, for the ancient MSS. clearly prove that it originally formed part of the "Expugnatio Hibernica."

Thanks, however, to the zeal and industry of Mr. Brewer, we are at present acquainted with another work of Girald, written at a later period than his historical tracts on Ireland. It is entitled "De Principis Instructione," and was edited in 1846 for the "Anglia Christiana" Society.

Now, in this treatise Girald refers to the confirmatory bull of Alexander III., but prefixes the following

[1] "Eccl. Hist.," cap. iv., 224.

remarkable words: "*Some assert or imagine that this bull was obtained from the Pope, but others deny that it was ever obtained from the Pontiff* (Sicut a quibusdam impetratum asseritur aut confingitur; ab aliis autem unquam impetratum fuisse negatur)." Surely these words should suffice to convince the most sceptical that the fact of the bull of Alexander being recited by Giraldus in his "Expugnatio Hibernica" is a very unsatisfactory ground on which to rest the argument for its genuineness.

So far, then, from supporting Adrian's grant, this bull, to my mind, is the strongest piece of evidence yet produced against it. For if Girald forged the second document —and any impartial observer will be forced to admit that it reads exceedingly like a forgery—there can be no doubt that his object in so doing was to bolster up the previous bull. And that Adrian's letter should have needed bolstering up at all is—as must be admitted—a very suspicious circumstance. A truthful historian would have no need to forge one bull in order to support another, if the latter were genuine. Dr. Moran and the editor of the "Analecta" appear to score a point here.

But, on the other hand, the argument is more ingenious than convincing. The basis of it all is a hypothesis, and one can hardly look for a firm superstructure on such a foundation. Neither, it is only fair to add, does the question of the genuineness of Alexander's bull *vitally* affect the authenticity of that of Adrian. The latter can stand without the former, though not *vice versâ*.

Dr. Lynch, apparently in a sudden outburst of passion, declares that the Irish race—priests and people alike—have never accepted Adrian's bull as authentic. Had this statement been true, there would have been some ground for the supposition that it was regarded with suspicion and mistrust from the first; but, unfortunately, the exact contrary was the case. In the year 1319—soon after the battle of Bannockburn, in fact—the Irish nation addressed a brief to Pope John XXII., calling upon him to rebuke Edward II. of England for his callous behaviour towards Ireland, and, as if to strengthen their case against him, quoting to the Pope the terms of Adrian's bull, which, as they allege, each succeeding English sovereign had failed to carry out. So far, therefore, were the Irish from repudiating the grant of Adrian, that they actually founded their protest on it.[1] The brief is written in the name of "Donaldus Oneyl, rex Ultoniæ, ac totius Hiberniæ hæreditatio jure verus herus," and claims to speak on behalf of Ireland as a nation, "nec non et ejusdem terræ reguli atque magnates ac populus Hiberniacus."

Similarly, the "Leabhar Breac," or "Book of the Four Masters," an interesting and exceedingly trustworthy compilation of the fifteenth century from earlier MSS., not only acknowledges the bull, but gives a most circumstantial reason why it was granted. The passage is worth quoting in full: "O'Annoe and O'Chelchin of Cill Mor,

---

[1] Fordun, "Scottichronicon," vol. iii., pp. 906-8; Hearne's edition.

O'Sluasti from Cuil O'Sluasti, O'Glesain. These were they who stole the horses, and the mules, and the asses, of the Cardinal who came from Rome to the land of Erin to instruct it, in the time of Domhnall O'Brian, King of Munster. And it was on that account the Cowarba (*i.e.*, successor) of Peter sold the rent and right of Erin to the Saxons; and that is the right and title which the Saxons follow on the Gaedhil (*i.e.*, Irish) at this day; for it was to the Cowarba of Peter, to Rome, used to go the rent and tribute of Erin until then."—" Leabhar Breac," fol. 51 b (now 41 b).

This passage is quoted by Robert King in his " Primer of the History of the Holy Catholic Church in Ireland " (supplementary vol., Appendix XI.), who adds some interesting comments.

The letter of the Irish nation, as also the Pope's reply, is worthy of careful attention. The following extract will give some idea of the temper in which it was conceived not less than of the manner in which it was written. ". . . At length your predecessor, Pope Adrian, an Englishman (although not so entirely English in his origin as in his temperament and connections), in the year of our Lord 1170 (*sic*), relying upon lying and iniquitous misrepresentations made to him by Henry, King of England (the very sovereign under whom, and perchance at whose instigation, S. Thomas of Canterbury was murdered, as you will remember, while defending the Church and upholding justice), made over the dominion of this realm, in a certain set form of words, to that monarch; while, for the enormity we have just recalled to your memory, his Holiness had done better to have taken away the kingdom that he already had; in fine, the Pontiff presented him *de facto* with that which he had no power to bestow, while utterly disregarding *de jure* the fairness or the equity of the proceeding. Anglican prejudice, it is sad to say, had so far blinded that estimable Pontiff. . . ."

Pope John XXII. read this brief, and forthwith wrote to Edward II. as desired. His letter is preserved by many historians, and may be found in Wilkins's "Concilia,"[1] where it is taken from a "Bullarium" published in Rome in 1583. After severely taking the King to task for his conduct, the Pope reminds him of the conditions upon which Adrian granted the island to his ancestor, Henry II., and warns him to be more careful for the future. "Finally," he adds, "in order that you may clearly understand what it is the Irish people rebel against, I am sending you their letters, *together with a copy of the grant which* Adrian, our predecessor, made to your ancestor, Henry II., regarding Ireland."

Thus, in 1319—less than a century and a half after Adrian's death—there was no suspicion of spuriousness attaching to his bull, either in the minds of the Irish people or of the authorities at the Vatican! The editor of the "Analecta," or any other hostile critic, will find it difficult to explain away these facts.

I mentioned two other authorities as having some-

[1] Vol. ii., p. 491.

times been quoted in support of Adrian's bull, to wit, the "Annales" of Cardinal Baronius and the various editions of the "Bullarium" published from time to time at Rome. With regard to the former, Dr. Moran has the following passage:

"During my stay in Rome," he writes, "I took occasion to inquire whether the MSS. of the eminent annalist (Baronius), which happily are preserved, indicated the special 'Vatican MSS.' referred to in his printed text, and I was informed by the learned archivist of the Vatican, Monsignor Theiner, who is at present engaged in giving a new edition and continuing the great work of Baronius, that the 'Codex Vaticanus' referred to is a *MS.* copy of the history of Matthew of Paris,[1] which is preserved in the Vatican Library. Thus, it is the testimony of Matthew of Paris alone that here confronts us in the pages of Baronius, and no new argument can be taken from the words of the eminent annalist. Relying on the same high authority, I am happy to state that nowhere in the private archives, or among the private papers of the Vatican, or in the 'Regesta' which Jaffé's researches have made so famous, or in the various indices of the pontifical letters, can a single trace be found of the supposed bulls of Adrian and Alexander."

Similarly, no reliance is to be placed on the authority of the "Bullarium." In one edition, the bull of Adrian is

---

[1] Matthew of Paris was a monk of S. Albans who took the hood in 1217. His history was compiled largely from other historians, and the best critics are now agreed that very little of his matter is original.

given, while that of Alexander is not; in another, Alexander's obtains a place, while Adrian's is wanting. The truth is, that the selection of the matter to be used in a "Bullarium" rests in the editor's hands, and an editor, being human, is as likely to err as a commentator.

I have thus briefly tried to run over the chief arguments that have been brought up, or that might be brought up, for and against Adrian's bull. On the one hand we have the testimony of Girald, of John of Salisbury, and of other contemporary writers; we have the fact that the Irish people themselves recognized the authenticity of the bull, a recognition which was endorsed by a succeeding Pontiff, John XXII., who undoubtedly had no suspicion of forgery in his mind; and, finally, we have the independent judgment of annalists, historians, and commentators (Baronius, Jaffé, Ciaconius, Lingard, Lanigan, Ussher, Dimock, O'Callaghan, and a score of others), everyone of whom declares unhesitatingly that it is genuine. On the other hand we have a mass of unsupported destructive criticism, founded on purely negative facts, which, however ingenious be its construction, must of necessity fail to convince. I think I have said enough to justify my previous assertion that the charge against Adrian's bull is not proven, and that, until definite proof is forthcoming, we must regard it as genuine.

It is impossible to expect an ancient document of this nature to be entirely above historical criticism.[1]

---

[1] I am indebted to Dr. Creighton, Bishop of Peterborough, for this view. In his opinion, "the evidence of John of Salisbury is unanswerable."

Moreover, as was often the custom in those days, the bull was probably private between Adrian IV. and the King—to be used if necessary, not otherwise—and never given to the secretaries to register.[1]

In this act Adrian was anticipating the grants which in after times were made by the Popes to the travellers and discoverers of the fifteenth century, and it may be noted that the claim over all islands was the principal, if not the sole basis on which he made the grant. For when the King of France besought him for a similar bull to enable him to wage an annexing war against Spain, it was refused by Adrian, who, recognizing the religious motives on which Louis VII. professed to base his claim—i.e., the expulsion of the Saracens from the peninsula—still withheld permission, pointing out that Spain was an independent state, and did not come under the scope of Constantine's will.

[1] As a matter of pure conjecture, it may also be argued that perhaps Henry did not use the bull when he got it on account of it laying too much stress on the temporal power of Rome; and I am inclined to believe this to be the real reason, but can find no evidence to support my view.

CHAPTER X

1155 TO 1156.

Growth and History of the Kingdom of Sicily—William II. of Sicily—Adrian's Letter to him—Attack on Beneventum—Adrian excommunicates William—Roman Defeats in Campania—Negotiations with Manuel I.—Proposed Treaty with William—Divisions among the Cardinals—Failure of Negotiations—William takes Brundisium and Bari—Appears before Beneventum—Terms of Peace with the Pope—Embassy from the Eastern Church—Proposed Reunion—Adrian goes to Orvieto.

DURING the early part of Adrian's reign there were important events occurring in connection with the kingdom of Sicily which render some account of the previous history of the papal relations with that country necessary.[1] During the ninth, tenth, and eleventh centuries all the southern part of Italy was constantly convulsed by internal wars and troubles, and by repeated invasions of Saracens and Greeks. The last of these convulsions was the conquest of the island of Sicily by the Normans under Roger, son of Tancred, in

[1] "The History of the Western Empire from its Restoration by Charlemagne to the Accession of Charles V." Sir R. Comyn. London, MDCCCXLI. Vol. i., pp. 224, 228, 235, 238. Also Muratori, vol. vii.

1058, who took the name and title of Roger I., Count of Sicily, in 1061.

In 1059, Robert Guiscard, also a Norman, and an elder brother of the Count of Sicily, was made Duke of Apulia, and his title was confirmed by Pope Nicholas II. He helped his brother, and, though he was excommunicated in 1074, he made peace and did feudal homage for his duchies of Apulia and Calabria to Pope Gregory VII. in 1080. His reign was eventful and celebrated for his wars against Henry IV., Emperor of Germany, and also the Greeks. He died at Cephalonia in 1085. Roger II., son of Roger I., succeeded his father under the regency of his mother at the end of the eleventh century, and when he came to rule by himself, he styled himself King of Sicily, and governed his little kingdom, no easy task, with skill and moderation.

In 1121, his cousin William, who succeeded the Duke of Apulia, died, and Roger entered Naples and took the titles of his dead cousin. This being done without the papal permission, led to a war with Pope Honorius II., who led an army against Roger and excommunicated him, but in the end, after the two armies had lain facing each other for forty days on opposite banks of the river Brentano, the Pope yielded, and confirmed Roger in the duchies of Apulia, Naples, and Calabria.

In 1130 Roger espoused the cause of the anti-Pope Anacletus, who was his wife's brother, and who confirmed his title of King of Sicily, helping him to incorporate the republics of Naples, Amalfi, and Gaieta. He then became King of the Two Sicilies. In 1137, Bernard of Clairvaulx urged the Emperor Lothair and the Kings of England and France to help the cause of the Pope Innocent II. against Anacletus. Roger II. was beaten at first in the war which ensued, and had to retreat before Lothair; but owing to a variety of causes, the principal one being a division between the Pope and the Emperor, he gradually won back all he had lost, and in 1139 he took the Pope himself prisoner, obtained the terms he wanted and recognition of his title. He passed the rest of his years in constant warfare, and died in 1154, being succeeded by his son William.

I think I have shown enough in the above sketch to point out that the southern part of Italy had, since its Norman conquest, been constantly in open dispute with the see of Rome. The difference rested on the following grounds, that the Popes always claimed the feudal sovereignty of the whole of South Italy, on the grounds that they inherited it from the Emperors, and so were entitled to the homage of its rulers. The Emperors of Germany also claimed the temporal rights over the whole peninsula, but were seldom able to insist on their claims. The Normans, who held the country by the right of conquest, did their best to play off Pope against Emperor, but on the whole were ready to agree with the former as the best geographical ally against any incursion, either from Germany, the Eastern Empire, or the Saracens.

William, the new King of Sicily, was a great contrast to his father, who was a great and wise ruler; he neglected the affairs of his country, domestic and foreign, being under the influence of a lowborn favourite of the name of Wrajo. He was crowned King of Sicily and Apulia on Easter Day, 1154, at Palermo, by Hugh, its archbishop; and at the end of the year, when Adrian was elevated to the papal chair, he sent ambassadors to Rome to congratulate him and to ask for the special papal privileges which had been given to his father to be granted anew. But he had mistaken his man. Adrian would not have been true to himself had he abated one inch of his ground of dignity or the smallest part of his papal prerogative. William had neglected to ask for papal permission to be crowned, and so had outstripped the bounds of that conduct which the Pope held as indispensably due to the Church.

He knew the past history of constant rebellion and trouble in the matters of the kingdom of Sicily, and as usual determined to assert himself in the same stern, unyielding way in which he treated Frederic and his rebellious Roman subjects, and so to put an end to the constant disaffection of his vassal.

He caused a letter to be prepared addressed to him as "Lord" of Sicily, and sent it to William by the hand of Henry, Cardinal of S. Nereus and S. Achilles.[1] William paid no attention to the Pope's missive, and remembering

---

[1] Muratori, vol. vii.

how his father had obtained his ends by waging a successful war against the Pope, he refused to receive Cardinal Henry, and gave orders to his chancellor, Ascletinus or Scitinus, to declare war against the papal dominions, to devastate the territory of Beneventum with an army, and lay siege to that town. The news of this audacity was carried to Adrian IV. As usual he struck his blow immediately and without hesitation. Just as he had laid Rome under an interdict, so he thundered out a bull of excommunication against William,[1] declaring him to be " a rebel and an enemy to S. Peter and his Church," and absolving all his subjects from their oath of allegiance.

The formula of excommunication was no less dreadful to the individual than an interdict was to the state, depriving him as it did, not only of all religious privileges, not even excepting the last rites of the Church, but of all social ones as well; though, great as was the terror which the sentence inspired, it never seems to have weighed much on the consciences of the Norman Kings of Sicily, and they generally regained their religious liberty at the point of the sword. William did not seem to be greatly affected at the news; he went back to Sicily on the pretext of quelling a disturbance in the island, and spent his time in pleasure and debauchery with his favourite Wrajo, leaving his general Ascletinus as governor of Apulia in his absence, with orders to carry on the war against the Pope. At the

[1] " Hist. B. Platinæ."

same time that this was happening, the Emperor of the East,[1] Manuel I., was employing secret agents in Apulia to stir up the nobles to resist William's forces, in order that he might eventually be able to regain some of the provinces which had been lost by the Greeks. This enabled the inhabitants of Beneventum to make such a strong resistance to the siege of their city, that after several attempts to take it, involving the loss of many of his men, Ascletinus was at length compelled to raise the siege; much to Adrian's disadvantage, for as he passed away from the successfully defended city, he poured his troops into southern Campania and ravaged the country by fire and sword, taking the towns of Cepperano, Bacano, Frusinone, and Acre, pillaging them, and leaving them in flames. He then marched back into Apulia, and on his way burnt and sacked the monastery of Aquino, the castle of Pontecorro, and a number of other places belonging to the monastery, which at that time was under the monks of Monte Cassino. All this was going on at the time that Frederic was advancing from the north, and before Adrian knew what would be the ultimate result of that great movement. We now see the full amount of the dangers which the Pope had to face in the first year of his pontificate: a rebellious Rome, with a fiery and popular agitator at its head; the Eastern Emperor plotting in some sinister way on the very borders of the papal dominions; war with all its terrors in

---

[1] Succeeded 1143.

the south, and the greatest monarch in the world advancing from the north with every incentive of success and glory to increase his arrogance ;—small wonder that Adrian complained to his faithful friend John of the anxieties which attended his exalted position! Now indeed, if ever, did the Church require firmness and courage in its chief. Adrian, in his interview with Barbarossa, endeavoured to persuade him to make common cause against William, but Frederic, while sympathizing with the troubles which were assailing the papal interests, declined on account of the effects the climate was having on his troops. Then, as we have seen, the Byzantine Emperor endeavoured also to persuade Frederic by a heavy bribe to enter into an alliance with him also against William, but with the same answer. Frederic was well content that the Pope and the King of Sicily should be opposed to each other, not wishing indeed to see Rome do that which he was unable to do himself, viz., become master of the peninsula.

A political situation as tangled and complicated as can well be imagined, and requiring a cool and masterly head to see the way clear through it to the attainment of the dignity of the Church without losing so powerful, but so jealous an ally as the ambitious warrior who guided the fortunes of the empire.

The action of Adrian in excommunicating William had led to his obtaining the support of several of the usually turbulent nobles of Apulia, who came and paid homage to him.[1]

[1] Oct., 1155, at St. Germano. Card. Arragon in " Vitâ."

Amongst the principal were Robert, Count of Loritelli, who was a cousin of the King, Andrew, Count of Rupi-Canino, Richard, Count of Aquila, and Robert, Prince of Capua, all of whom, with many others, were disgusted with the conduct of their feudal chief in neglecting the internal affairs of his kingdom, so well governed by his late father Roger, and wasting his life and kingly responsibilities in debauchery and low living. Encouraged by these adhesions Adrian determined to test William, who remained in Sicily, and whose very existence was doubted by some, by taking action himself. He judged, and rightly, that however the King might affect to despise his sentence, it must in time weigh heavily on his conscience, and holding in his hands, as he did, the power of releasing him from the ban, he hoped by a successful campaign to obtain a treaty of peace restoring Rome and her Church once more to the undoubted ascendency in Italy which he wished eventually to see her occupy in the whole of Christendom. This would be turning the tide against William which he had hoped to use against the Pope. Adrian therefore, Rome being fairly quiet, left the city and accompanied his army towards Beneventum, invading the Terra di Lavoro, and after a short campaign took up his quarters at Beneventum, where he remained for some time, during which he occupied himself with domestic affairs and Church matters, and received the long visit from John of Salisbury which I have mentioned. While Adrian was thus employed, William gradually lost many of his possessions, and it seemed as if he was going to make no effort for his crown. At the beginning of the year 1156 Manuel I. sent a magnificent embassy to congratulate Adrian on his position as head of the Western Church, and offered an alliance against William on the following terms: the Emperor was to pay five thousand pounds' weight of gold, and to supply an army to operate against the King of Sicily, on condition that three seaport towns in Apulia were to be handed over to the Greek Empire. This news on reaching William thoroughly alarmed him; he at once sent ambassadors to Adrian, praying to be absolved from his sentence of excommunication. His anxiety was increased at hearing that Adrian had sent a letter to Frederic asking for his assistance as well, and against such a combination of enemies he would be powerless. This was exactly the effect which Adrian desired to produce, and the terms which William offered sufficiently indicate the state of alarm he had been placed in. He sailed from Sicily to Salerno, and landing there despatched his ambassadors to Adrian with the following proposals in addition to the prayer for release: he undertook to restore to the Pope all the cities he had taken, and to add three seaport towns in addition, as an indemnity for the raid on the Campagna; Ascletinus also to pay a sum equivalent to the amount promised by Manuel I., and to help Adrian if ever he required assistance in quelling the ever-turbulent community in Rome. In return for these concessions, his sentence of excommunication to be removed, and his title as King of Sicily and

Apulia to be recognized on his undertaking to comply with the Pope's demands as to doing homage and swearing fealty to him as the liege lord of Sicily. The embassy arrived; but Adrian could hardly believe that his diplomacy had achieved such a marvellous success, and half-suspected that there must be some condition attached as to which the King had neglected sufficiently to instruct his envoys. So he sent three cardinals, Hubald of S. Praxed, Julius of S. Marcel, and Roland of S. Mark, the Chancellor,[1] to William to ascertain the truth. And now, as if the difficulties and troubles hemming in the Pope were not enough, he was called upon to deal with a division among his cardinals. The position of the Pope in respect to the cardinalate was in a small degree analogous to that of a constitutional ruler of the present day, having almost the powers of a dictator, but nevertheless so placed in regard to his senate that he could not view an adverse expression of opinion with respect to his individual action with indifference, and it has often happened in history, that just at the moment when the strong man should have a perfectly free hand an interfering or divided senate has fettered his action and marred his plans. And in this manner was Adrian hampered now. There was and always had been a strong German party among his cardinals, and they viewed an alliance with William and possibly Manuel as a move in direct opposition to the interests of the Emperor Frederic, which indeed it would have been; so

[1] The signatures of all these three may be seen in the Bull reproduced in this book.

when they met to consider the terms of the proposed treaty, they suggested that Adrian should not hear of the terms offered, but carry on the war against Sicily with renewed vigour. Adrian did his best to persuade them to his views, but faction and cabal had its way, and the Pope was not the first nor the last man in history to find that the worst hindrances were they of his own household. He had no intention, however, of surrendering the helm of the ship of state to the factious opposition in his cabinet. He simply decided to shape his plans in a different mould, and to try and obtain the best results he could, having regard to the German party in the cardinalate. Therefore he refused the terms which William had offered, and declined to consider the question of his title. William seems to have been thoroughly roused by this and the sense of danger, and sending his fleet round through the Straits of Messina, he laid siege to Brundisium [1] by sea and land.

This important city had been captured by Manuel, and was held by a Greek general of distinguished fame, named Ducas. It was one of the ports by which the Greek armies acting against the soldiers of William were to be poured into Italy. At the time when William arrived at Brundisium, the fort or citadel garrisoned by Sicilian troops was still holding out against Ducas, and the garrison was already considering on what terms it should agree to the surrender which famine and sickness was making more

[1] Brindisi.

imperative every day. William, however, gave them fresh hopes. He drew off the troops of the Greeks, and forced Ducas to a pitched battle outside the town, which raged for a long time without any advantage to either side; but after a stubborn fight the Sicilians were victorious, and William once more took possession of Brundisium. By a stroke of good fortune he found here the gold intended by the Emperor Manuel for the Pope. He also made an immense capture of ships, stores, and munitions of war, besides a number of wealthy Greeks, whom he sent to Palermo, some for ransom, but the greater number to be sold into slavery.

There were also in the city a good many of the Apulian nobles who had revolted against him, and these met with the awful severity of those times, when "væ victis" had a real and terrible meaning; a great many were executed on the spot, while torture and mutilation were inflicted on all those remaining who were not fit for the slave market.

This great stroke practically determined the issue of the war; for although one more lesson was still to be taught William's rebellious subjects, the awful severity of his treatment of Brundisium sufficiently warned the inhabitants of Apulia what to expect, and many laid down their arms. The other lesson referred to was even more cruel and harsh than the first. Brundisium had resisted the troops, and William entered in all the excitement of conquest. But at Bari, whither he next marched, there was no resistance; the army was met by a crowd of its principal citizens coming out to prostrate themselves with all the humiliating customs of the age at the feet of the powerful King and to pray for his mercy. To be impartial in criticising William's action on this occasion, I should mention that they had added to their offence of siding with his opponents the great one of destroying the citadel of Bari while it was garrisoned by his troops, who refused to betray their trust. The only answer they received was that the King in consideration of their non-resistance would spare them the horrors of giving up their town to be sacked immediately; but would only allow them forty-eight hours to make their arrangements, during which time they should be free to pass his lines with their families and their goods. After this, he added, the city would be given up to the soldiers and reduced to ruins, for as they had dared to destroy his house in their town, so would he in return revenge himself by destroying theirs.

The conditions of life in these towns was sufficiently precarious, and one wonders how trade and commerce could develop at all under the change of rulers constantly resulting from the fortune or chance of war. The inhabitants were always in a dilemma. If they did not bow to the party in power their homes were desolated, and if they did, there was every chance of their city being burnt and destroyed at the next change of authority. Certainly the houses of those days were easily rebuilt, for the majority of them were made of mud or clay, baked hard under the Italian sun; but still all the interests of home, and the associations attaching to such things as household furniture and goods must have suffered in those shocks in an irreparable way—not to mention the added horrors of starvation and pillage, of the knife and the firebrand in the hands of the fierce troops who had no mercy for young or old, at whose hands neither man's life nor woman's honour were safe. Bari was fortunate in her two days' respite. The inhabitants did all they could to comply with the peremptory decision of their conqueror—a decision which was carried out to the letter; the entire city was destroyed, even to its walls, and vengeance was completed. This crowning lesson confirmed the movement already begun in William's favour, and all his subjects returned to his allegiance.

William now determined to march his victorious forces against the Pope, and turned in the direction of Beneventum, where, as we have seen, Adrian IV. was, together with the Prince of Capua and other rebel nobles, who now were beginning to feel somewhat less secure. Several left the city and retired to the fastnesses of the hill country for safety. Some fell into the hands of William's soldiers, and were treated with incredible ferocity. The most unfortunate was Prince Robert of Capua. He left the city with his son and daughter, and had made good his escape, when, by the treachery of a neighbour, Richard, Count of Fondi, he was waylaid and captured, the traitorous friend thereby securing his own safety with the King, who gave him a free pardon. The unfortunate prince was delivered up bound to the King, and after being exposed to the insults of the court, was sent off to Palermo, where he was thrown into prison and his eyes destroyed. Fortunately for him, death put an end to his suffering within a few months. Such were the terrible examples made in these turbulent times!

William now invested Beneventum, and prosecuted the siege with all the vigour which a successful army was able to give him. It was now in the month of May, 1156, one year after the exciting times attending the approach of the Emperor Frederic. Again we find Adrian faced with difficulties, this time with the enemy at his gates and the road to Rome cut off.

To any weaker character the position would have seemed hopeless; but Adrian had that strong determination, that powerful will, which can literally force a man through difficulties and dangers, and bring him to the result he intends to arrive at in spite of the apparently immovable nature of the obstructions in the way. The Pope never for one moment lost his head; he remembered the success with which his great predecessor and model, Hildebrand, had used the power of the anathema,[1] and he knew that its weight was pressing with increasing power on William every day. It must not be forgotten that this awful sentence was not only confined to the individual, but, in the case of a prince, the subjects who paid him allegiance were virtually also under the ban, and men, however brave, however cruel or reckless, little cared to be

[1] See Milman, "Latin Christianity," vol. iv., bk. vii., cap. 1 and 2.

fighting in a campaign where death meant the loss of absolution, and their souls, as they considered, deprived of the privileges of Heaven, and even of the more doubtful benefits of Purgatory. So they counselled William to use his position as a successful conqueror to bring Adrian to his knees and dictate the price of peace. But the king was not living who could frighten this great man. Adrian had not only foreseen this situation, but to some extent he had prepared it. He was no longer the new Pope, on whom all sorts of experiments were to be attempted. He had increased his reputation enormously by the eventful year during which he had occupied the chair—men knew of his iron will and realized his strength of character. His first step was, so to speak, to carry the matter into the enemy's country; he sent to William first, to request that those rebel princes who were still in Beneventum might have their lives spared to them, plainly inferring that this must be a preliminary to any negotiations which might be afterwards entered into. William knew the Pope's character, and that in agreeing to this he was paving the way towards a prospect of getting what he himself required. Moreover, he was quite satisfied with the vengeance he had already executed, and was inclined to see his kingdom settle down into a more peaceable, and therefore more lucrative state, as soon as he had stopped all chance of further rebellion. So he agreed to the Pope's preliminary offer; the revolted nobles in Beneventum were pardoned on the condition that they left the country, and though this involved some of them leaving ancestral homes, the majority of them were soldiers of fortune, to whom a change of country was nothing new and little hardship. It may be assumed pretty certainly that the hereditary nobles of Apulia managed to escape from Beneventum by the help of their clansmen, and also that many never came to that city at all.

Thus did Adrian show not only his firmness, but the fact that he was loyal to those who served him. Nothing would have been easier than to surrender the nobles to William as a means of getting his terms agreed to; but this idea the English Pope would have scorned. It probably never entered his head to treat his allies otherwise than honourably and fairly. A deed like this would add to his reputation in those days almost more than anything else, and probably produced a deep impression on William himself.

The next step was also taken by the energetic Pope. He sent another embassy to William, with proposals for a treaty of peace and alliance based on the proposals of the King which had been rejected on account of the action of the German section of the cardinals.

And here let us pause and look at the accurate and wonderful game Adrian was playing. Thwarted by the countermove of the German cardinals, he waits till the enemy is actually under the very walls of the city in which is the papal court, and then he triumphs over his cabal by making what terms he can; and who could cavil at an alliance instead of a sack?

After some negotiation, the King practically agreed to

the Pope's proposals; a treaty of alliance was concluded, in which the Pope consented to withdraw his sentence of excommunication and to invest William with the crowns of Sicily and Apulia, the principality of Capua, the territories and states of Naples, Salerno, and Amalfi, the march of Ancona, and all the other cities which he then possessed. The Pope agreed also to an addition to the original treaty, by which he undertook not to receive appeals from William's subjects except through the King, not to send any legate to Sicily without his permission, and to leave the choice of clergy in his hands. In return, King William agreed to stop all hostilities forthwith, to swear allegiance to the see of Rome, also to pay a yearly tribute to the Pope from Apulia, Calabria, and the march of Ancona as feudatory of the Church, and to defend the city of Rome against its enemies.

This treaty was sealed and confirmed by a papal bull, and on 9th June, 1156, Adrian opened the gates of Beneventum and issued forth in state, attended by his cardinals, bishops, and clergy, and proceeded to the church of S. Marcian outside the walls. Here he received William, absolved him from his sentence of excommunication, and while the monarch knelt before him solemnly declared him King of Sicily and Apulia, Prince of Capua, Duke of Naples, and Lord of all the other places included in the treaty; after which they embraced. High mass was celebrated; after the mutual exchange of presents they separated, and King William started on his way to Palermo. Adrian had again got his way; he had bent Italy to the control of the Church, and had dictated the terms of peace to his virtual conqueror! Some writers have said that Adrian's ambition was thwarted by the additions made to the treaty by the King; but when one reflects that these were, after all, points of quite minor importance, and that the Pope actually obtained from William, when successful, the same terms substantially which the same King had sued for to avoid defeat, one must admire the genius of the man who so successfully reinstated the power of the Church in the face of such tremendous odds.

Adrian now made preparations to leave Beneventum, where he had spent such an eventful time, and was on the point of starting when an embassy arrived from Jerusalem, consisting of the Patriarch Fulcher and six bishops of the Eastern or Greek Church, to complain of the conduct of the Knights Hospitallers, who had been granted certain privileges by Anastasius IV., which the bishops and their chief declared had been greatly abused. This is interesting as showing the reputation for justice which Adrian must have had. These Greek bishops would not have undertaken so perilous a mission to the domains of the Western Church had they not had a high opinion of the man they had come to consult!

The complaints of the bishops were that their devotions were hindered by the interruption of the Knights; that the freedom of the order from tithe, which was amongst the privileges conferred by Anastasius, was a great hardship on the clergy; that the Knights received excommunicated persons in their church, and many other similar charges, amongst which was the absurd one that the hospital of S. John at Jerusalem was a finer building than the church of the Holy Sepulchre opposite which it stood.

Adrian listened carefully to all the charges, and eventually decided not to revoke the liberties granted by his predecessor to the Knights; but no doubt he wrote a homily to them on the duty of not disturbing your neighbour; for one of Adrian's favourite aspirations was to see a reconciliation between the Eastern and Western Churches, and he had much correspondence with both the Patriarch at Constantinople and the Byzantine Emperor on the subject. Basil, Bishop of Salonica, wrote to the Pope an important letter in the course of these negotiations, which, in the light of modern views, is most interesting. He asserts in it that the principles and doctrines of the two Churches are practically the same, that he did not at all consider himself as separated from the Catholic Church, but as belonging to a branch only differing from that of Rome in points of ceremony and ritual—discrepancies which he says belonged entirely to the Pope to remove, and that if he only removed them there would be nothing to prevent the union of the churches. We have heard much the same answer to the suggestion of reunion put forward more than seven hundred years later!

There is little question, however, that had Adrian not been so hampered in the next and last two years of his life by differences with the Emperor Frederic and other troubles, he would have done much towards a reconciliation between the Churches of the East and West.

After leaving Beneventum, the Pontiff made a progress through the papal dominions, redressing grievances, consecrating churches, and blessing monasteries, passed through Narni, probably stopping at the monastery of S. Casciano, whose ruins may still be seen, and finally reaching as far north as Orvieto,[1] where he was received with the liveliest expressions of loyalty and regard. He took a great fancy to the lovely Umbrian town, perhaps the most picturesque site in central Italy, overlooking miles of classical ground, stayed there some while, founded some new churches, and gave the city many privileges; so that the traveller to Orvieto will to this day hear his name spoken of by those who are fond of antiquarian research or who are acquainted with the history of their town. Adrian passed the winter of 1156-1157 at Viterbo, the last period of anything like calm in his stormy pontificate. It was no doubt at this time that he wrote some of the books which are attributed to his pen. While at Viterbo he received a deputation from the Romans, and arranged a satisfactory agreement with them. At the beginning of 1157 he returned to the papal city.

Either while Adrian was at Orvieto or Viterbo he received a visit from the old friend of his legatine days,

---

[1] In "Days near Rome," vol. ii., pp. 118-33, is a very good description of Orvieto; and, indeed, nearly all the places near Rome mentioned in this work may be found in Mr. Hare's delightful book.

Eskill, Archbishop of Lund, with whom he must have spent many pleasant hours of conversation. The archbishop left Italy on his return to Danemark before the end of 1156, and we shall hear further on how Frederic's treatment of him led to the breach in the friendly relations between Emperor and Pope which occurred in 1157.

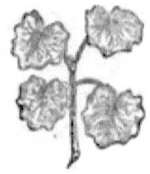

CHAPTER XI.

1156 TO 1158.

Frederic's Dissatisfaction at the Pope's Conduct—The Capture of the Archbishop of Lund—Diet at Besançon—Reception of Adrian's Envoys—The Pope's Letter—Cardinal Roland—The Dispute about "Beneficium"—Frederic's Proclamation to the German Church—Preparations for the Second Invasion of Italy—Adrian's Second Letter to the German Bishops—The Answer—Frederic at Augsburg—The Pope sends two Cardinals to the Emperor—Their Misfortunes—Their Reception—Temporary Reconciliation.

FREDERIC BARBAROSSA, after his return from his expedition to Rome in 1154-55, had been much occupied by the internal affairs of his empire, which his campaign had caused him to neglect. It must not be supposed, however, that he did not keep a sharp look-out on events in the south—a process in which he was assisted by the cardinals who took the German side in the papal council, and who kept the Emperor well informed of their progress. Frederic considered that his authority should be as unquestioned over Italy as over Germany, and he further regarded himself and not the Pope as feudal lord of William of Apulia and Sicily. He not only asserted this as an inherited right dating back to Charlemagne,

FREDERIC I. (BARBAROSSA),
EMPEROR OF GERMANY.

but he claimed that the custom of paying the feus had been exercised down to recent times.

And certainly there was some foundation in fact for his theory. In former years the Emperor Lothair II. had compelled Roger II. of Sicily to own the feudal claims of Germany over Apulia. It is true that this was imposed as the condition of peace after the ordeal of war, and it should be added that the Pope Innocent II. made a protest at the time, and tried to persuade Lothair to acknowledge the justice of the pontifical claims. But all that was arrived at was, an agreement that the Pope and Emperor should be joint lords over Apulia, and that when the banner of the duchy was handed to the King of Sicily, the Pope and the Emperor should each hold the flagstaff with one of their hands.

Frederic himself in the last year of the Pope Eugenius III. had stipulated for the observance of this custom, and had agreed not to make any treaty with the King of Sicily without the consent of the Pope.

It will easily be seen that there was much to be said on both sides, and ample debatable ground whereon to stir up a quarrel. And thus it was that, when Barbarossa heard of Adrian's treaty with William, which, it will be remembered, brought about the very state of things which the German party among the cardinals had tried to prevent, he looked with suspicion and distrust on the alliance, and regarded it as a distinct breach of faith on the part of the Pope. What he expected Adrian to do, however, it is difficult to conjecture, for the Pope had asked for the

Emperor's help, and that refused he was by all the rules of war entitled to make the best terms for himself. Perhaps Frederic was looking forward to difficulties in his next march to the south, which doubtless he had in his mind already; but, whatever the cause, he chose to take offence, and the friendly relations with Adrian were suspended, never again to be genuinely renewed.

It is impossible here to pick up all the tangled threads of the complicated history of this time, to trace the course of each intrigue, or to follow the diplomacy of the various rulers of the world. It was in truth not for this reason or for that that these great differences came about, nor was it to any discussion as to this particular feudal right or that particular form or ceremony that the constant heat was due. It was indeed the sole result of the friction of the two great causes working ever one against the other, the spiritual and the temporal. Again to quote from Dean Milman,[1] " These two powers, the Empire and the Papacy, had grown up with indefinite and necessarily conflicting relations; each at once above and beneath the other; each sovereign and subject, with no distinct limits of sovereignty or subjection; each acknowledging the supremacy of the other, but each reducing that supremacy to a name, or less than a name. As a Christian, as a member of the Church, the Emperor was confessedly subordinate to the Pope, the acknowledged head and ruler of the Church. As a subject of the Empire,

---

[1] Milman, " Latin Christianity," vol. iv., bk. vii., chap. 11, pp. 37, 38.

the Pope owed temporal allegiance to the Emperor. The authority of each depended on loose and flexible tradition, on variable and contradictory precedents, on titles of uncertain signification, Head of the Church, Vicar of Christ; Patrician, King of Italy, Emperor; each could ascend to a time when they were separate and not dependent on each other. The Emperor boasted himself the successor to the whole autocracy of the Cæsars, to Augustus, Constantine, Charlemagne; the Pope to that of S. Peter, or of Christ himself."

This is the keynote of all papal and imperial history at this period, and it is only when this central fact is fully realized that we can trace with some meaning the bewildering and conflicting accounts of the motives which led to some of the most important actions on the part of Emperor or Pontiff.

The Emperor, occupied as he was with German affairs, could not come to overawe either Pope or King in person. Various edicts insulting in their terms, and calculated to still further open the breach between himself and the Pope, were however issued; no allowance for Adrian's position at Beneventum was made, and, considering Italy to have slipped from his control, it was not long before Frederic proceeded to acts of overt hostility against the papacy. He forbade any German ecclesiastics to journey to Rome, and he appointed one Albertus de Moray to the bishopric of Verdun without consulting or asking the Pope. This and various other incidents passed without comment from

Adrian, who had no wish to provoke the Emperor to wrath, and certainly did not want to see him south of the Alps again except as a friend and ally. But at last he received news which appealed to his strong sense of loyalty to his friends, and provoked a letter from him which proved to be the spark required to start the smouldering quarrel into life and earnest. Eskill, Archbishop of Lund, on his way home from Rome to Danemark, had been set upon in German territory by independent knights of the German Empire, and, after having been plundered of all his property, including presents from the Pope himself, was imprisoned in one of the castle strongholds of his assailants, and heavy ransom demanded for his release.

This was no uncommon incident of these lawless times; but it became of great importance when, upon Eskill managing to communicate with the Pope, the latter, staunch to his friend, wrote to Frederic asking for his release, and pointing out the crime of seizing one of his rank in the Church. Whatever the Emperor's feelings may have been in regard to the Sicilian treaty, he ought certainly for his credit, and in common justice, to have procured the release of the captive. But to Frederic's lasting shame he declined to interfere. This naturally enraged the Pope, who determined to send a special embassy to the Emperor to complain, and also to call his attention to other matters. The year was already far advanced, and it was September before the embassy started. Adrian calculated that the envoys would reach Frederic at a great meeting he was to hold at Besançon in October, and determined to produce all his complaints in public at that place. Frederic, anxious to confirm his title of King or Duke of Burgundy, had determined to hold a diet of unusual magnificence at Besançon. He invited representatives from all parts of Europe to attend, and envoys came from England and France, from Italy, Venetia, and Spain, to the glory of the court of the successor of Charlemagne. All the chivalry of Germany was there; the veterans who had accompanied Frederic to Rome, and who were perhaps still chafing under what they considered their lord's submission to the Pope in 1155. The festivities were unexampled in their splendour, and everything combined to add to the grandeur and spectacular effect of the brilliant gathering.[1] Adrian, never backward at rebuke when he thought it necessary, selected with great care two cardinal legates, in whose loyalty, even to death, he could place absolute reliance. They were Roland, Chancellor and Cardinal of S. Mark, afterwards Pope Alexander III., and Bernard, Cardinal of S. Clement.

The envoys arrived at the brilliant scene and presented their credentials. They were received with the courtesy and honour due to the magnate whom they represented. Roland was the chief of the embassy, a man who feared no one, upright and dignified. His pride in the Holy Church had been deeply wounded, not only by the action of the Emperor in not complying with the demand of its pontiff

---

[1] Milman, *ibid.*; Comyn's "W. Empire," *ibid.*, p. 235; Radevicus Frisingensis, lib. i. (in Muratori, tom. vi., pp. 746, 747).

to release the Archbishop of Lund, but also at the insult he had offered by refusing to allow his prelates to go to Rome—a course of action which not only offended the pride of the papal state, but deprived the Church of a large part of her lawful revenues. The legates were presented by the Count Reinold, Chancellor of the Empire, at a sitting of the council convened for the special purpose of hearing the letter from the Pope. Cardinal Roland was the spokesman; a worthy representative of Adrian, in after years destined to succeed his master in the papal chair—one of the stern school of S. Bernard.

He read the letter, which of course was in Latin, and had to be interpreted as he went on for the benefit of those of the German nobles who did not understand the language; so the ceremony took some considerable time, and was constantly interrupted by questions and arguments between the interpreter and the unlettered knights. Roland's calm, haughty mien angered the followers of the Emperor from the first, and the opening words of the letter provoked the first murmurs of excited feeling.

"His Holiness the Pope," read Roland, "and the cardinals of the Roman Church salute you—he as a father, they as brothers." At once there was a burst of indignation from the assembly. The mighty Emperor bearded in all his splendour by two priests, who not only dared to put the Pope in a position of superiority to him, but had the audacity to claim for themselves and their brother cardinals an equality with the mighty monarch Barbarossa, and therefore superiority to all of less degree than the Emperor himself. Some of the nobles rose from their seats, swords were loosened, and an angry clamour arose; but Frederic, whatever his feelings may have been, kept them under control, and calming the assembly, obtained a hearing for Roland, who, undismayed, preserved his lofty bearing, and proceeded to read on.[1] The letter was lengthy, and dealt with a number of subjects. After a long preamble, it reproved the Emperor in severe terms for his neglect to punish those of his subjects who had laid hands on the sacred person of the Archbishop of Lund. It reminded Frederic, after recapitulating the distinct charges against him of breaches of faith, of the events in the plain of Sutri two years before, when he had received his crown at the hands of the Pope with all majesty, pomp, and honour, and then came a passage in the letter which ran as follows[2]: "That the Holy Roman Church had conferred the imperial crown on the Emperor, with the plenitude of all power and honour, and the Pope would rejoice had he conferred even greater benefits (beneficia) on him." At the word "beneficia" the storm broke. The Pope had used the word solely in the sense which is here given, of "benefits," and he certainly had no ulterior motive for its

---

[1] It may be read at length in Radevicus, Muratori, tom. vi., p. 747.

[2] "... et qualiter Imperialis insigne coronæ libentissime *conferens*, benignissimo gremio suo tuæ sublimitatis apicem staduerit confovere ... si majora *beneficia* excellentia tua de manu nostra suscepissit ... non immerito gauderemus" (*ibid.*).

use. But the word had then another meaning, and to the feudal nobles present it only conveyed the meaning of the word "beneficium" in feudal law. The beneficium was a form by which property was held, and was first created by the Franks when they settled in Gaul. The later term for this particular kind of title was the better known one of fief or feoff. It arose in this way[1]: After taking forcible possession of territory, the chiefs rewarded their followers by gifts out of the spoil, and later on these gifts or beneficia took the form of grants of land. But the usual character of a beneficium was that of absolute dependence on the feudal lord who was the "grantor," and this brought with it various conditions according to ever-changing custom or the exigencies of time or country. Moreover, although beneficia were often hereditary, they were generally of the nature of a modern life-interest, and on the death of the holder either reverted to the lord or could only be renewed for the next generation by a fine. I have explained this at length, as it is important to realize the effect of the word on the minds of the angry German nobles. To them the last sentence which Roland had read was the crowning insult of the Pope's intolerable letter, and plainly meant that Frederic was only a feoff or holder of a beneficium from the Pope. It had been hard to admit even the spiritual authority, it was impossible to endure the assumption of absolute temporal authority.

[1] Montesquieu, "Esprit des Lois," liv. xxx., xxxi.; Guizot, "Histoire de la Civilisation en France," Paris, 1829-32, tom. iii.; Hallam's "Middle Ages."

The knights sprang to their feet, angrily shouting and half-drawing their swords; and among them all the most furious was the Count Otho of Wittelsbach.

This noble, Otto or Otho, Count of Wittelsbach, was a devoted follower of Barbarossa, and ever jealous of anything affecting his dignity or his honour. He afterwards was made Duke of Bavaria by Frederic,[1] and this accounts for an error into which many writers have been led. For the incident I am about to relate is generally described as having been provoked by the Count Palatine of Bavaria, who at this time was Henry the Lion,[2] ancestor of the house of Brunswick; doubtless he also was at Besançon.

It was Otho,[3] then, who rose at the head of the nobles on hearing the objectionable word. Half-drawing his sword he tramped down the room, faced Roland, and angrily demanded if he meant to imply that Frederic held his empire as a mere feoff of Adrian.

There was silence for a space. It was a crucial moment, and much might depend on the cardinal's words.

But the man who was brought up in the school of S. Bernard, and was the friend and colleague of the now

---

[1] In 1180. Dollinger, "Studies in European History."

[2] Henry, Duke of Burgundy, restored by Frederic to his dukedom, but deprived of it again in 1180, on account of his siding against the Emperor. He married Maud, daughter of Henry II. of England, and died 1190 (*ibid.*).

[3] Born 1126, made Duke of Bavaria 1180, died 1183; ancestor of the royal house of Bavaria.—"Allgemeine Deutsch Biographe."

renowned Adrian, was not to be abashed. With lofty scorn he let the words bear the meaning the barons thought them to have, disdaining to correct their impression. In calm, quiet language he said to Otho: " And of whom then does he hold his empire, except it be of our Lord the Pope?" This was the signal for Otho to draw his sword, and, rushing at Roland, he would have cut him down had it not been for the direct personal intervention of Frederic, who had himself to quell the tumult and restore calm amongst his angry lords. Indeed, he had actually to hold back Otho with his own hands. But Frederic, if he had his temper better under control than the rest of his court, was hardly less incensed with the Pope for the letter; not that he did not understand the meaning of the disputed word, but he deeply resented those portions of the epistle conveying rebuke and the Pope's displeasure.

Much to his discredit he allowed the error as to " beneficia " to go uncorrected, and he put the two legates to the indignity of close arrest, had them searched, all their papers taken from them, and ordered them to return to Rome direct, without stopping anywhere on the way. The order was pronounced nominally because the envoys were found to have blank documents with the papal seal, which were suspected to be intended for use against any of the German churches who were biassed against the Pope or who refused to back up his authority against the Emperor, and to be filled in with pains and penalties accordingly.

This was merely an excuse. A trusted legate such as

ALEXANDER III,
CARDINAL ROLAND BANDINELLI.

Roland was, would be sure to have blank forms for purely formal use, such as the charter of a monastery, the certificate for relics, and numerous other instruments by the use of which the delay consequent on sending to Rome would be saved. The real reason was that Frederic was not absolutely sure of his German bishops, and did not want the insulted though undaunted Roland to start on a campaign of agitation and complaint amongst the prelates of the empire. And here again I must refer to the complicated relations and opinions which were all working at the same time. It must be remembered that while Adrian had, as we have seen, those among his followers who were not wholly sincere in backing his views to the extreme; so, in Frederic's case, there were many among the German bishops who were not prepared to admit the full extent of his claims. So, again, with respect to his own personal opinion, Frederic had no wish to upset the power of the Pope, his real desire being to attain, if it were possible, his own absolute supremacy over the empire, and to the full extent of his claims, without interfering with the papal rights. As regards Italy, I have not hitherto said anything as to the feelings of Lombardy, Tuscany, and the other states he had swept over in 1155. This work is a history of Adrian, not of Frederic; but it is necessary to point out that, although the country had been cruelly laid waste and impoverished, a strong spirit of opposition was rising, which survived the next invasion, and eventually defeated him in 1174. The germs of the North Italian republics of the Middle Ages were fructifying, and a spirit was abroad which, growing in strength of resistance and power, was first exhibited in the varied life of Milan, Genoa, and Venice, Florence, and Bologna, and the other states of the later Middle Ages, and reappearing centuries later became concentrated and realized in the United Italy of our own time. It is often the case that we are apt to judge the actions of men as if they had the fuller knowledge which we possess of the events going on round them. The life of a man occupies a very small space in the history of a great movement. Those near the picture can certainly see details which escape our more distant eye, but they cannot see the whole design—a fact which must be allowed for in attempting to criticise the actions of men in these early days, whose ideas were largely influenced by the environment of circumstances lost to us, or only very faintly visible; leading us, as it often does, to condemn them for not acting in accordance with principles which may seem to us to be perfectly plain and clear, but which were hidden from their eyes by the narrow limits of their vision. Thus, that the German bishops took Frederic's side is not so much a sign that they were opposed to the domination of the Pope, as that they were unconsciously taking their part in the development of national spirit in Germany. These considerations will enable us to account for many apparent inconsistencies of action on their part, and also for their so frequently playing fast and loose with the spiritual directions of the Pope.

After the legates had been escorted to the frontier of

the papal states, they made their way with all despatch to Rome and informed Adrian of their reception at Besançon and the insult offered to them by Otho of Wittelsbach. In the meantime Frederic deemed it necessary to be beforehand with the Pope, and issued a proclamation[1] to all the bishops of the empire, in which he described the insults (as he considered them) he had received from the Pope, and stated that the blank authorities found on the legates were intended to be used for the purpose of spoiling the churches of the empire, by laying excessive papal taxes on their revenues, and even taking away their plate and sacred vessels to Rome. It seems hardly credible that Frederic should have circulated so monstrous an accusation quite gratuitously, and it may be that there was some very slight foundation in fact for the statement. It is very possible that the legates really were going to collect some church dues, and this served as a groundwork for exaggeration amounting to falseness.

Frederic was playing a desperate and high-handed game. His unbounded ambition was leading him roughshod over all considerations, even those of simple accuracy and justice.

His letter went on to accuse the Pope of trying to stir up enmity and hostility between the Roman Church and the empire. He repeated his declaration that he held his empire from God alone, on whose servant, the Pope, simply

---

[1] Roderic, i. 8, 10; Gunther, vi. 800.

devolved the duty of performing the ceremony of coronation, and he dwelt also on the unlucky word "beneficia," declaring that man to be a liar who stated that he held his crown as a beneficium of the Pope. He wound up by informing the bishops that he and he alone stood between their liberties and the oppression of the Roman see, and repeated his edict that there should be no communication with Rome on the part of his clergy except by express permission.

Thus did Frederic throw down the challenge to the Pope; but Adrian in spite of the provocation kept his temper under complete control. His anxieties were great; he could not carry out the negotiations for reunion with the Eastern Church on which he had set his heart; he did not feel at all sure as to how far William of Sicily could be depended upon, and he was quite aware that any day might see trouble in Rome itself. During his stay in Rome Frederic had noticed a picture which greatly displeased him, representing the Emperor Lothair prostrate at the feet of the Pope, with the following lines underneath:

> "Rex venit ante fores, jurans prius urbis honores
> Post homo fit papæ sumit quo dante coronam."

Adrian had promised to have it destroyed, but Frederic had used the incident to inflame his nobles, who probably did not read the lines, but understood the picture. All this Adrian heard soon after the return of his legates.

But he also knew of a further design on the part of Frederic, viz., his intention to undertake another campaign to the south in the summer of 1158. There was every cause to expect the second invasion to be as successful as the first, and if so, what form would the meeting of Pope and Emperor take?

The former would no longer be able to use the threat of refusal to crown Frederic as a weapon. There was no common enemy like Arnold of Brescia to unite them, and Adrian had settled with William of Sicily. If they met not as friends, but as antagonists, the interests of the Church would suffer, and perhaps all the results of the success of 1155 destroyed. Adrian had no intention of surrendering any right, nor did he, as some writers have said, fear the Emperor.

The fear of God was the only kind of fear that Adrian ever showed, or indeed knew. That he would not shrink from the severest and most uncompromising measures if he felt them to be necessary he had already shown, and later actually proved, as we shall see. But he had a marvellous tact, and he was now determined that if Frederic and he should meet again that summer, it should be in peace. As soon as he became possessed of the full account of the Besançon affair he called his cardinals together and calmly discussed the situation. There was an animated debate; the German interest in the conclave, not daring to blame the stern figure who sat in the chair of state, tried to throw discredit on Roland and Bernard by accusing them of mismanagement. This Adrian would not permit, and though he felt the insult of the Emperor keenly, he did not allow any remarks to pass his lips which disaffected rumour on its way to Frederic might distort into either insult or cowardice. Adrian closed a heated discussion by announcing that he would write a circular letter himself to the German Church. The letter commenced with the statement, treated as incontestable, that, whenever anything happens in the Church which is against the honour of our Lord and the reputation of Catholicism, it is the duty of the Pope, bishops, and all who have the charge of men's souls, to chastise and rebuke the offenders without regard to rank or position.

The Pope proceeds to recite how "Our illustrious son, Frederic, Emperor of the Romans," has committed an act unprecedented in the history of the Church by allowing the legates of the Holy See to be insulted and almost murdered when receiving them at his council; that he had burst into passion about a passage in the Pope's letter, had allowed the envoys to be ill-treated and searched, and their documents seized, and that he added to these insults the crowning one of ordering them back to Rome.

Adrian made no explanation of the word beneficium, which he presumably reserved for use later if required. He also complained of the Emperor's edict forbidding the bishops to go to Rome, and finished the brief by exhorting them to be loyal to the apostolic see and their Holy Father, pointing out that this was a case in which the honour of Christ's Church was involved, calling on them to do their duty by the Church in persuading the Emperor from his infatuation and exhorting him to "return to the right path" from which he had "strayed," and to ordain that public satisfaction be made by the Chancellor Reinold and Otho of Wittelsbach for their personal share in the insults to the legates. The last sentence of all declares that however much the Church may be shaken by the winds, she will yet "endure throughout all ages under the Lord's protection."

This able and dexterous letter produced great effect on the German bishops, who found it difficult to please two masters, and were much exercised as to how to answer it to the approval of the Pope without giving offence to Frederic. This was exactly the effect which Adrian intended it should produce. Most of the bishops of the empire had become rather German nobles and soldiers than peaceful prelates, but there were those among them who counselled peace. They ended by answering the Pope's missive in a letter which was a curious mixture of servility and arrogance, in effect throwing the responsibility of action on Adrian. This was an attitude which Adrian both expected and welcomed, recognizing him as it did as head of the Church, and enabling him to preserve the calm and dignified attitude with which he had met the passionate outburst of the Emperor.

The arrogance in the answer was probably due to the fact of the letter having been laid before Frederic for his final approval. The substance of the letter was as follows. After equivocating about the edict, and stating that the Emperor never meant to deter pilgrims or people having ecclesiastical business from going to Rome, but merely alluded to what they vaguely termed " papal encroachments," the bishops affirmed that their lord was indignant at the picture he had seen at Rome, with the offensive lines underneath, which Frederic regarded as a good ground for his fear that the Church sought to overthrow the state; that he wished to protect his churches from excessive taxation; and further that the Emperor was indignant at the treaty being made with the King of Sicily, against whom he was allied, without his interests being consulted in the matter. The chancellor, they added, was then preparing for the Emperor's campaign to Italy in the summer, and they accordingly besought the Pope to do all he could, and to be as conciliatory as possible, so that the Church might continue in peace and the Empire preserve its dignity. This letter was duly received by Adrian, and though he must have been somewhat amused at its feebleness in comparison with his vigorous brief, and the irrelevant answers to his telling points, he determined to send an embassy to the chancellor and to Frederic with becoming dignity. At this time Frederic was at Augsburg with his army, having concluded some military operations along the frontiers of Italy, and was preparing for his second descent into Lombardy.

Adrian selected Cardinal Henry of S. Nereus and S. Achilles, and Cardinal Hyacinth to go to Augsburg and request an audience of the Emperor.

These unfortunate dignitaries were attacked while on

their journey across the Alps by some robber-knights who owned allegiance to the Duke of Bavaria, and who, knowing of the quarrel between the Emperor and the Pope, thought they would not be punished for imitating in their own fashion the conduct of their lord—an instance of the danger of travelling in those days, as well as of the responsibility attaching to the action of high authorities. The envoys were plundered and imprisoned. Fortunately, however, for them, the brother of one of these wild counts gave himself up as a hostage for their ransom, and they were at length permitted to continue their journey without further hindrance. Henry, Duke of Bavaria, on hearing what had taken place, rendered every assistance and severely punished their captors. The cardinals were received with high honour at the camp at Augsburg on January 29th, 1158, both by the chancellor and by Otho of Wittelsbach, who took them into the presence of Frederic, to whom they handed a letter from Adrian containing an explanation of the word " beneficium," [1] namely, that the word was used in its scriptural sense, and was not intended to bear the feudal interpretation that Frederic's nobles had applied to it. The Pope also disclaimed any other intention but that of peace, and assured the Emperor that any other expressions which had been taken exception to had not been employed otherwise than with the highest motives and with all goodwill.

[1] "Ex beneficio Dei, non tanquam ex feudo, sed velut ex benedictione" (Radivicus, *ibid.*).

The Emperor professed himself satisfied with these explanations, and requested a settlement of one or two minor points, on which the deputation agreed. He then embraced the cardinals as a token of reconciliation, expressed regret at the discomforts they had gone through, and gave them handsome presents for themselves and others for transmission to the Pope.

The cardinals returned to Rome, and Adrian had reason to be satisfied with the results of his diplomacy. He had again succeeded in his negotiations, and if the reconciliation was only of a short duration, it at any rate preserved the dignity of the Church, and gave him some months of peace in which to go on with his charitable and domestic duties in Rome.

CHAPTER XII.

1158 TO 1159.

Causes which led to the Second Invasion of Italy—The Countess Matilda's Possessions—The History of the Guelph Claim—State of Lombardy and Tuscany—Frederic's Army enters Italy—Surrender of Brescia—Siege and Capture of Milan—Diet of Roncaglia—The Case of the Archbishop of Ravenna—Adrian writes again to the Emperor—Frederic's Declaration at Roncaglia—Adrian's Repudiation of the Imperial Claims—Revolt of Milan—Adrian's Courage—Frederic's last Insult—The Embassy of the four Cardinals—Adrian's Ultimatum—Frederic's Vacillation—Adrian retires to Anagni—War—Preparations for Excommunication of the Emperor—Adrian's Death—His Funeral—His Tomb.

BEFORE relating the history of the next difference with the Emperor—a difference which developed into open rupture—it is necessary to examine the causes which led to the second invasion of Italy, for which Frederic was preparing at Augsburg in Bavaria.

Besides the constant jealousy between the two powers, which showed itself in the dispute after the Besançon incident, Adrian had an independent and serious cause of complaint against Frederic in the matter of his dealings with the property of the late Countess Matilda, the history of which is interwoven with events in North Italy at that time, and cannot be separated from the second Italian campaign.

In addition to the Emperor's public acts, there was also a personal question arising out of his second marriage and the repudiation of the first Empress, which will be dealt with later.

The Countess Matilda was born in 1046, and was the daughter of Beatrice of Lorraine, whose mother, Matilda, was a sister of Gisla, mother of the Emperor Henry III. Matilda and Gisla were daughters of Herman V., Duke of Swabia; and in this way the Countess Matilda was a cousin of the Emperor Henry IV. of Germany. She was celebrated for her virtue and piety, and was always a staunch adherent of the Popes. She married Godfrey V., Duke of Brabant, called the "Crooked," and by her marriage became interested in extensive property in Tuscany, her husband's mother[1] having been the widow of Boniface, Duke of Tuscany.

She led an unhappy married life, from which she was released by the murder of her husband. By his death and that of her father, she succeeded to immense property in Italy and Lorraine—the latter through her father's family, her brother and sister predeceasing her.

At that time a fearful war was raging between the Emperor Henry IV. and Pope Gregory—a war one of the incidents of which was the capture and sack of Rome

---

[1] His father was Godfrey IV., d. 1069.

itself. The city was taken by Henry in 1084, Robert of Sicily acting as his ally and pouring his troops, including a body of Saracens, into the town. Matilda sided with Gregory in this struggle, and her domains were wasted in the course of the war. Gregory died in 1085, and was succeeded by Pope Victor III.

I must rapidly pass over the stirring history of the intrigues and wars which took place in the next few years between Emperor, Popes, and Anti-popes; suffice it to say that more than once was the unfortunate Matilda's property again overrun by the imperial troops and given up to fire and sword.

In these events Matilda sacrificed everything to the interests of the Church, and while many women in her day took the vow of celibacy for the sake of religion, Matilda surrendered her liberty for the welfare of the Roman Church by marrying a lad scarcely twenty years of age, of the influential house of Guelph, thus securing a powerful ally against the imperial house of Henry.

This happened in 1088, and is the keynote to Frederic's interest in her property. We must be careful therefore to follow closely the complications of interest and relationship caused by the marriage. For the moment indeed it caused a fresh outbreak of war, combined with dissatisfaction and budding revolution among her vassals. But the victory of Canossa ended the war in her favour, and after the death of the Emperor Henry IV. in 1106, she made terms with the Emperor Henry V.[1] and was present at his coronation in Rome in 1111, being herself left in comparative peace as vice-regent of Italy. She died in 1115, and by her will left all her immense estates to the papal see. Henry V. immediately claimed them as an imperial fief, and so began a fresh difference between the empire and Rome. After constant struggles with the popes Henry V. died in 1125, a few years after the celebrated treaty of the Diet of Worms,[2] by which the Emperor conceded to the Pope almost all the powers which in later years Frederic tried to usurp from Adrian. Lothair II., the next emperor, conceded to the Pope his powers as suzerain over Matilda's property on the annual payment of 100 marks in silver, and purported to grant the reversion to Henry VIII., Duke of Bavaria and Saxony. Lothair II. died in 1137, being succeeded by Conrad III., brother of Frederic II., Duke of Swabia,[3] and uncle to Frederic Barbarossa; but nothing happened in his reign with reference to the property of the Countess Matilda. He, as we know, died in 1152. Now, whatever we may think as to the claims of the Pope to temporal power in the empire, or to possessions in southern Italy, there can be no two opinions as to the justice of the papal claims to Matilda's property, which were founded on her will, and were admitted by both the Emperors Henry V. and Lothair "the Saxon." But Frederic chose to consider that Lothair had the right to dispose of the reversion in the

[1] Henry V. married Matilda, daughter of Henry I. of England.
[2] 1122.
[3] Died 1147.

GENEA MATILDA AND FREDERIC'S RELATIONSHIP

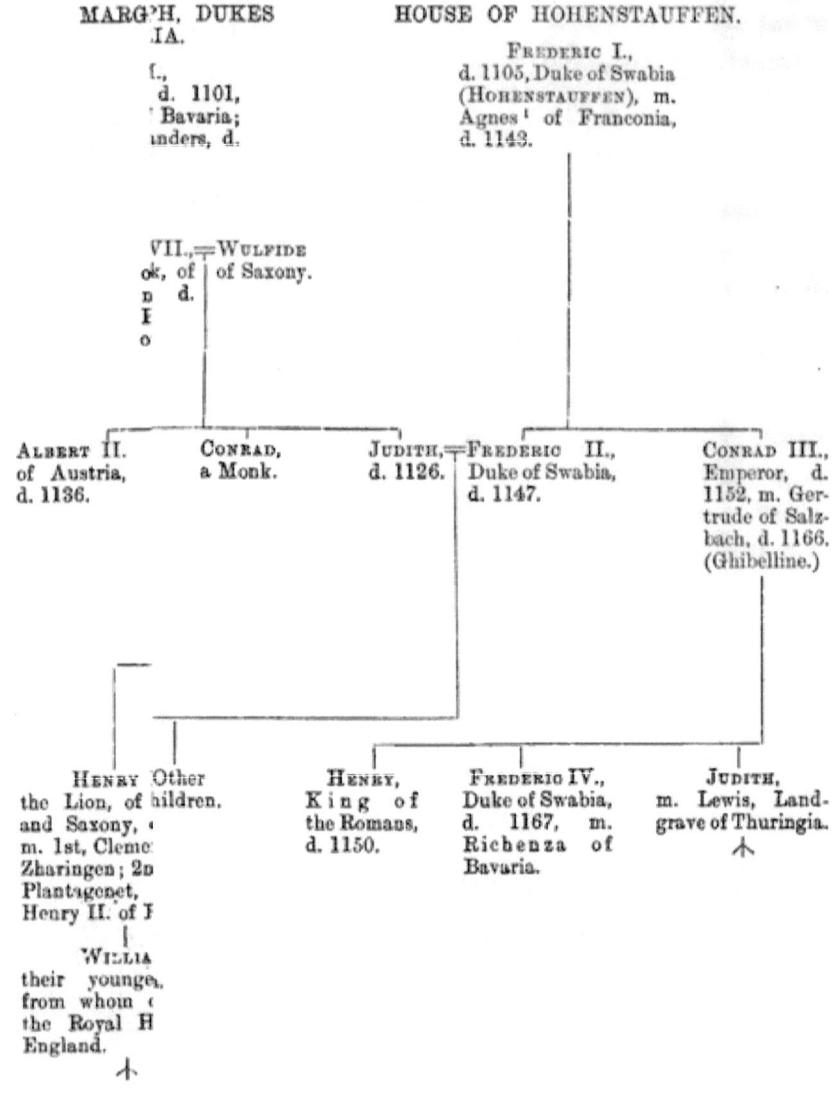

way he did, and claimed the domains for his uncle, Guelph VIII.[1] Here we must pause to pick up the threads of the complicated relationships of Frederic.

Henry Guelph, the Proud, Duke of Bavaria, was the son of Henry VII., the Black (from whom our present royal family are descended), brother of Guelph VII., who married the Countess Matilda.

He married Gertrude, the daughter of Lothair II., who died in 1143. The Emperor Conrad III. hated this man as having been the supporter of Lothair, the constant opponent of the house of Hohenstauffen, and forfeited his duchies on account of his claiming the throne as heir to Lothair, giving Bavaria to Leopold IV., Margrave of Austria, and Saxony to Albert, Margrave of Brandenburg. Henry the Proud was, however, able by the loyalty of his subjects to keep Bavaria till his death in 1139. It was in the wars which ensued from these acts that the warcries of Guelph and Ghibelline first were used—the latter derived from Conrad of Hohenstauffen, Lord of Wiblingen.

After the death of Henry the Proud, Conrad restored the duchy of Saxony to his son, Henry, called the "Lion," but on the death of Leopold bestowed Bavaria on his brother, Henry of Austria, who married Henry the Lion's mother, the widow of Henry the Proud.

When Frederic came to the throne he took the duchy of Bavaria away from Henry, Margrave of Austria,[2] whom he

[1] Often called Guelph VI.
[2] Henry of Austria was Frederic's uncle by marriage.

compensated by making Duke of Austria, and bestowed it again on Henry the Lion, who was the Duke of Bavaria who rescued Adrian's legates from the robbers, as related in the last chapter, and he made restitution to his uncle, Guelph VIII.,[1] by granting him Tuscany, Spoleto, Sardinia, and all the Countess Matilda's possessions.

In later years Frederic took Bavaria away again from Henry the Lion, and gave it to Otho of Wittelsbach.

We must now look at the state of Italy; and it is chiefly with the part which forms the modern Lombardy that we are concerned. In the ninth, tenth, and eleventh centuries the peninsula was, roughly speaking, divided between four dynasties or powers: Lombardy, Venice, Rome, and Naples. I have already mentioned the growth of Naples into the kingdom of Sicily, and with Venice we have nothing to do. Lombardy at the time of which I am writing had become more limited on the side of the northern borders of Italy, and, with the exception of some southern districts, occupied much the same geographical position as the ancient Cisalpine Gaul.

The principal cities of Lombardy were Milan and Pavia. Milan had led the way in the direction of independence, which the communities of North Italy were already beginning to show, by converting itself in 1107 into a republic—an example which was soon followed by Lodi, Cremona, Verona, Genoa, and Pavia. In this way a number of

---

[1] Son of Henry the Black.

different states were gradually formed, each consisting of a walled city and its environs. Genoa, of course, with her sea power, forms a history by herself; but the others were constantly at war with each other, and showed themselves intensely jealous rivals both in their military and commercial aims.

The strong oppressed the weak, and so soon as a strong power became weakened by war, the others were ready to take advantage of the weakness. In this way Milan crushed Lodi and Como, and in 1136, 1139, and 1150, was in her turn beaten by Pavia.

Verona and Padua kept up a constant war with each other; so did Modena and Bologna. Thus the history of northern Italy at this time was the history of the rise of petty rival republics, whose constant differences made it easy for the emperors to destroy them in detail whenever they descended with their armies. The towns of Tuscany to the south were developing themselves in a somewhat different manner. The system they adopted of choosing two or more citizens to rule as consuls resulted none the less in a series of petty wars between the states. Tuscany was at this time the most unsafe part of Italy for travellers, and all historians agree that the condition of the country was unexampled. Her cities, however, began to be celebrated, Pisa rivalling Genoa in importance and sending her fleets all over the Mediterranean. She captured Sardinia and Majorca from the Saracens, and gradually became one of the most important cities of Italy.

Arezzo, Lucca, Siena, and Pistoja were all struggling separately for liberty. Florence was becoming known, but her greatness was of a later date. Venice was asserting her powers, and had recently taken and sacked Padua, and extended her authority down the coasts of the Adriatic.

This, then, was the state of affairs which confronted Frederic. He had concluded his marriage with Beatrice, the rich heiress of Rinaldo, Duke of Burgundy, and by so doing had added the vast domains of her inheritance to his already large empire. To effect this he had annulled his marriage with Adelaide, and for their joint coronation at Rome he hoped to receive or extort the papal sanction.[1] He was reconciled with the hereditary enemy of his house, Henry the Lion, who when in Rome in 1155 had saved his life, either during the attack on the Vatican or afterwards, and he united in his own person the blood of Guelphs and Ghibellines through his mother, who was a daughter of Henry the Black, Duke of Bavaria. All seemed well in Germany; but what of Italy? The whole of Lombardy was restless and rebellious, beginning to see the advantages that a league between the republics would give them against their powerful foe, who by his whole course of action in Italian affairs was working up the country to exasperation; the Pope doubtfully reconciled, ready to take offence with a strong hand; William, King of Sicily, as powerful as his father had been before him, and an ally of the Pope.

[1] Hallam's "Middle Ages."

Frederic determined to select Milan, and humble the growing pride of that city, the most important place in Lombardy, on the ground that the Milanese had in 1157 sacked and destroyed Lodi, which he considered an imperial fief. At last his army was collected, and through every pass in the Tyrolean Alps poured down upon the fertile plains of Italy. The leaders were, besides the Emperor himself, Ladislaus, King of Bohemia; Frederic's cousin, Frederic IV., Duke of Swabia; his brother Conrad, Count Palatine of the Rhine; Duke Bernard of Zahringen, and a host of others. Frederic himself crossed by the Brenner, and descended the valley of the Adige to Trent; but his host was so numerous that all the passes leading to Friuli and Chiavenna and the distant Bernardino were choked with the passage of what was perhaps the largest army which had ever descended on the plains of Lombardy. Most of the villages and towns surrendered before his advance, and at last he appeared before Brescia, the inhabitants of which paid a heavy indemnity, and obtained peace. The first resistance was made by the Milanese troops at the passage of the river Adda at Cassano. At first it seemed as if the army was checked, but the King of Bohemia and his men swam across the river, losing 200 men in the affair, and turned the flank of the Milanese, who fled to their capital.

Frederic advanced, and, reinforced by Italian troops from Como and Lodi anxious for revenge against their rival, laid siege to Milan with no less than 100,000 men. Within a month the proud city had fallen, and the haughty conqueror made his terms. Lodi and Como were to have their liberty, and the former, which had been destroyed, was to be rebuilt; a ransom of 9,000 marks in silver was levied; 300 hostages were to be given; while the Emperor was to have the free coinage of the city, an acknowledgment of him as their lord; and then came the crowning humiliation—the imperial camp was pitched four miles from the city, and all the nobles had to walk past bareheaded, with halters round their necks.

Frederic had reduced Milan. He was destined to do it with greater severity a second time in 1163, and then the Milanese were to have their reward in hurling him back defeated from Alessandria in 1176.

After this stern display of power, Frederic descended to the plain of Roncaglia and held another of his famous diets. And now we come again to the actual relations between the Emperor and the Pope.

Adrian viewed with misgiving the action of the Emperor, and while preparing to strengthen his alliance with William he sent a legate to attend the diet at Roncaglia.

In November, 1158, the Emperor appointed Count Guido of Blandrada, one of his German nobles, to be Archbishop of Ravenna. This Guido was actually a subdeacon of the Roman Church, and Adrian declined to approve of the appointment, writing a courteous letter, in which he said that he could not part with so beloved a friend, as he had reserved him for promotion in the Church of Rome. But his letter does not seem to have had any reply. It was evident that relations had again become strained, and this time certainly the sole cause was the arrogant and interfering attitude of the Emperor himself. The open rupture came soon. Arrived at Roncaglia, whither a vast concourse had flocked of bishops, prelates, princes, and nobles, besides the papal legate, Frederic determined to decide once for all by what laws the people of Lombardy should be governed, and he called in some learned doctors from Bologna to consider and report to him. With great servility they drew up a long list of laws, amongst which were the following:—that all monopolies of fisheries, mines, customs, taxes, and other dues fell under the head of regalities, and were due to the Emperor; that homage was also due to him from all the bishops and nobles; that forage was to be supplied free to his troops; and many other equally imperious decrees were framed by the doctors and promulgated by Frederic. The various towns and chapters, frightened by these proceedings, appealed to the Pope. Frederic now sent the Bishop of Vercelli to Rome to obtain the confirmation of his appointment of the Archbishop of Ravenna, which Adrian promptly refused. A second letter of the Emperor, pressing him to grant the point, provoked one of Adrian's characteristic missives, severe, though moderate in tone, complaining of the want of respect shown to the papal legate; of the insolence of the imperial troops; of the pillage of papal castles; and drawing his attention to the fact that he had broken the treaty of Worms made by his predecessor, and had also violated his own coronation oath. The letter also forbade the Emperor to proceed with the settlement of a dispute which he had taken into his own hands between the churches of Brescia and Bergamo. It is said that this letter was sent by a ragged messenger, who put it in the Emperor's hands and ran away. The truth probably is that Adrian had no intention of again exposing his cardinals to insult, and sent the letter by an officer of lower rank, who, knowing the too often unhappy fate of messengers of evil tidings in those times, made good his departure for fear of becoming the first object of the Emperor's rage.

It was now June, 1159, Frederic having spent the intervening time in proceedings characterized by the utmost cruelty. He had sent his chancellor to arrange the new constitution of Milan, and that imperious servant of his master provoked the Milanese by exceeding the terms on which they had surrendered. The principal cause of complaint was that the town of Monza was declared free, although it had been expressly promised that only Lodi and Como should be taken from them. A revolution ensued; and as Frederic was now in winter quarters at Bologna, and many of his followers had left him, the Milanese took advantage of his apparent weakness, and, breaking out into open hostility, drove the imperial chancellor out of their city.

They next attacked and recaptured the castle of Frezzo, on the Adda, one of the keys to North Italy. Barbarossa was furious; he was not strong enough just then to reduce

Milan a second time, but he levied a war with guerilla troops, declared Milan to be under the ban of the empire, and wasted all the country round the city. He also executed some of the Milanese hostages in sight of their city, and laid siege to Crema. He conducted his operations with unparalleled severity, and rendered the whole of the Milanese plain desolate.

Murder, torture, and plunder were his weapons; lust and cruelty the guiding forces of his soldiers. Never perhaps had Lombardy been so miserable as it was in the early months of 1159. Adrian was aware of the terrible sufferings of the country, and made up his mind to quietly encourage the Milanese in their resistance; to strengthen his position, and eventually, perhaps, with the help of the Sicilians, to wage a successful war against the Emperor, for which he considered he had ample grounds. In reserve he held the terrible weapon of excommunication—a weapon which, as he had proved in his dealings with William of Sicily, he would not hesitate to use if he found it necessary. Relying thus upon the spiritual as well as upon the material forces at his command, the Pope from this point onwards took up an attitude of firm opposition to the encroachments of Frederic.

He no doubt saw the advent of the Italian struggle for freedom against Barbarossa with prophetic eye, and he was aware that, even amidst all the troubles and griefs of Lombardy, a secret treaty had already been framed between Brescia, Crema, and Milan, which bound these cities to conclude no peace with the Emperor without the consent of the papal see—a treaty destined to bear full fruit years afterwards at Legnano. To this end, then, Adrian occupied himself in fortifying and strengthening the castles and military posts in the Campagna and the neighbourhood of Rome, and judging from his actions and letters, expected to be ready for war by the end of 1159. We must now go back to the Emperor, who had just received Adrian's letter. He was furious at what he regarded as a personal insult, and showed his rage by answering Adrian in a letter purposely offensive, in that it commenced with the singular number instead of the plural, the style of address usually adopted by the Emperors in letters to the Pope, though the Popes always used the singular number; he at the same time directed his chancellor to adopt this fashion in all future correspondence. On receiving this fresh insult Adrian at once wrote to the Emperor a dignified but extremely severe letter, which reached the Emperor at Bologna on June 24th, 1159, in which in stately language he reproved Barbarossa for his want of reverence to the representative of Christ.

"My son in the Lord," he says, and proceeds to marvel at his conduct. "The law of God promises long life to those who honour, threatens death to those who speak evil of their father and mother.

"He that exalteth himself shall be abased." He goes on to add that the Emperor by his conduct incurs the guilt of insolence, and reminds him of the fealty he had sworn to S. Peter, telling him that by insulting the bishops, "saints of the Most High," and closing the cities and churches of the empire against them, he is incurring the risk of forfeiture at the Pope's hands of that which the Pope had granted, and warns him to be prudent.

Thus did Adrian speak out. Frederic had no hope of inspiring him with fear; unflinching and courageous the Pope stood firmly on his rights, and no shadow of yielding could be detected in his actions. As may be supposed from the character of Frederic, he did not take this letter quietly. Flushed with his victories, furious at the new insurrection in Milan, which he ascribed entirely to the machinations of the Pope, the indignant Emperor wrote him a letter teeming with insult and couched in the most arrogant terms.[1] In this outburst he told the Pope to confine himself to the humble doctrines of Christ. It was his bounden duty to pay full honour to the memory of his predecessor by preserving the dignity of the imperial crown and keeping intact the dominions of the German empire. He informed the Pope in disdainful language that he required feudal oaths from all the bishops of the Church, and defended this view by pointing out that Christ Himself paid taxes to Cæsar for Himself and S. Peter, whose chair the Pope occupied, and quoted the text, "Learn of Me, for I am meek and lowly of heart."

[1] Baronius, sub anno 1159.

After this sanctimonious commencement he proceeds: "The churches are closed, the city gates will not open to the cardinals, because they are not preachers, but robbers; not peacemakers, but plunderers; not the restorers of the world, but greedy rakers-up of gold.[1]

"When we shall see them, as the Church enjoins, bringing peace, enlightening the land, maintaining the cause of the lowly in justice, we shall not hesitate to provide them with proper entertainment and allowances." He proceeds to ask whether Pope Sylvester possessed any temporal power in the time of the Emperor Constantine, and whether subsequent Popes had not owed all the temporal powers they possessed to the magnanimity and generosity of successive Emperors, including the writer of the letter.

"We cannot but return such answer when we find that detestable monster pride to have approached the chair of Peter. As far as ye are peaceful, so may ye always prosper."[2]

Even under the bitter provocation of this arrogant message Adrian did not let his temper get the better of his calm judgment. The temporal power might disgrace itself by unseemly rage and petulance; the Church could not act otherwise than with dignity.

Her example was necessary. All Europe was gazing on the quarrel; nothing must be done to impair the high

---

[1] "Auri insatiabiles corrasores."
[2] "Paci bene consulentes bene semper valete."

office of the spiritual guide of mankind. Frederic should have every chance, and the dread sentence of excommunication should only be used when all other means had failed.

Adrian selected with care four of his cardinals,[1] personal friends of his own. They were: Octavian of S. Cecilia, Henry of S. Nereus and S. Achilles, William, cardinal deacon, formerly Archdeacon of Pavia, and Guido of Crema. He consulted the German party in his conclave, and obtained their consent to this course, which was to send the four as an embassy to the Emperor, but he himself drew up the terms they were to offer. These amounted to an ultimatum, and were such as Frederic could not possibly accept without a complete and final surrender of all his claims and pretensions. Such a surrender would inevitably undermine, if not destroy, his power and influence in Italy. There is no question as to Adrian's meaning; no longer is there a quibbling correspondence as to the meaning of words or phrases, but there is put forward the final issue of war and spiritual disgrace on the one hand, and peace on conditions involving, as I have said, absolute surrender on the other. Let us examine the proposals, which were five in number.

1. The absolute dominion of the city of Rome to be acknowledged. The Emperor was to send no officers to represent him in the papal city without permission of the

---

[1] Ciaconius, *ibid*.

Pope, and all the monopolies and royalties were to belong to the papal see.

2. No levies of any sort for forage or otherwise were to be made by the Emperor on the papal domains, saving only on the occasions of the coronation of each successive Emperor, and the imperial armies therefore were prohibited from entering the Roman domains.

3. The bishops and clergy in Italy might swear allegiance to the Emperor, but were not to do homage to him.

4. The custom of lodging the imperial envoys in episcopal palaces was to be discontinued.

5. The whole of the domains of the Countess Matilda were to be taken from Guelph VIII., and, together with the duchy of Spoleto, the islands of Sardinia and Corsica, the territory from Acquafundente to Rome, and the revenues of Ferrara, Massa, and Fighernola, to be handed over to Rome, while the Emperor was to do homage for all his possessions in Italy.

Such was the ultimatum addressed to the loftiest monarch in Europe from the sturdy Englishman who held the papal see! The Emperor at first absolutely refused even to listen to them; but, better counsels prevailing, he answered that certain points he would reply to at once, and upon others he would take counsel. The points he answered at once were the following. He would waive the homage of the bishops if they would restore to the empire the fiefs they held of him in Italy, and if they declined to obey the Pope in matters involving disobedience to the Emperor.

"As for the city of Rome," said he, "by the grace of God I am Emperor of Rome," and he declined to admit the Pope's power in temporal matters in the city. He would not require his envoys to be lodged in episcopal palaces when those palaces stood on their own land, but he demanded the right if they stood on imperial property.

He then complained again of the papal legates entering the empire without his permission, also of the treaties of Adrian with William of Sicily and the Eastern Empire, and proposed a conference of six cardinals to be chosen by himself and six by the Pope, whose decision on the remaining points was to be accepted and honourably observed by both parties.

But Adrian had as usual meant exactly what he said and no less, and indignantly refused to consider any answer short of a complete acceptance of his terms. He reminded the Emperor of his concordat with Eugenius III., and called upon him to stand to the compact. In the meantime, while these pourparlers were going on, Adrian had retired to Anagni, so as to be nearer the King of Sicily, and was accumulating his troops in readiness for war.

Frederic replied to this last demand that he was exonerated from the treaty with Eugenius III. by Adrian's own act in concluding the peace with the King of Sicily in 1156, a totally unwarranted assertion, and persisted in again pressing for a council of arbitration.

The citizens of Rome now thought they saw their

opportunity, and in the absence of the Pope they sent a deputation to Frederic, who received them favourably; but this disaffection had no effect in shaking the steadiness of Adrian, who sent a letter exhorting Lombardy to rise and shake off the yoke of the tyrant.

He communicated no more with Frederic, but sent a fiery proclamation to the Archbishops of Treves, Mentz, and Cologne, in which he said: "Glory to God in the highest that ye remain faithful, whilst the flies of Pharaoh swarming from the abyss of hell and driven about by the whirlwind are turned to the dust of the earth.

"Thanks be to God, who doubtless hath enabled you to perceive that betwixt us and the King there can be no more fellowship.

"This schism caused by him will yet rebound upon his head. . . . Take heed that ye be not involved in the sins of Jeroboam; and, behold! a worse than Jeroboam is here. Was not the empire transferred from the Greeks to the Teutons by the Pope? The King of the Teutons is not Emperor before he is consecrated by the Pope.

"Before his consecration he is but King; . . . from whence then the Emperor but from us? . . .

"That which we bestowed on the faithful German we may take away from the disloyal German. It is in our power to grant what we will. . . .

"So great is the power of S. Peter, that whatsoever is done by us worthily and rightfully must be believed to be done by God. Do ye admonish him after this manner, and reclaim him to the right path; for you also will be involved in ruin if there be schism between Church and State."

Having delivered himself of this message, Adrian prepared to excommunicate the Emperor as well for the causes above mentioned as for his marriage with Beatrice of Burgundy after putting away his lawful wife.

The man was ready. He was on the point of opening the campaign and waging a war to the knife in support of the claims of that Church of which he was so loyal and so staunch a servant, when the summons came to him that his day's work was over and his earthly troubles at an end. No more was Christendom to hear his powerful voice, no more was the Church to feel his strong support.

Frederic for the time was to be freed.

Overtaken at Anagni by an attack of quinsy, the great Pope, the true, honest man breathed his last on September 1st, 1159. He died at his post, a glorious representative of the Church militant, face to the foe, upholding the standard of his master, faithful to his principles, staunch to his supporters, and, above all, true to himself.

Many legends have been circulated about his death. The usual accusation of poisoning was made, but it has never had a shadow of evidence to support it. The followers of Frederic invented a story that he was choked while drinking at a fountain by a fly; but this probably was merely a distorted account arising from the nature of his illness, about which there is no doubt. It is also added, as a matter of course, by his enemies, that it was the judgment of God for his attempted excommunication of Frederic. His body was carried to Rome and entombed in a red marble sarcophagus, beside that of Eugenius III., in the nave of the old basilica of S. Peter. His funeral was attended by the ambassadors of Frederic, who, it is pleasant to relate, with chivalrous feeling which does him credit, desired all respect and honour to be paid at the obsequies of his staunch opposer.[1]

In 1607, when the old church was demolished to make way for the modern cathedral, his tomb was removed, and is now in the crypt of S. Peter's[2]—a large sarcophagus of red marble, with the deer's skull, the sign of S. Albans, and two roses to represent England, in basrelief, with the simple inscription, "Hadrianus Papa IIII."

[1] Muratori, *ibid.*; Ciaconius, *ibid.*   [2] See frontispiece.

CHAPTER XIII.

John of Salisbury on Adrian's Death—Adrian's Character—Boso's Estimate of him—Pictures of Adrian IV.—High Altar Screen at S. Albans —His Literary Works—Improvements in Orvieto and Rome—Concluding Remarks.

JOHN OF SALISBURY,[1] continuing the record of Adrian which I have endeavoured to translate in Chapter VIII., refers in touching language to the death of his beloved friend. Even his staunch spirit seems to sink under this unlooked-for blow to the Church just when it was hoped that the English Pope was about to rise, a majestic figure, above the mass of danger and difficulty around him. John writes evidently at the time when, after Adrian's death,[2] the Church was rent asunder by Frederic's insolent support of the Anti-pope Octavian. For the sentence of excommunication against Barbarossa was carried out from the steps of the cathedral of Anagni by the faithful Roland,[3]

[1] Joan. Sar., vol. v.; "Metalogicus," lib. iv., cap. 42, p. 205-6.
[2] Those who wish to follow the events immediately after Adrian's death should read chap. i., vol. v., Milman's "Latin Christianity."
[3] 24 March, 1160.

who had been elected Pope as Alexander III., while the German party put up a rival in the Anti-pope Octavian. The latter received all the German and the German-Italian support; France, Spain, England, Sicily, and the rest of Italy being for Alexander III., who did not become supreme till 1165. Thus John of Salisbury had everywhere before his eyes schism and division, wars and rumours of wars, and none can doubt the genuineness of his feeling that the devoted friend who had held him in such high esteem has left a space no other man can fill. He writes:

"I have said enough, and now I am constrained to weep rather than to write. My argument has proved clearly enough that the whole world is given over to vanity. We looked for peace, and lo! a storm has burst over Tolosa, raising strife between England and France. Kings whom we once saw living lovably together now pursue each other with hatred implacable. Our Lord, Pope Adrian, is dead, and his death has thrown every Christian nation into confusion. This England of ours, the land which gave birth to him, is plunged into the depths of grief, and the country is flooded with tears. His death will be wept by all good men, but by none more than by myself.[1]

"He had his own mother and brother, but he loved me more than them. He used to say, both publicly and privately, that I was more dear to him than any man. Indeed, he held me in such esteem that, whenever the

---

[1] "Omnibus ille bonis flebilis occidet, sed nulli flebilior quam mihi."

opportunity occurred, he laid bare his inmost heart for my scrutiny. When he became Pope, nothing delighted him more than to have me as a guest at his private table; indeed, he would fain have me—unworthy as I was—eat out of the same dish and drink out of the same cup with himself.

"At my entreaty he conceded to Henry II., most illustrious King of England, a bull delivering Ireland into his hands of hereditary right, as his letters show to this day. For all the islands, according to ancient right, belong to the Church of Rome, being the gift of Constantine, who founded and endowed her. And he also sent a ring by me, a beautiful emerald, in a gold setting, by which the King was invested with right to govern Ireland. The ring is still kept by command in the public archives of the court. But if I were to try to enumerate its many virtues, I could write a volume of immense size on this subject alone.

"At the moment men's minds are exercised at the schism in the Church, which has come upon us as a punishment for our sins. When our holy father was taken away, Satan himself brought it about that he might sift the Church like a riddle of wheat, and by another traitorous Judas' act spread broadcast bitterness and dissension. Quarrels have arisen, worse by far than civil war, for they are feuds of priests and brethren. Now judgment falls on the world, and I fear that the heavens themselves may be involved in the downfall of this self-seeking traitor. Woe to him, I say, who brought this scandal on the Church. Better had it been, by far, if he had never been born."

I think that those who have followed me so far will agree that Nicholas Breakspear was no ordinary man; the mere fact of his wonderful rise from his penniless condition to his ultimate glory is sufficient to tell us that. One of the most remarkable traits in the character of the man is his marvellous power of responding to the demands of each successive position he was called upon to fill and his absolute fitness for his post. His character has stood the test of centuries; no breath of scandal or of dishonour has come down to us. On the contrary, the worst his enemies could say was that he was too sparing in his expenditure. In an age of very slender morality as to the rights of any kind of property, he remained absolutely just; when bribery and corruption was the established custom of the day, his honour remained unstained.

He was true to his Church, to his friends, and to himself. He has been accused of being haughty and overbearing, but his ideal was a lofty one—the supremacy of the Church, and as it was high, so were his principles, which were no more arrogant, for the manners of the times in which he lived, than those of any great simple-minded leader of our present age.

It is impossible to attempt a forecast of all he might have done for the Church had he lived. He would certainly have taken rank as the most prominent churchman of his century, and who shall say but that he might not have purged the Church of many of the abuses which were gathering round her? What the effect would have been on the Church in England we cannot venture to surmise, but it is at least probable that had Adrian lived to old age, and remained true to the absolute integrity he showed in his short pontificate, his success would have ensured there being more than one Pope to chronicle as chosen from our country; and possibly, when we remember his desire for union with the Eastern Church, we should not be far wrong in supposing that the influence of a line of English Popes modelled on the record of Adrian IV. might have changed the whole history of the Church.

His life was typical of the best traditions of our race, and the features of the national character which kept him firm and successful in difficulties were the same features that in later centuries have developed the magnificent heritage of which Henry II.'s island kingdom was but the commencement.

His secretary, Boso, in the life of him already alluded to,[1] thus sums up his attainments: "He was a man of surpassing kindness, gentle and patient, thoroughly versed in the English and Latin tongues." Other writers tell us he also was accomplished in French and Norse. "A ready speaker of brilliant eloquence, a sweet singer, and a worthy preacher, slow to anger, quick to forgive, a cheerful giver,[2]

---

[1] Muratori, *ibid.*
[2] "Hilaris dator."

liberal in charities—in a word, a man renowned for every good quality."

The portrait of Adrian at page 65 is taken from the "Historia B. Platina de vitis Pontificum Romanorum," published at Cologne by P. Cholinus in 1610, and professes to be "Vera effigies summo studio emendata et correcta," but it does not mention the source from which it was derived. The head of him in the frontispiece to this book is from a painting, which, by the courtesy of Monsignor Stonor of the Vatican, was allowed to be taken for the purposes of the present work from an old mosaic in the Vatican collections. The other prints are from Ciaconius, "Vitæ Pontificorum," and from the collection of prints in the British Museum.

In the beautiful high altar screen of S. Alban's Abbey, a representation of which I have been enabled, by the kind permission of Lord Aldenham, to reproduce from the drawing in his "Account of the High Altar Screen in the Cathedral Church of St. Albans,"[1] there is a statue of

---

[1] See "An Account of the High Altar Screen in the Cathedral Church of Saint Albans." By Henry Hucks Gibbs (Lord Aldenham). Gibbs and Bamforth. S. Albans, 1890. This most interesting pamphlet—the proceeds of the sale of which go to the repair fund of the abbey—gives a most complete history of the high altar screen, once the chief glory of the abbey, almost completely destroyed in the seventeenth century, but now nearly restored to its former grandeur and beauty by Lord Aldenham. Adrian IV.'s statue is the second from the right in the upper tier.

Most of the Anglican saints are also represented, both those before and after the Roman mission of S. Augustine. S. Alban is on the left of the altar, and S. Augustine on his left again. Above S. Augustine is S. Cuth-

HIGH ALTAR SCREEN,
S. ALBAN'S.

Adrian IV. In the drawing the screen is shown as it is hoped some day it will appear; though it is difficult to realize what the great champion of the Church would think were he to see his statue adorning it and his Master's conspicuous by its absence!

We are told by various writers that he was of great personal beauty and had a commanding presence.

He wrote several literary works which are lost to us, or are buried in the precious hoards of the Vatican. To his letter to Henry II. about Ireland, Stowe tells us he appended two translations into English of the Apostle's Creed and the Lord's Prayer. These are so beautiful that I give them here, though some doubts have been thrown on their authenticity. They are, at any rate, of his period, and I believe myself implicitly in their genuineness.

" This that followeth is ioyned to the former epistle of Adrian the fourth, beeing an English manne, written to King Henry the Second."[1]

---

bert, and above him King Edmund; above S. Alban is S. Benedict, and above him S. Edward the Confessor. To the right of Adrian is the Venerable Bede, to the left S. Hugh of Lincoln, beneath whom is S. Patrick.

The beautiful design for the central crucifix has not been executed, for reasons into which I need not enter; perhaps some day we may see it completed. I would recommend anyone interested to read the above-mentioned pamphlet.

Note.—The expressions " right " and " left " refer to the spectator's right and left hand.

[1] "The Annales or General Chronicle of England." Stowe, 1615, p. 150.

"*Petrus.* I belieue in God Fadir almichty Shipper of Heuen and Earth.
  Andreas. And in Ihesus Crist his onelethi son vre Louerd.
  Iacobus. That is iuange thurch the holy Ghost: bore of Mary Maiden.
  Iohannes. Tholede pine vnder Pounce Pilat picht on rode tree, dead and yburiid.
  Thomas. Licht into helle, the thridde day from death arose.
  Iacobus Alphei. Steich into heauen, sit on his fadir richte honde God Almichty.
  Philippus. Then is cominde to deme the quikke and the dede.
  Bartholomeus. I beleue in the holy gost.
  Mattheas. All holy Chirch.
  Simon. Mone of alle hallwen: forgiuenis of sine.
  Thadeus. Fleiss vprising.
  Mathias. Lif withuten end. Amen."

And in the same simple old English language we have:

"*Paternoster in Anglico.*
" Vre Fadir in heuene riche,
Thi name be haliid euerliche,
Thou bring vs to thi michilblisce
Thi will to wirche thee vs wisse,
Als hit is in heuene ido,
Euer in earth ben hit also,
That holi bred that lasteth ay,
Thou send hit ous this ilke day,
Forgiue ous all that we hauith don,
Als we forgiuet vch other mon,
He let vs falle in no founding,
Ak scilde vs fro the foule thing. Amen."

He wrote a history of his mission to the north, catechisms of Christian doctrine for the Swedes and Norwegians, various homilies, and a treatise on the immaculate conception of the Blessed Virgin, written before his pontificate, and dedicated to Peter Pontiniacus.

He is also said to have written the following epitaph for himself: " Adrianus hic situs est qui nihil sibi infelicius in vita, quam quod imperaret, duxit." Of all those works the greatest loss is that of his account of his mission to the north, which must have contained some description of England at a period about which our knowledge is most scanty. Perhaps some day it will come to light in the Vatican Library (like his letter to Frederic Barbarossa, which was discovered at Frankfort in 1585), when we shall learn more of the character and doings of our English Pope, and possibly clear up some of the mists which envelop his origin.

Adrian IV. did much building during the period of his pontificate; he added to the Lateran palace, erected many new edifices in Rome, and added to several of the churches. Those who are familiar with Rome may find a relic of Adrian in the church of SS. Giovanni e Paolo, which stands a short way from the gate leading out of the Parco di S. Gregorio on the left hand, and close to the church of S. Gregorio. The portico of SS. Giovanni e Paolo was built by Adrian in 1158. The church is said to stand on the spot where two officers of those names in the service of the Princess Constantia were martyred. The portico in question is well worth a visit, as is the church and convent adjoining. The eight granite columns of the portico are particularly simple and grand, and the pavement of the interior of the church is the very pavement which must have been trodden by our English Pope. It is very beautiful. The railed-in space in the centre is said to be the spot, marking the place in their own house, where the saints were executed, their remains being interred beneath the high altar. The campanile of this church was not in existence at the time of Adrian IV., not being built till the thirteenth century. He was the first Pope who ever went to Orvieto, and he built some churches there, and a palace. He also largely helped in the expenses of erecting the Norwegian cathedral of Hammer. S. Alban's Abbey received many marks of his favour, as also did Canterbury, to which province[1] Girald of Wales tells us he gave especial privileges, among them a confirmation of its authority over Wales. An account of his bulls, and a list of the cardinals he created, will be found in Appendix III.

The task I set myself, which was that of trying to piece together the various fragments of information which have come down to us about Nicholas Breakspear, is now ended, and I have failed in my purpose if I have not left my readers with the feeling that his life may be placed with the highest of those known to us for strength, honesty, and purity of motive. It is by studying the lives of men like him that we feel the influence which they leave behind them to succeeding generations. They teach us, in grand, simple language, not to despair if the way seems hard and weary, but to

---

[1] "Rerum Britannicarum Mediævi Scriptores." Girald Camb., Opera, vol. iii., lib. i., cap. 1, pp. 13, 17.

boldly step out on our journey, remembering that lofty motive and high ideal will lead us on and bring their reward, if not in earthly fame, yet in the satisfaction of feeling that one has tried to do one's duty, that feeling which, if a man but has, he can lay down his pilgrim's staff at the end of the journey and know that his labours have not been in vain.

L L

APPENDIX I.

THE bull here reproduced was addressed to one Rodulfus, prior of the monastery of the Camalidotes in the valley of Camalduli, between Florence and Arezzo. This order of monks was founded by S. Romualdo as a branch of the Benedictine order, of which he was a brother, in the early part of the eleventh century. It was a very strict order, habited in white, and is in existence to this day. In the twelfth century it was very extensive, and enjoyed many privileges, most of which were granted by papal bulls. Adrian IV. issued three in his short pontificate, of which this one is the first. It is, I believe, almost the only document in private hands bearing the autograph of Adrian, and is in a perfect state of preservation. The text and translation given here speak for themselves. The leaden seal is reproduced on the title-page of this book, and a full size facsimile of Adrian's signature is reproduced beneath his portrait at page 196.

The handwriting is that of Roland Bandinelli, Chancellor at that time, and, as I have already mentioned, Adrian's successor as Alexander III. He was the Pope who canonized S. Thomas à Beket. Another signatory, Hubald Alloingoli, succeeded Alexander III., in 1181, as Lucius III.

The date requires some explanation. The year as given is that of the Florentine Incarnation, which was one year earlier than the ordinary reckoning, and makes the right date of the bull 1155, and not 1154.

The words, "in the third indiction," refer to the system of marking time by indictions, which originated in the third century, and had reference to the imperial census, which was taken every fifteen years, or at the end of each three "lustres." The rule for finding the exact indiction is as follows: To the ordinary figures of the year add 3, and divide by 15; the remainder marks the indiction. If there is no remainder the indiction is 15. Thus, in the present case, $1155 + 3 \div 15$ leaves 3, viz.,

$$
\begin{array}{r}
15\overline{)1158}(77 \\
105 \\
\hline
108 \\
105 \\
\hline
3
\end{array}
$$

The year for the purpose of reckoning the indiction begins on September 1st. It must be noted that an indiction only marks a cycle of time relatively to certain periods, and not in absolute relation to the whole. Thus in old writers it is usual to find the indiction qualified by the names of the consuls of the time. A full notice of the subject will be found in Smith and Cheetham's "Dictionary of Christianity."

I now proceed to the text of the bull, which measures 30 inches by 24 inches, and, as may be gathered from the reproduction, is most beautifully written.

"Adrianus Episcopus, servus servorum Dei, dilectis filiis Rodulfo Camaldulensium Priori, ejusque fratribus, tam presentibus quam futuris, regularem vitam professis, in perpetuum. Officii nostri, nos ammonet et invitat auctoritas pro Ecclesiarum statu satagere et earum quieti et tranquillitati salubriter, auxiliante Domino, providere. Dignum namque et honestati conveniens esse dinoscitur, ut qui ad earum regimen, Domino disponente, assumpti sumus, eas et a pravorum hominum nequitia tueamur, et Beati Petri atque Sedis Apostolicæ patrocinio muniamus. Eapropter, dilecti in

Domino filii, vestris justis postulationibus, clementer annuimus, et predecessorum nostrum felicis memoriæ Pascalis, Eugenii et Anastasii, Romanorum pontificum, vestigiis inherentes, præcipimus, et presentis decreti auctoritate sanccimus, ne cuiquam omnino personæ, clerico, monacho, laico cujuscumque ordinis aut dignitatis, presentibus aut futuris temporibus, liceat congregationes illas et loca illa quæ Camaldulensis heremi sive cenobii disciplinam et ordinem susceperunt, quæque hodie sub illius regimine continentur, ab ejus ullomodo subjectione et unitate dividere, quæ videlicet loca et congregationes conservandæ unitatis gratia singularibus visa sunt vocabulis annotanda. In Episcopatu Aretino, monasterium Sancti Salvatoris Berardingorum, Sancti Petri in Rota, Sanctæ Mariæ in Agnano, Sancti Quirici in Rosa, heremus Fleri, monasterium Sancti Viriani, Sancti Bartholomei in Anglare; juxta Balneum monasterium Sanctæ Mariæ in Trivio. In Galiata, monasterium Sanctæ Mariæ in Insula. In episcopatu Montis Feretrani, monasterium Montis Herculis. In episcopatu Forumpopiliensi, Hospitale Almerici. In episcopatu Pansauriensi, monasterium Sancti Decentii, heremus Fajoli. In episcopatu Bononiensi, monasterium Sancti Archangeli juxta castrum Britti, Sancti Felicis. In episcopatu Florentino, monasterium Sancti Petri in Luco, Sancti Salvatoris juxta civitatem. In episcopatu Fesulano, monasterium Sanctæ Mariæ in Poplena et ecclesiam Sanctæ Margaritæ. In episcopatu Vulterrano, monasterium Sancti Petri in Fontiano, Sanctæ Mariæ in Policiano, Sancti Petri in Cerreto, Sancti Justi prope civitatem. In episcopatu Pisano, monasterium Sanctæ Mariæ de Morrona, monasterium Sancti Stephani in Cinctoria, Sancti Savini in Montione. In ipsa civitate, monasterium Sancti Michaelis, Sancti Fridiani, Sancti Zenonis. In episcopatu Lucano, monasterium Sancti Salvatoris in Cantiniano, Sancti Petri in Puzeolis. Item in Sardinia, in archiepiscopatu Turritano, monasterium Sanctæ Trinitatis de Saccaria, ecclesiam Sanctæ Eugeniæ in Samanar, ecclesiam Sancti Michaelis et Sancti Laurentii in Vanari, ecclesiam Sanctæ Mariæ et Sancti

Johannis in Altasar, ecclesiam Sanctæ Mariæ in Contra, ecclesiam Sancti Johannis et Sancti Symeonis Salvenaro, ecclesiam Sancti Nicholai de Trulla, ecclesiam Sancti Petri in Scano, ecclesiam Sancti Pauli in Contrognano, ecclesiam Sancti Petri in Olim. Item in Tuscia, in episcopatu Clusino, heremum Vivi in Monte Amiato, cum omnibus supradictorum locorum pertinentiis, villam preterea de Mojona quam emistis ab Enrico proposito et reliquis canonicis cum omnibus pertinentiis suis; villam de Montione quam emistis ab Abbate Sanctæ Floræ, quemadmodum in vestris cartulis continetur, et vobis a predecessore nostro bonæ memoriæ Papa Anastasio mediante justitia adjudicata est, et scripti sui sententia confirmata. Omnia igitur supradicta monasteria cum omnibus ad ipsa pertinentibus statuimus, et Apostolicæ Sedis auctorite sanccimus, tanquam corpus unum sub uno capite, id est sub Priore Camaldulensis heremi, temporibus perpetuis permanere, et in illius disciplinæ observatione persistere, sub illo, inquam, Priore qui ab ipsius congregationis abbatibus sive prioribus et ab eremitis regulariter electus, præstante Domino, fuerit. Porro congregationem ipsam ita sub Apostolicæ Sedis tutela perpetuo confovendam decernimus, ut nulli episcoporum facultas sit aliquod ex his monasterium absque Prioris conniventia, vel Apostolicæ Sedis licentia excommunicare, vel a divinis officiis interdicere. Fratribus autem ipsis licentia sit, a quo maluerint Catholico episcopo consecrationum seu ordinationum sacramenta suscipere. Decernimus ergo ut nulli omnino hominum liceat præfata monasteria temere perturbare, aut eorum possessiones auferre, vel ablatas retinere, minuere, seu quibuslibet vexationibus fatigare, sed omnia integra conserventur eorum pro quorum gubernatione et sustentatione concessa sunt usibus omnimodis in futura. Salva Sedis Apostolicæ auctoritate.

"Si qua igitur in futurum," etc.

"Oculi mei semper ad Dominum. Sanctus Petrus, Sanctus Paulus, Adrianus Papa IV.

"Ego Adrianus Catholicæ Ecclesiæ Episcopus.

"Ego Ubaldus Presb. Card. tit. Sanctæ Praxedis.

"Ego Aribertus Presb. Card. tit. Sanctæ Anastasiæ.

"Ego Julius Presb. Card. tit. Sancti Marcelli.

"Ego Joannes Presb. Card. Sanctorum Joannis et Pauli tit. Pamachii.

"Ego Henricus Presb. Card. tit. Sanctorum Nerei et Achillei.

"Ego Joannes Presb. Card. tit. Sanctorum Sylvestri et Martini.

"Ego Rodulfus Diac. Card. Sanctæ Luciæ in Septa Solis.

"Ego Wido Diac. Card. Sanctæ Mariæ in Porticu.

"Datum Romæ apud Sanctum Petrum, per manum Rolandi Sanctæ Romanæ Ecclesiæ Presb. Card. et Cancellarii, ii. idus Martii, indictione iii., Incarnationis Dominicæ anno 1154,[1] Pontificatus vero domini Adriani Papæ IV., anno primo."

"Adrian, Bishop, servant of the servants of God, to his beloved children Rodulf, prior of Camalduli, and all his brethren invested with the monastic hood, now and in the future, for all time to come.

"Inasmuch as we are admonished, nay urged, by the authority of our office to look carefully to the state of the Church, and with God's help to provide for her the blessings of peace and tranquillity: it now seemeth right and truly meet that we, who have been called by the disposition of the Lord to ward over her interests, should hereby protect her from the wiles of all wicked men and accord to her the fostering tutelage of S. Peter and the Apostolic Chair. To which end, well-beloved children in the Lord, we gladly accede to your just demands, and following in the footsteps of our predecessors in the pontificate of Rome, Paschal, Eugenius and Anastasius of happy memory, we do decree, and by these presents do ratify our decree, that it shall be unlawful for any person whatsoever, be he cleric, monk, or layman, of any rank or dignity,

[1] Anno Incarnationis Florentino.

either now or at any future time, to sever from Camalduli or to subvert from the authority thereof any one of those congregations or places which have ever come under the rule of its cloister or have been added to its estate, and are at the present time under such authority; all which congregations and places for the better conservance of their unity are hereinafter mentioned singly by name.

"In the see of Arezzo—the monasteries of S. Salvator of Berardhingi, S. Peter de Rome, Our Lady of Agnano, S. Cyr-aux-Roses, S. Vivian, S. Bartholomew d'Anghiari, and the hermitage of Fleri; also the monastery of Our Lady of Trivio near Bagni. In Galeata, the monastery of Our Lady of the Isle. In the see of Montefeltro, the monastery of Mount Hercules. In the see of Forlimpopoli, the Hospital of Almerici. In the see of Pesaro, the monastery of S. Decentius and the hermitage of Fajoli. In the see of Bologna, the monastery of S. Archangel near the village of Britti, and of S. Felix. In the see of Florence, the monasteries of S. Peter of Lucca, and of S. Saviour by the city. In the see of Fiesole, the monasteries of Our Lady of Poplena and the Church of S. Margaret. In the see of Volaterra, the monasteries of S. Peter of Fontian, Our Lady of Policiano, S. Peter of Cerreto, and S. Justus by the city.

"In the see of Pisa, the monasteries of Our Lady of Morona, of S. Stephen of Cinctoria, and of S. Savin of Montion. In the city of Pisa the monasteries of S. Michael, S. Fridian, and S. Zeno.

"In the see of Lucca, the monasteries of S. Saviour at Cantiniano, and S. Peter at Puzzuolo. In Sardinia, in the archiepiscopal see of Torre, the monastery of the Holy Trinity de Saccaria, and the churches of S. Eugénie at Samanar, of SS. Michael and Lawrence at Vanari, of S. Mary and S. John at Altasar, of S. Mary in Contra, of SS. John and Symeon at Salvenaro, of S. Nicholas de Trulla, of S. Peter in Scano, of S. Paul in Contrognani, and of S. Peter in Olim.

"In Tuscany, in the see of Chiusi, the hermitage of Vivi on

Mount Amiato, with all the appurtenances thereto; also the villa de Mojona which you bought from the afore-mentioned Henry, together with all such appurtenances thereto as are rightly yours; and the villa de Montion which you bought from the Abbot of S. Flora—as the deeds you hold will show—and which our predecessor Pope Anastasius of happy memory, when called on to adjudicate, declared to belong to you, confirming his judgment under writing of his own hand. All the afore-mentioned monasteries, therefore, with the appurtenances thereto, we do hereby declare and decree, by the authority of the Apostolic Chair, to be as one body under one head; and that head to be the Prior of the hermitage of Camalduli, under whose authority the whole body shall remain and whose discipline they shall maintain, for all time to come; and he alone, we add, is Prior who shall have been elected in due form by the abbots or priors and brethren of the order, God being their guide.

"Furthermore, we do hereby so far extend the fostering tutelage of S. Peter over the brotherhood that no Bishop shall for the future have power to excommunicate any monastery of the order, or to interdict it from the performance of holy rites, without the connivance of the Prior, or without the express sanction of the Apostolic Chair. And the brethren shall be entitled to receive the sacraments of consecration or ordination at the hands of any Catholic Bishop they may choose.

"Let none, then, presume to harass the said monastery, either by robbing it of its possessions, or by retaining such possessions after they have been taken, by weakening its power, or by annoying it in any vexatious way; but let all its property be preserved intact to those for whose guidance and sustentation it has been given. This we decree by the sacred authority of the Apostolic Chair.

"So let no one in the future, etc.

"My eyes raised ever to God. S. Peter, S. Paul, Adrian IV. Pope."

APPENDIX II.

A BIBLIOGRAPHY

OF WORKS OF REFERENCE TO THE LIFE AND TIMES OF NICHOLAS BREAKSPEAR (ADRIAN IV.).

ANTIQUARIES (SOCIETY OF)	*Collecteana Topographica et Genealogica*	London, 1838.
ARCHDALL (MERVYN)	*Monasticon Hibernicum*	London, 1786.
BAKER	*Chronicles of the Kings of England*	London, 1720.
BARONIUS (CÆSAR)	*Annales Ecclesiastici*	Lucæ, 1738, etc.
BLESIENSIS PETRI	*Opera Omnia*, ed. by J. A. Giles	Oxon., 1847.
BREYER (ROBERT)	*Die Legation des Kardinalbischofs Nicolaus von Albano in Skandinavien*	—— 1893.
CAMDEN (WILLIAM)	*Britannia*	London, 1586.
CIACONIUS (ALPHONSIUS)	*Vitæ et Res Gestæ Pontificorum Romanorum*	Rome, 1687.
COMYNS (SIR R.)	*History of the Western Empire*	London, 1841.
FORDUN (JOHANNIS DE)	*Scottichronicon*, ed. by Thomas Hearne	Oxon., 1722.
FULLER (THOMAS)	*Worthies of England*	London, 1662.
	The Church History of Britain	London, 1656.
GASQUET (F. A.)	*Adrian IV. and Ireland.* Vide in *Dublin Review*, July—October, 1883	Dublin, 1883.
GIBBON (EDWARD)	*Decline and Fall of the Roman Empire*, ed. by W. Smith, D.D.	London, 1855.
GIESEBRECHT (WILHELM VON)	*Geschichte der Deutschen Kaiserzeit*	Brunswick, 1874.
GIRALDUS CAMBRENSIS	*Opera Omnia*, ed. by J. F. Dimock and J. S. Brewer	London, 1867.

GUIZOT (FRANÇOIS P.G.)	Histoire de la Civilisation en France, from Histoire Générale de la Civilisation en Europe	Paris, 1828.
HALLAM (HENRY)	History of the Middle Ages	London, 1855.
JAFFÉ (PHILIPPUS)	Regesta Pontificorum Romanorum	Lipsiæ, 1885.
JOHN OF SALISBURY	Opera Omnia, ed. by J. A. Giles	Oxon., 1848.
KEANE (WILLIAM)	Beauties of Middlesex	Chelsea, 1850.
KOHLRAUSCH (FREDERIC)	History of Germany	London, 1844.
KORTUEM (J. F. G.)	Kaiser Frederich der Erste, etc.	Haran, 1818.
LINGARD (JOHN)	History of England	London, 1849.
LYSONS (DANIEL)	Historical Account of those Parishes which are not described, etc.	London, 1800.
MACQUIN (NICHOLAS)	La plus grand gloire des Anglais, etc.	Paris, 1854.
MALONE (SYLVESTER)	Adrian IV. and Ireland. Vide in Dublin Review, Jan.—April, 1884	Dublin, 1884.
MATTHEW PARIS	Chronica Majora, ed. R. H. Luard	London, 1872.
MIGNE (J. P.)	Patrologiæ Cursus Completus	Paris, 1849, etc.
MILMAN (H. H.)	History of Latin Christianity	London, 1864.
VON MOSHEIM	Institutes of Ecclesiastical History, etc.	London, 1863.
MÜNTER (D. F.)	Magazin für Kirchengeschichte und	
MONTESQUIEU (BARON)	De l'Esprit des Lois	Paris, 1749, etc.
	Kirchenrecht des Nordens	Altona, 1792-6.
MURATORI (L. A.)	Rerum Italicarum Scriptores	Mediolani, 1729.
NEWCOME	History of the Abbey of S. Albans	London, 1795.
NORDEN (JOHN)	Speculum Britanniæ	London, 1593.
RABY (RICHARD)	Pope Adrian IV.	London, 1849.
REDFORD (GEO.)	History of Uxbridge	Uxbridge, 1818.
ROBERTSON (J. C.)	History of the Christian Church	London, 1858.
ROGER DE WENDOVER	Flores Historiarum, ed. by H. O. Coxe	London, 1841.
ROHRBACHER (F. R.)	Histoire Universelle de l'Église Catholique	Paris, 1868.
SACCHI (BARTHOLOMÆUS)	Historia B. Platinæ de vitis Pontificorum, etc.	Cologne, 1610.
	The Saxon Chronicle, trans. and ed. by Rev. J. Ingram	London, 1823.
STOWE	The Annales or General Chronicle of England	London, 1615.

Torfæus (Thormodus)	*Historia Rerum Norvegicarum* . . .	Hafniæ, 1711.
Trollope (E.) . . .	*Memoir of the Life of Adrian IV.* .	London, 1857.
Tyrell (James) . .	*General History of England* . . .	London, 1700.
Walsingham (Thomas)	*Chronica Monasterii S. Albani*, etc., ed. by E. Riley	London, 1867.
William of Newburgh	*Historia*, ed. by Thomas Hearne . .	Oxon., 1719.

Note.—In the compilation of this bibliography the works have been cited of those authors (1) who are quoted as authorities in this volume, and (2) of those whose opinions have directly or indirectly influenced me in forming my judgment. Original records of the middle ages are so widely distributed throughout Europe, and, for the most part, are so inaccessible to the student, that anything like a complete bibliography of all books and MSS. relating to Adrian IV. may be regarded as impracticable. It is hoped that the list of works named here—all of which may reasonably be looked for in a large, well-equipped library—will prove of some assistance to the reader who desires to study the time of the only English Pope with more minuteness. It will be observed that some works which are quoted do not appear in this bibliography. These and many others not mentioned are the usual authorities for this period of history, which would naturally be consulted, but which have no special bearing on Adrian's life, such as the standard histories of England, France, Rome, etc., and a number of works bearing on the history of the Papacy and the Church.

For a more detailed account of the feudal meaning of the word *beneficium* (chap. xi., p. 212), the best work to consult is Guizot's "Histoire Générale de la Civilisation," an excellent translation of which was made by William Hazlitt, London, 1846, under the name of "The History of Civilization from the Fall of the Roman Empire to the French Revolution," 3 vols.—*vide* vol. iii., pp. 24-37.

APPENDIX III.

CARDINALS LIVING AT THE TIME OF ADRIAN'S CREATION.

BISHOPS.

IMARUS	Episcopus Cardinalis Tusculanus		(*Innocent II.*)
GUARINUS	,, ,,	Prænestinus	(*Lucius II.*)
HUGO	,, ,,	Ostiensis	(*Eugenius III.*)
NICOLAUS (BREAKSPEAR)	,, ,,	Albanensis	,,
GREGORIUS	,, ,,	Sabinensis	(*Anastasius IV.*)
CENTIUS	,, ,,	Portuensis et S. Rufinæ	,,

CARDINALS PRESBYTER.

GUIDO	Presb. Card. tit. S. Chrysogoni		(*Innocent II.*)
GREGORIUS	,, ,, ,, S. Mariæ Transtyberim tit. Callisti		,,
RAINALDUS	,, ,, ,, SS. Marcellini ac Petri		,,
HUBALDUS	,, ,, ,, S. Praxedis		,,
MANFREDUS	,, ,, ,, S. Sabinæ		(*Cœlestine II.*)
ARIBERTUS	,, ,, ,, S. Anastasiæ		,,
JULIUS	,, ,, ,, S. Marcelli		,,
HUBALDUS	,, ,, ,, S. Crucis in Hierusalem		(*Lucius II.*)
GUIDO	,, ,, ,, S. Pudentianæ tit. Pastoris		,,
BERNARDUS	,, ,, ,, S. Clementis		(*Eugenius III.*)
JORDANUS	,, ,, ,, S. Susannæ		,,
OCTAVIANUS	,, ,, ,, S. Cœciliæ		,,
ASTALDUS	,, ,, ,, S. Priscæ		,,
ROLANDUS	,, ,, ,, S. Marci, S.R.E. Cancellarius		,,
GERARDUS	,, ,, ,, S. Stephani in Celio monte		(*Anastasius IV.*)

JOHANNES	. .	Presb. Card. tit.	SS. Laurentii et Damasi	.	(*Anastasius IV.*)
JOHANNES	. .	,, ,,	,, SS. Johannes et Pauli, tit. Pamachii		,,
HENRICUS	. .	,, ,,	,, SS. Nerei et Achillei . . .		,,
JOHANNES	. .	,, ,,	,, SS. Sylvestri et Martini in montibus, tit. Equitii . .		,,

CARDINALS DEACON.

OTHO	. . . .	Diac. Card.	S. Georgii in Velabro	. . . .	(*Innocent II.*)
RODULFUS	. .	,, ,,	S. Luciæ in Septisolio	. . . .	(*Cœlestine II.*)
GUIDO	. . .	,, ,,	S. Mariæ in Porticu	. . . . .	(*Lucius II.*)
HIACINTHUS	.	,, ,,	S. Mariæ in Cosmedin	. . . .	,,
JOHANNES	. . .	,, ,,	SS. Sergii et Bacchi	. . . . .	(*Eugenius III.*)
HILDEBRANDUS		,, ,,	S. Eustachii	. . . .	,,
GERARDUS	. .	,, ,,	S. Mariæ in via lata	. . . .	,,
OTHO	. . . .	,, ,,	S. Nicolai in carcere	. . . . .	(*Anastasius IV.*)

LIST OF CARDINALS CREATED BY ADRIAN IV.[1]

PRIMA CREATIO CARDINALIUM HADRIANI IV. PAPÆ.

A.D. 1155, pontificatus secundo, mense Decembri, Adrianus IV. Romanus Pontifex primo creavit Cardinales, qui fuerunt:

HILDEBRANDUS GRASSUS, Bononiensis, ex Diacono Cardinali Sancti Eustachii, Presbyter Cardinalis Basilicæ Sanctorum Duodecim Apostolorum.

JOHANNES PIZZUTUS, Neapolitanus, Diaconus Cardinalis S. Mariæ Novæ.[2]

JOHANNES alter, Neapolitanus quoque, cujus cognomen ac titulum nescitur. Hic legatione S.R.E. ad Gulielmum Siciliæ regem Alexander III. papa functus est.

BOSO BREAKSPEAR, natione Anglus, Hadriani IV. nepos, Diaconus Cardinalis SS. Cosmæ et Damiani, ac S.R.E. Camerarius.

[1] I have adhered to the original Latin in this list, and for the sake of uniformity have also kept the footnotes in Latin.

[2] Apud Ciaconium. Apud Aubery autem S. Mariæ in Porticu. Haud est dubium quin hic in errore sit.

BONADIES DE BONADIE, Romanus, Diaconus Cardinalis S. Angeli.
ARDICIO RIVOLTELLA (quem Baronius modo Ardericum nominat, modo Adricionem), Mediolanensis, Diaconus Cardinalis S. Theodori.
ALBERTUS SARTORII de Mora, Beneventanus, Diaconus Cardinalis S. Adriani.
GUILIELMUS MATENGUS, Papiensis, Diaconus Cardinalis S. Mariæ in via lata.

SECUNDA CREATIO CARDINALIUM.

A.D. 1158, pontificatus quarto, mense Martio, Romæ Adrianus IV. Papa iterum creavit Cardinales, qui fuerunt:

GUIDO CREMENSIS, ex Diacono, Presbyter Cardinalis S. Mariæ Transtyberim tit. Callisti.
JOHANNES PIZZUTUS, ex Diacono, Presbyter Cardinalis tit. S. Anastasiæ.
BONADIES DE BONADIE, ex Diacono, Presbyter Cardinalis tit. S. Chrysogoni.
ALBERTUS DE MORA, ex Diacono, Presbyter Cardinalis tit. S. Laurentii in Lucina.
GULIELMUS MATENGUS, ex Diacono, Presbyter Cardinalis S. Petri ad vincula tit. Eudoxiæ.
CYNTHIUS, de regione Transtiberim, Diaconus Cardinalis S. Adriani.
PETRUS, DE MISO dictus, Diaconus Cardinalis S. Eustachii.
RAIMUNDUS, Schismaticus postea, Diaconus Cardinalis S. Mariæ in via lata.
JOHANNES, Diaconus Cardinalis S. Mariæ in Porticu, vel in Aquirio.
SIMEON, Abbas Benedictinus, schismaticus postea, Diaconus Cardinalis S. Mariæ in Dominica.

TERTIA CREATIO CARDINALIUM.

A.D. 1159, Pontificatus quinto, Adrianus tertio creavit Cardinales, qui fuerunt:

HUBALDUS Allucingolus Lucensis, ex Presbytero Cardinali tit. S. Praxedis Episcopus Cardinalis Ostiensis et Veliternus, postea Lucius III. Papa.
JULIUS, ex Presbytero Cardinali tit. S. Marcelli Episcopus Cardinalis Prænestinus.
BERNARDUS, ex Presbytero Cardinali tit. S. Clementis Episcopus Cardinalis Portuensis et S. Rufinæ.
GUALTERUS Episcopus Cardinalis Albanensis.
HUBALDUS[1] Presbyter Cardinalis tit. S. Luciæ.

[1] Apud Ferdinandum Ugbellium.

PETRUS Presbyter Cardinalis tit. S. Cœciliæ. Hic postea in schismate electus Pseudopontifex dictus est Victor IV.
JACOBUS Presbyter Cardinalis tit. SS. Johannis et Pauli legatus ad Fredericum Imperatorem processit.
GREGORIUS Diaconus Cardinalis S. Mariæ in Porticu, legatus ad Fredericum supradictum alter.
GERARDUS Presbyter Cardinalis tit. S. Pudentianæ, iisdem legationibus quibus supradicti Jacobus et Gregorius functus est.
BONIFACIUS Diaconus Cardinalis SS. Cosmæ et Damiani.
GERARDUS Diaconus Cardinalis S. Nicolai in carcere Tulliano.
HUBERTUS Presbyter Cardinalis tit. S. Priscæ in Aventino.

Adrianus IV., Romanus Pontifex tribus ordinationibus, mensibus Martio ac Decembri factis, creavit ex Ciaconio tredecim, ex Panuinio quatuordecim Cardinales.

ADRIAN'S BULLS.

I append here a list of the Bishops, Cardinals Presbyter and Cardinals Deacon who subscribed to the bulls in Adrian's reign.

BISHOPS.

GUALTERUS .	Ep. Albanensis	. . .	a 27 Feb., 1159,	ad 30 Jul., 1159.
HUGO . . .	„ Ostiensis	. . . .	„ 19 Dec., 1154,	„ 19 Apr., 1155.
HUBALDUS .	„ „	. . . .	„ 1 Jan., 1159,	„ 25 Jun., 1159.
CENCIUS . .	„ Portuensis et S. Rufinæ	. . . .	„ 19 Dec., 1154,	„ 13 Jun., 1157.
GUARINUS .	„ Prænestinus	. . .	die 19 Apr., 1155.	
JULIUS . .	„ „	. . .	a 22 Sept., 1158,	„ 13 Mai., 1159.
GREGORIUS .	„ Sabinensis.	. . . .	„ 19 Dec., 1154,	„ 30 Jul., 1159.
IMARUS . .	„ Tusculanus	. . .	„ 19 Dec., 1154,	„ 7 Mart., 1159.

CARDINALS PRESBYTER.

ARIBERTUS .	tit. S. Anastasiæ	. . .	a 19 Dec., 1154,	ad 28 Dec., 1155.
JOHANNES .	„ „	. . .	„ 16 Apr., 1158,	„ 30 Jul., 1159.

ILDEBRANDUS	tit. basilicæ XII. Apostolorum	a 4 Jan., 1157,	ad 30 Jul., 1159.
OCTAVIANUS	„ S. Cœciliæ	„ 19 Dec., 1154,	„ 14 Mart., 1159.
GREGORIUS	„ S. Calixti	die 19 Apr., 1155.	
GUIDO	„ „	a 19 Mart., 1158,	„ 23 Mai., 1159.
GUIDO	„ S. Chrysogoni	„ 19 Dec., 1154,	„ 13 Jun., 1158.
BONADIES	„ „	„ 14 Mai., 1158,	„ 13 Mai., 1159.
BERNARDUS	„ S. Clementis	„ 19 Dec., 1154,	„ 26 Jun., 1158.
HUBALDUS	„ S. Crucis in Hierusalem	„ 20 Jan., 1155,	„ 30 Jul., 1159.
JOHANNES	„ SS. Johannis et Pauli tit. Pamachii	„ 19 Dec., 1154,	„ 1 Mai., 1159.
ALBERTUS	„ S. Laurentii in Lucina	„ 13 Apr., 1158,	„ 13 Mai., 1159.
HUBALDUS	„ S. Luciæ	„ 15 Oct., 1156,	„ 3 Jun., 1157.
JULIUS	„ S. Marcelli	„ 24 Dec., 1154,	„ 24 Feb., 1159.
HENRICUS	„ S. Nerei et Achillei	„ 19 Dec., 1154,	„ 29 Jan., 1159.
GUIDO	„ S. Pastoris	„ 20 Jan., 1155,	„ 15 Jun., 1157.
GULIELMUS	„ S. Petri ad Vincula	„ 14 Mai., 1158,	„ 14 Mart., 1159.
HUBALDUS	„ S. Praxedis	„ 19 Dec., 1154,	„ 6 Nov., 1158.
ASTALDUS	„ S. Priscæ	„ 23 Dec., 1154,	„ 30 Mai., 1159.
MANFREDUS	„ S. Sabinæ	„ 19 Dec., 1154,	„ 28 Sept., 1157.
JOHANNES	„ SS. Silvestri et Martini	„ 19 Dec., 1154,	„ 30 Mai., 1159.
GERARDUS	„ S. Stephani in Celio Monte	„ 20 Jan., 1155,	„ 26 Jan., 1158.

CARDINALS DEACON.

ALBERTUS	tit. S. Hadriani	a 16 Feb., 1157,	ad 11 Mai., 1158.
CINTHIUS	„ „	„ 14 Mai., 1158,	„ 30 Mai., 1159.
BONADIES	„ S. Angeli	„ 20 Jan., 1158,	„ 18 Mart., 1158.
BOSO	„ S. Cosmæ et Damiani	„ 4 Jan., 1157,	„ 28 Jan., 1159.
ILDEBRANDUS	„ S. Eustachii juxta templum Agrippæ	„ 27 Dec., 1154,	„ 31 Dec., 1156.
PETRUS	„ „	„ 24 Apr., 1158,	„ 30 Jul., 1159.
ODDO	„ S. Georgii ad velum aureum	„ 17 Apr., 1155,	„ 30 Jul., 1159.
RODULFUS	„ S. Luciæ in Septisolio	„ 14 Mar., 1155,	„ 12 Jun., 1158.
GUIDO	„ S. Mariæ in Aquiro	die 13 Jun., 1157.	
LACINTHUS	„ S. Mariæ in Cosmidin	a 28 Dec., 1155,	„ 23 Mai., 1159.

Guido . . .	tit. S. Mariæ in Porticu.	a 19 Dec., 1154,	ad 18 Mart., 1158.
Gerardus . .	„ S. Mariæ in via lata	„ 11 Feb., 1155,	„ 21 Jul., 1155.
Raimundus . .	„ „ „	„ 24 Feb., 1158,	„ 12 Mai., 1159.
Oddo . . .	„ S. Nicolai in carcere Tulliano	„ 19 Dec., 1154,	„ 30 July, 1159.
Abdicio . . .	„ S. Theodori . . .	„ 27 Dec., 1156,	„ 28 Jun., 1159.
Centius . . .	„ S.R.E.	die 19 Mart., 1158.	

Between the dates December 12th, 1154, and September 11th, 1157, and, again, from December 30th, 1157, to August 17th, 1159, all bulls are given *per manum* of Roland, Cardinal Presbyter and Chancellor of the Church; during the interval between September 26th and December 1st, 1157, when Roland was absent on the German mission, the functions of Chancellor were discharged by Albert, the Cardinal Deacon of S. Adrian.

Some half-dozen bulls of various dates in the year 1159 are given by one Hermannus, who appears to have been a subdeacon and private clerk to his Holiness.

The Florentine year of Incarnation[1] is commonly employed with the Cæsarean indiction in dating Adrian's bulls, and in nearly every case the Pope adds the motto:

"Oculi mei semper ad Dominum."

Altogether some 650 bulls have come down to us, many of course in a mutilated form. Of the originals the greater part are in the Vatican, a large number in the Bibliothèque Nationale in Paris, a few in the British Museum, and a moderate number in various Continental collections, while the only one known to be in private hands is that described in Appendix I.

The exhaustive research of Jaffé, a second edition of whose "Regesta," under able editorship, appeared in 1888, has probably brought to light all that is known for certain up to the present time of the diplomatic records of Adrian, and in these admirable

[1] *Vide* Appendix I.

volumes¹ will be found every known instrument of his, carefully classified and indexed.

Of these the great majority will be found reproduced *verbatim et in toto* in Migne,² and in the various editions of the Bullarium, the works of the annalists (such as Baronius), etc.; while authorities for the rest, with, as far as possible, original sources, will be found in the "Regesta."

It would occupy too much space and be a very doubtful benefit to reproduce here anything like a complete set of the bulls of Adrian IV. The student will find them in any large well-stocked library, and such information would be of but little interest to the general reader. The following general statement will show the immense amount of such work done in his short pontificate.³

Adrian was elected on December 4th, 1154, and his first bull is dated eight days later. Jaffé apportions the succeeding instruments as follows:

In 1154	25 bulls.
" 1155	144 "
" 1156	124 "
" 1157	88 "
" 1158	60 "
" 1159	54 "

in addition to the following which are given approximately:

From 1154-1157 and 1154-1158	2 bulls.
" 1155-1158	9 "
" 1155-1159	4 "
" 1156-1158	29 "

---

¹ "Regesta Pontificorum Romanorum," tom. ii.
² "Patrologiæ Cursus Completus," tom. 188.
³ It is worthy of note that these bulls issued at an average rate of between two and three a week!

From 1156-1159 . . . . 2 bulls.
„ 1157-1158 . . . . 13 „

and undated, to which no time can be affixed, 25.

The majority of these are granted to abbots and priors, dealing with the management of monastic business, the confirmation of clerical property, the apportionment of disputed claims, etc.

A very cursory glance at these is sufficient to impress the reader with the varied and heavy responsibilities of the head of the Church in those days, while a more detailed study reveals most forcibly the power and strength of character which Adrian brought to bear in all his dealings. His grave and dignified style is full of a quiet consciousness of the majesty of his office.

Sometimes he breaks through his habitual reserve, and speaks forcibly and in no measured terms, censuring high and low with equal impartiality. For instance, he is "pained" at the Archbishop of Canterbury, whose remissness is the cause of many abuses in the English Church; but when Henry II. attempts to subvert the authority of Rome, he leaves his own feelings out of the question, and tells the monarch very plainly that such conduct must not be. At the same time, he never stints his praise when he considers it to be merited.

The events leading up to the more important bulls, such as the rescript by which Ireland was made over to the English king, and the instruments of negotiation between himself and Frederic Barbarossa, the King of Sicily, etc., are fully dealt with in the text.

INDEX.

ABBEY of Clairvaulx, 71.
—— Clugny, 80.
—— Pisa, 41.
—— S. Albans, lands of, 25; High Altar Screen at, 252-3, 252-3 n.
—— S. Denys, 27; Abelard at, 76.
ABBOT of Clairvaulx. See S. Bernard.
—— Geoffrey of S. Albans, 129.
—— Peter of Moutier la Celles, 138.
—— Richard of S. Albans, tomb of, 4; 19, 129.
—— Robert of S. Albans, 2, 6; his journey to Rome, 129, 133.
—— William of S. Rufus, 39.
ABBOTS LANGLEY, 10, 11-25.
ABELARD, his birth, early life, 75; and Heloise, 76; compared with S. Bernard, 77; his character, his persecution, 77; effects of his teaching, 78; his trial, 79; appeals to Rome, 80; his death, 80, 81; result of his teaching, 81, 82.
—— John of Salisbury a pupil of, 137.
ACQUAFUNDENTE, 242.
ACRE, 187.
ADDA, river. Passage of, by Barbarossa, 1158, 233; 236.
ADELAIDE, first wife of Frederic Barbarossa, 232.

ADIGE, valley of the, 233.
ADOUR, river, 26.
ADRIAN IV. See Breakspear.
ADRIATIC, 232.
ÆDGAR THE ATHELING, 22.
Æsop, fable of belly and the members, 148.
AFFRANCHISSEMENT des Communes, 26.
ALBANO, 87.
ALBERT, Margrave of Brandenburg, 229.
ALBERTUS DE MORAY, 207.
ALESSANDRIA, 234.
ALEXANDER II., 31, 161.
ALEXANDER III., 94, 95, 166; and Henry II., 169; Papal bulls of, 173-175; 209, 248, 258.
ALICE, daughter of Geoffrey de Clare, 15.
ALPS, Adrian's envoys attacked in crossing the, 222-3.
AMALFI, 184, 199.
ANAGNI, 94, 243, 245, 247.
ANACLETUS, Anti-Pope, 88, 183, 184.
ANALECTA, the, 170.
ANASTASIUS IV., 4; his benevolence, treatment of Breakspear, 64; his death, 65; 90, 91, 128, 200.
ANATHEMA. See Excommunication.
ANCONA, 125; march of, 199.
ANDREW, Count of Rupi-Canino, 189.

ANGLICAN Church, 108.
—— Saints, 252-3 n.
ANGLO-SAXON Church, 31, 32.
ANJOU, 26; earldom of, 128.
APOSTLE of the North, Breakspear styled, 64.
APOSTLE'S Creed, 254.
APSLOE, 58.
APULIA, 140, 183, 187, 188, 193, 198, 199, 205.
APULIAN nobles, the, fate of, at Brundisium, 193.
AQUINO, monastery of, 187.
AQUITAINE, 26, 163.
—— Duke of, 33.
ARCHBISHOP of Canterbury, Lanfranc, 32, 56.
—— Theobald of ——, 138, 171.
—— of Cologne, envoy to Adrian IV., 1155, 102.
—— Eskill of Lund, created Primate of Sweden, 61, 203; plundered and imprisoned, 208; 209, 211.
—— of Palermo, Hugh, 185.
—— of Ravenna, envoy to Adrian IV., 1155, 102.
—— Guido, 234.
ARCHDEACON of Pavia, 241.
AREZZO, 232, 258.
ARGENTEUIL, Convent of, 76.
ARLES, 6, 36; kingdom of, 34.
ARNOLD, Bishop of Greenland, 58.
—— of Brescia, 45, 48, 68, 75, 82; birth and early life of, 83; opinions of, 83, 84, 85; sentenced at Sens and escapes, 86; his influence and power, 86, 87; invites Barbarossa to Rome, 90; his attempt to rule Adrian IV., 93; his preaching in 1155, 94, 96; banished from Rome by Adrian IV., 97; his flight from Rome, 1155, 101, 102; captured by Barbarossa, 104; prisoner in Rome, 105; execution of, 106, 107; reflections on his character, 107, 108.
ARNULF, Roman agitator, 83.
ARTHUR, King. Barbarossa compared to, 114.
ASCLETINUS, 186: **ravages the Papal dominions**, 187.
ASHBY, Elizabeth, 16.
—— family, 16.
—— Margaret, 17.
—— Robert, 16.
ASSHEBY, George, 16.
—— Margaret, 16.
AUGSBURG, 222, 223, 225.
AVIGNON, 37.

BACANO, 187.
BACHWORTH, Sir Roger, 15.
BALDWIN de Clare, 15.
—— FitzGeoffrey, 14.
BANDINELLI. *See* Roland.
BANNOCKBURN, 169, 176.
BARBAROSSA. *See* Frederic.
BARFLEUR, 20, 26.
BARI, capture and destruction of, by William of Sicily, 193-195.
BARONIUS. *See* Cardinal Baronius.
—— and the grant of Ireland, 180.
BASIL. *See* Bishop.
BAVARIA, 225, 229.
—— Duke of, 213, 223.
BEATRICE de Bollers, 14.
—— of Burgundy marries Frederic Barbarossa, 232, 245.
—— of Lorraine, 226.

INDEX.

BELLY and the members, fable of, 146-148.
BENEFICIA, 211.
BENEFICIUM, meaning of feudal term, 212, 268.
BENEVENTUM, 131, 133, 140, 186; siege of, 187, 189; besieged by William of Sicily, 195, 196; 197, 198; William of Sicily crowned at, 199; 200, 202, 207.
BERGAMO, 236.
BERGEN, 58.
BERNARD. *See* Cardinal.
—— of Clairvaulx. *See* S. Bernard.
—— Duke of Zahringen, 233.
—— of Pisa. *See* Eugenius III.
—— de Rennes, 143.
—— *See* S.
BERNARDINO, Pass of, 233.
BESANÇON, 208. *See* Luxeuil.
BIBLIOGRAPHY, Appendix II., 266-8.
BISHOP of Albano. *See* Breakspear.
—— of Chartres. *See* John of Salisbury.
—— of Evreux, 130.
—— of Lincoln, 133.
—— of Luxeuil, 130.
—— of Mans, 130.
—— of Præneste, 144.
—— of Rouen, 30.
—— of Sabina, 64.
—— of Salonica, Basil, 201.
—— of Vercelli, 235.
—— of Verdun, 207.
BLANCHE Neuf, 19.
BLANDRADA. *See* Guido.
BOHEMIA, 233.
BOLOGNA, 216, 231, 235, 236, 238.
BONIFACE, Duke of Tuscany, 226.
BRAKSPEAR. English family in Paris, 17.
—— W. H., 17.

BREAKSPEAR, Nicholas. Birthplace, 1; or Brekspere, 1; or Hastafragus, 1 *n.*; or Brekespere, 2; his father 3; Bales' allegation concerning, 6; his mother, 8; traditions of his birth, 10; Fuller's account of, 12, 13; Bishop of Albano, 13; error in date of his death, 13; name de Camera accounted for, 15; connection with Breakspears, 15, 16, 17; birthplace, 18; family, 18; refused at S. Albans, 18, 19; goes to France, 19; boyhood, 23; reaches France, 26; at Paris, 27; life at S. Denys, 33, 35; leaves Paris, goes to Arles, to Avignon, enters S. Rufus, becomes a monk, 36-38; made a prior, 39; becomes Abbot of S. Rufus, 40; rigid rule of, at S. Rufus, 40; first visit to Rome, 41; and the monks of S. Rufus, 41-45; and Eugenius III., 42-44; second visit to Rome, 44; Cardinal-Bishop of Albano, 45; accompanies Pope to S. Denys, 46; his power of languages, chosen for Scandinavian mission, 47, 49; appointed papal legate, his instructions, visits England, 53, 54; in England, 55; arrives in Norway, settles Norwegian affairs, 56, 57; reforms the Church in Norway, 58; national saint of Norway, 59; his affection for Norway, leaves Norway, goes to Sweden, 60; his action with the Swedish Church, leaves Sweden, goes to Danemark, 61; his diplomacy in Danemark, 62; endeavours to prevent the war with Sweden, 63; styled "The Good," 64; leaves Danemark, returns to Rome, 64; elected Pope, 65-66; aspect of affairs in

Rome on his accession, Arnold of Brescia, 90; his fitness for Pope, 91, 92.

BREAKSPEAR. ADRIAN IV., his dealings with the Republic, 1155, 93-94; Boso's description of his government, 94-97; enters Rome, Easter, 1155, 97; lays Rome under an interdict, 98-99; at Viterbo, 100; sends an embassy to Barbarossa, 1155, 102; at Civita Castellana, 103, 105, 108; negotiations with Barbarossa, 1155, 111-113; first meeting with Barbarossa, 116-119; second interview with Barbarossa, 119, 120; crowns Barbarossa, 121; merciful treatment of prisoners, 123; parting with Barbarossa, 125, 129; conversation with Abbot Robert, 131-133; and John of Salisbury, 139-152; and Ireland, 149, 150; on the position of the Pope, 152; grant of Ireland to Henry II., Chapter IX., 153, 161, 166, 168, 169, 174, 175; refuses bull to the King of France similar to the grant of Ireland, 181; his letter to William, King of Sicily, 185; excommunicates the King of Sicily, 186; his difficulties in 1155, 187, 188; negotiations with William of Sicily at Beneventum, 189; campaign against Ascletinus, visit from John of Salisbury, 189; negotiations with Manuel I., 190, 191; his difficulties with the German party among his Cardinals, 191-192; at Beneventum, 1156, 195; his difficult position in May, 1156, 196; negotiations, 197; and treaty with William of Sicily, 198, 199; absolves William of Sicily from excommunication and crowns him, 199; brings Italy under control of the Church, 200; receives embassy from Eastern Church, 200; his wish for Church union, 201; at Orvieto, quiet life at Viterbo, return to Rome, 1157, 202; receives visit from Eskill, Archbishop of Lund, 202-203; sends embassy to Frederic I. at Besançon, September, 1157, 208, 209; his letter to Frederic at Besançon, 210, 211; and Frederic I., 217; his difficulties with Frederic I., in 1157, 218; preparation for Frederic's second invasion of Italy, 219; his letter to the German Church, 1157, 220, 221; receives answer from the German Bishops, 222; his explanation of the "beneficia" difficulty, 223, 224; and the bequest of the Countess Matilda, 225, 228; letter to Barbarossa about Archbishop of Ravenna, 234; correspondence with Barbarossa, 1158, 235, 236; sympathy with Lombardy, 237; preparations for war with Barbarossa, 238; letter to Barbarossa, 1159, 238-9; sends embassy to Barbarossa, 241; ultimatum to Barbarossa, 241-243; retires to Anagni, 1159, 243; proclamation to the German Church, 243, 244; prepares to excommunicate Barbarossa, 245; his death, funeral, 245-6; account of his death by John of Salisbury, 248; his character, 250; accomplishments, 251; epitaph, 255; literary works, 253-256; architectural works, 255; concluding remarks, 257.

BREAKSPEAR, Adrian, 17.
—— Anne, 17.
—— farm in Hampshire, 56; farm in

Kent, 56; farm near S. Albans, 56 n.
BREAKSPEAR, Robert, 15, 18.
BREAKESPEARE, or Breakspear, 18 n.
BREAKSPEAR, or Briselance, 1 n.
BREAKSPEARS, 11, 12.
—— or Breakspeare, 12.
—— records of, 16.
—— site of, 14.
BREIFNY, 162.
BREKESPERE. See Breakspear.
—— William of Brekespere, 16.
BREKSPERE. See Breakspear.
BRENNER pass, the, 233.
BRENTANO, river, 183.
BRESCIA, revolution in, 86; submits to Barbarossa, 1158, 233; 236, 237.
BREWER on Giraldus Cambrensis, 174.
BRILL-ON-THE-HILL, 17.
BRISELANCE. See Breakspear.
BRITTANY, 25, 75.
BRUIS, Peter de, 82, 83.
BRUNDISIUM, siege of, 192; siege of by William of Sicily 193.
BRUNSWICK, 213.
BULLARIUM, the, of 1583, 169, 178, 179, 180.
BULL, of Adrian IV. granting Ireland to Henry II., text of, 157-159; translation of, n. 159, 160; facsimile, of Adrian IV., Appendix I. 259-265.
BULLS issued by Adrian IV., Appendix III. 269-276.
BURGUNDY, King of. See Frederic.

CALABRIA, 183, 199.
CALIXTUS II., 29, 82.
CAMALDULI, the Bull granting privileges to, Appendix I., 259-265.

CAMDEN account of Breakspear, 11, 12; on Alexander's bull, 174.
CAMERA de, supposed name of Breakspear, 15; Robert de, 3.
CAMPAGNA, the, 105, 238; rescue of Arnold by, 101; the nobles of, 102; captured and released by Barbarossa, 104.
CANOSSA, victory of, 227.
CANTERBURY, 138; province of, 256.
CAPUA, 199.
—— Prince Robert of, his treatment by William of Sicily, 195, 196.
CARDINAL of Aragon, 5.
—— Baronius, 169.
—— —— and Matthew Paris, 179.
—— Bernard, 219.
—— Boso, 5, 9, 55, 65; his life, 94-96; his literary merits, 95; probable meeting with Breakspear on his way to Norway, 96; his account of Adrian IV. and the interdict in 1155, 96-97; 100; left in charge of Rome, 105; 121, 142; on Adrian IV., 251.
—— of Castello, 87.
—— Gerhard of S. Nicolas, 101.
—— Guido of Crema, 241.
—— —— Clement of S. Potentienne, 143.
—— —— of S. Potentienne, murder of, 96-98.
—— Henry of S. Nereus and S. Achilles, 222, 241.
—— Hubald of S. Praxed, 191, 259.
—— Hyacinth, 222.
—— Julius of S. Marcel, 191.
—— Octavian, 120; of S. Cecilia, 241.
—— Roland of S. Mark, Chancellor, Envoy to King of Sicily, 191.

CARDINAL of S. Clement, Bernard, 209.
—— of S. Còmo et S. Damien (Boso), 94.
—— of S. Como and S. Damien, 143.
—— of S. John and S. Paul, envoy to Barbarossa, 102.
—— of S. Maria in Portico envoy to Barbarossa, 102.
—— of S. Mark, Roland. *See* Roland.
—— of S. Nereus and S. Achilles, 185.
—— of San Pudenziana (Boso), 94.
—— of S. Pudenziana envoy to Barbarossa, 102.
—— William, Deacon, 241.
Cardinals, list of at Adrian's accession, 269, 270; created by Adrian, 270-272.
CARLOS, Prince of Sweden, 62.
CASHEL, Synod of, 172.
CASSANO, battle of, 233.
CATHOLIC Church. *See* Church.
—— religion, continuity of, preserved by the English Church, 32.
CELESTINE II., his reign and death, 87.
CEPHALONIA, 183.
CEPPERANO, 187.
CHAMPAGNE, 71.
CHARLEMAGNE, 110.
CHARLES VIII., King of France, 34 n.
CHIAVENNA, 233.
CHRISTIANITY in Danemark, 50.
—— introduction into Norway and Sweden, 52.
CHRISTINA, Prioress of Markgate, 131.
CHURCH and State, 221.
—— divisions in the, 74.
—— of the Blessed Martyr Alban, 5.
—— of Norway, 51.
—— of Rome, Countess Matilda's liberty sacrificed to, 227.

CHURCH the, in Scandinavia, 49.
—— of Sweden, 51; state of the, 60.
—— organization of the, 69.
—— state of the at Breakspear's accession, 68.
—— supremacy of the, 29.
—— Catholic, learning and literature, 28, 29; proposals for union in, 201.
Ciaconius, 6; account of Cardinal Boso, 95; and the grant of Ireland, 180.
CILL MOR, 176.
CIVITA CASTELLANA, 101; Adrian IV. at, 103, 118.
CLAIRVAULX, 71, 76.
CODEX, Vaticanus and Matthew Paris, 179.
COLNE, river, 14.
—— Valley, 14.
COMO, 231; helps Barbarossa in 1158, 233; 236.
CONNAUGHT, 162.
CONRAD, Bishop of Sabina, 64.
—— Count Palatine of the Rhine, 233.
—— II., Emperor, 34, 46, 87; his death, 90; 114.
—— III., Emperor, 228, 229.
—— of Hohenstauffen, Lord of Wiblingen, 229.
CONSTANTINE, Emperor, 240.
CORSICA, 242.
COUNCIL of Rheims, 29.
—— of Sens, 83, 85.
COVENTRY Cathedral, 56.
CREMA besieged by Barbarossa, 237.
CREMONA, 230.
CRUSADES, 70.

DANEGELT, the, 50.
DANEMARK, 49, 50, 62-64.

INDEX.

DANUBE, river, 115.
DENMARK. *See* Danemark.
DERMOT MACMURROUGH, King of Leinster, 162; petition to Henry II., 163; his death, 164.
DESMOND, 162.
DIMOCK, Rev. J., on the grant of Ireland, 153-154, 180; on Alexander's bull, 174, 175.
DISCONTENT amongst the monks of S. Rufus, 40.
DIVORCE questions, the, and the Roman Church, 128.
DOMHNALL, O'Brian, King of Munster, 177.
DRONTHEIM. *See* Nidrosia.
DUBLIN, 164.
—— Review, extracts from, *n.* 155, 156.
DUCAS, Greek general, 192, 193.

EASTERN church, 200.
EDWARD II., King of England; and Ireland, 176.
ELEANORA, heiress of the Duke of Aquitaine, marriage and divorce, 33.
ELEANOR, divorced queen of Louis VII., 128.
EMPERORS, the authority of, 82.
EMPRESS Matilda. *See* Maltida.
ENGLAND, state of, in twelfth century, 21-23; population of, 24; temporal power of the Popes weakened in, 31; under Stephen, 48; monastic movement in, 70; envoys from at Besançon, 209; 248.
ENGLISH Church, antiquity of, 32; separated from the Pope, 32.
—— churchmen, temper of, 32.

ENGLISH kingdom, extent of in twelfth century, 25.
—— language, 24.
—— missionaries in Sweden, 52.
ETAMPES, 26.
EUGENIUS III., 13; his character, 41, 42; at S. Denys, 46; 49; creates the Archbishoprics of Ireland, 52; 64; riot at his election, 88; reconciliation with the senate, 88; enters Rome 1145, 89; flies from Rome, 89; his influence in Rome, 90; his death, 90; 128, 138, 143, 205, 243; tomb of, 246.
EUROPE, effects of second crusade on, 47.
EVA, daughter of Dermot, King of Leinster, 164.
EXCOMMUNICATION, effect of, 196, 197.
EYSTEIN, Prince of Norway, 57.

FAGRSKINN, Archbishop of Lund, 64.
FAROE islands, 58.
FERRARA, 242.
FIGHNEBOLA, 242.
FINLAND, 63.
FLORENCE, 216, 232, 259.
FLORENTINE Incarnation, the, 259.
FONDI. *See* Richard, Count of.
FORSA, convent of, 88.
FRANCE, state of in twelfth century, 26, 27; English interest in, 33; state of affairs in 1118-1138, 33; monastic movement in, 70; envoys from at Besançon, 209; 248.
FREDERIC I., Barbarossa, Emperor, 46; decides to cross the Alps, 90; his character, 91, 114, 116; crosses the Alps, 1154, advances into Lombardy, 91; at Pavia, advances on Rome, 101; sends envoys to Adrian IV., 1155, 102; at

Viterbo, 105; receives deputation from Rome, 108, 109; his reply to the Roman senate, 110; negotiations with Adrian IV., 1155, 111, 113; his position amongst monarchs of Europe, 115; affair of the Pope's stirrup, 119, 120; crowned at Rome, 121; quells riot in Rome, 122; reasons for leaving Rome, 1155, 123, 124; negotiations with Greek Emperor, 125; his claims to authority in Italy, 204; his action about William of Sicily's treaty with the Pope, 205, 206; rupture with Adrian IV., 1157, 206; provokes Adrian IV., 207; declines to interfere with imprisonment of Eskill, 208; as King of Burgundy, 209; his arrangements at Besançon, 209; treatment of the Papal Envoys to Besançon, 214; and the German bishops, 215; proclamation to the Bishops, 217; and the "beneficia" difficulty, 217, 218; and the portrait of Emperor Lothair, 218, 222, 244; preparation for second invasion of Italy, 219; at Augsburg, 1157, 222; receives Adrian's envoys at Augsburg, 1158, his temporary reconciliation with Adrian, 223-224; his second marriage, 226, 232; and the Countess Matilda's possessions, 227; 228; and the duchy of Bavaria, 229; his relations with the Guelphs, 229; grants the Countess Matilda's possessions to Guelph VIII., 230; second invasion of Italy captures Milan, 1159, 233; Diet of Roncaglia and the Archbishop of Ravenna, 234; and the laws of Lombardy, correspondence with Adrian IV., 1158, 235, 236; insulting letter to Adrian, 1159, 238; letter to Adrian, June, 1159, 239, 240; answer to Adrian's ultimatum, 242, 243; proposes conference of Cardinals, 1159, 243; sends ambassadors to attend Adrian's funeral, 246; excommunicated by Alexander III, 1160, 247.

FREDERIC II., Duke of Swabia, 228.
FREDERIC IV., Duke of Swabia, 233.
FREZZO, castle of, 236.
FRIARS, dress of, 38.
FITZ REDBEARD. *See* Frederic I.
FRIULI, 233.
FRONTIER of Spain, 26.
FRUSINONE, 187.
FULCHER, Patriarch, 200.

GAIETA, 184.
GENOA, 216, 230; her sea power, 231.
GEOFFREY de Clare, 15.
—— of Gorham. *See* Abbot Geoffrey.
—— Plantagenet, 33, 127, 128.
GERMAN Bishops, the effect of Adrian's letter on, 221; their answer to Adrian's letter, 221.
—— Ecclesiastics, forbidden by Frederic I. to journey to Rome, 207.
—— interest in the papal conclave, 219.
—— popes, 31.
GERMANY, monastic movement in, 70.
GERTRUDE, daughter of Lothair II., 229.
GHIBELLINES. *See* Guelph.
GIRALDUS Cambrensis, on the grant of Ireland, 153, 168, 171-175, 180.
GISLA, 226.
GODFREY the Crooked, Godfrey V., 226.
GODFREY IV., Duke of Brabant, 226, *n.*
GOTHLAND, 52, 60.

GREEK empire, 183.
GREENLAND, 58.
GREGORY VII., 183; war with Henry IV., 226; and the Countess Matilda, 227.
—— XVI., 170, n.
GUELPHS and Ghibellines, war cries of first used, 229.
GUELPH, the house of, 227.
—— VII. marries the Countess Matilda, 227, 229.
—— VIII. and the Countess Matilda's possessions, 229; 230, 242.
GUIDO, Count of Blandrada, 234.
GUIENNE, 33.

HADRIAN. *See* Adrian.
HAMBURG, See of, 49, 51.
HAMMER, 58, 60.
—— Cathedral, 256.
HAMPSTEAD, 24.
HARALD, King of England, 25.
—— IV., King of Norway, 52, 57.
HAREFIELD, 10; ancient names of, 14; manor of, 15.
HARROW, 24.
HASTAFRAGUS. *See* Breakspear.
HEBRIDES, 58.
HELOISE, 76.
HENRY of Anjou, 56, 127.
—— III., Emperor, 226.
—— IV., Emperor of Germany, 183, 226; capture of Rome, 226, 227.
—— V., 227; and the Countess Matilda's possessions, 228.
—— the hermit, 83.
—— I., King of England, 21; his reign, 22, 30; and Ireland, 155, n. 228.
—— II., 115; sends an embassy to Adrian IV., 127; and his father's will, 128; petition to the Pope, 128; message of congratulation to Adrian IV., 130, 134, 137; and John of Salisbury, 138, 139; and Ireland, 149, 155-157, 164; and Strongbow, 164-166; his invasion of Ireland, 165; and Roderick, King of Connaught, 167; and Alexander III., 169; his support of Octavian, 171.
HENRY VII., the Black, Duke of Bavaria 229, 232.
—— VIII., Duke of Bavaria and Saxony, 228.
—— Guelph, the Proud, Duke of Bavaria, 229.
—— the Lion, Duke of Bavaria, 123, 213; rescues Adrian's envoys, 1157, 223; 229, 230, 232.
—— Margrave of Austria, 229.
—— Plantagenet. *See* Henry II.
—— ——, 128.
—— of Winchester, 56.
HERMAN V., Duke of Swabia, 226.
HIGHGATE, 24.
HILDEBRAND, 31; Adrian IV. compared to, 196.
HOHENSTAUFFEN. *See* Frederic I.
—— of Swabia, house of, 114, 229.
HOLY SEPULCHRE, Church of the, 201.
HONORIUS II., 183.
HOXTON, 24.

ICELAND, 58.
INDICTION, Method of reckoning time by, 260.
INGE, Prince of Norway, 57, 58.
INNOCENT II., 38, 75, 80; and Brescia, 86; and Rome, 87; death of, 87; 205.

INNOCENT III., 95, 170 n.
INTERDICT, Rome laid under an, 96; description of, 98-100.
IRELAND and Eugenius III., 52; 127, 149.
—— State of, in eleventh and twelfth centuries, 154-156, 162.
ISLE OF DOGS, 25.
ISLE OF MAN, 58.
ISLINGTON, 24.
ITALY, Monastic movement in, 70; Envoys from, at Besançon, 209; growth of modern, 216; second invasion of by Barbarossa, 225, 233-237; Countess Matilda's possessions in, 226; state of in twelfth century, 230-231.

JAFFÉ, his regesta, 179; and the grant of Ireland, 180.
JERUSALEM, embassy from to Adrian IV., 200.
JOHN, Bishop of Stavanger, 58.
—— PITS. See Pits.
—— Prince of Sweden, 62, 63.
—— of Salisbury on Breakspear's family, 8; 133, 134; his life and character, 137-139; conversation with Adrian, 140-148; mission to Adrian about Ireland, 149, 157; on the position of the Pope, 150-152; and the Irish grant, 161, 166-170, 180, 189, 249; his record of Adrian's death, 247, 248.
JOHN XXII., 169, 176; letter to Edward II, 178; and the grant of Ireland, 178, 180.

KEY OF ETRURIA. See Sutri.
KING Edmund, 253 n.

KING, Robert, his history of the Irish Church, 177.
KINGS Langley, 11, 25.
KNIGHTS Hospitallers of Jerusalem, 200.
—— of S. John of Jerusalem, 201.
KNUT the Great, King of Danemark and England, 50.
—— V., King of Danemark, 51.
KYFFHAUSEN, 114.

LADISLAUS, King of Bohemia, 233.
LANGLEY, 2, 17.
LANGUAGE, English, 24.
LANIGAN, Dr., criticism of the Irish grant, 174, 180.
LAMBETH, 25.
LATERAN, council of, 1139, 38.
——, the, 97.
LEA, river, 24.
LEABHAN BREAC, the, 176, 177.
LEGNANO, 238.
LEINSTER, 162.
LEOPOLD IV., Margrave of Austria, 229.
LIEGE, Council of, 75.
LINGARD, and the grant of Ireland, 180.
LINGKOPIN, synod of, 61.
LISMORE, 172.
LODI, 230, 231; helps Barbarossa in 1159, 233; 236.
LOIRET, department of, 26.
LOMBARD cities, 82.
LOMBARDY, 86, 101, 164, 215, 222, 230, 232; condition of in 1159, 237; supported by Adrian IV. against Barbarossa, 237-238, 244.
LONDON, 19; declared capital of England, 25; in twelfth century, 24.
LORD'S Prayer, 254.

LORRAINE, Countess Matilda's possessions in, 226.
LORITELLI, 189.
LOTHAIR II., Emperor of Germany, 184, 205; his portrait at Rome, 218; and the Countess Matilda's possessions, 228; 229.
—— the Saxon. *See* Lothair II.
LOUIS VI. (Le Gros), King of France, 26, 30; relations with Henry I., 33.
—— VII. (le Jeune), 33; and second Crusade, 46; at Sens, 79; 115, 181.
LUCCA, 232.
LUCIUS II., 87; riots in Rome—his death, 88.
—— III., 95, 259.
LUND, see of, 51, 52.
LUXEUIL, or Luxens. *See* Bishop of.
LYNCH, Dr., criticism of Giraldus Cambrensis, 171, 172; on Adrian's grant of Ireland, 176.

MAJORCA, 231.
MALCOLM, King of Scotland, 22.
MANUEL I., Greek Emperor, and the Sicilian War, 187; embassy of, to congratulate Adrian IV., offers of alliance, 190; 192, 193.
MANSI, 157.
MARGARET of Anjou, 16.
—— wife of King Malcolm, 22.
MASSA, 242.
MATILDA, Countess, her parentage, first marriage, disputes with the Popes, 226, 227; her second marriage, submits to Henry V., her death, 227, 228; her legacy to the Church, papal claims to her property, Guelf claims to her property, 228; her possessions granted to Guelph VIII., 230; possessions of, 242.
MATILDA, Empress, marriage of, 33; flight from England, 56; invasion of Ireland, 161.
—— mother of Beatrice of Lorraine, 226.
—— Princess, daughter of Henry I., *n.* 228.
—— wife of Henry I., 22.
MATTHEW Paris, on the origin of Pope Adrian, 2; on Breakspear's rejection at S. Albans, 6, 7; 179.
—— of Westminster, 169.
MAUD, Empress, 128.
MAZARIN, Suger compared to, 27.
MELUN, 26.
MESSINA, Straits of, 192.
METALOGICUS, 140, 170.
MIGNE, 157.
MILAN, 216; republic of, 230; conflicts with Lodi, Como and Pavia, 231; 232; besieged and taken by Barbarossa, 1158, 233; Barbarossa's terms with, 1158, 234; revolt against Barbarossa of, 236; 237, 239.
MILANESE, the, sack Lodi, resist Barbarossa, 1158, 233; revolt against Barbarossa, 236; hostages executed by Barbarossa, 237.
MILFORD, 165.
MILMAN on position of the Popes, 29, 30; on Eugenius, III., 43; on monasticism, 72-74; on the relations between Empire and Papacy, 206, 207.
MODENA, 231.
MONASTERIES, arrangements of, 39; revival of, 70.
MONASTIC orders, jealousy of in twelfth century, 1.

MONASTIC system, 69.
MONASTICISM, sudden rise of in twelfth century, 72.
MONKS, their learning, 29.
MONTE Cassino, 187.
MONZA, 236.
MOORFIELDS, 25.
MOOR Hall, 14.
MORAN, Dr., criticism of the Irish grant, 172-175, 179.
MOUTIER la Celles, 138.
MUNSTER, 162.
MUNTER, 49.
MURATORI, lives of Adrian, 5.

NANTES, 75.
NAPLES, 183, 184, 199, 230.
NARNI, 202.
NEPI, 108, 116, 119.
NICHOLAS BREAKSPEAR. *See* Breakspear.
—— Daccomb, 15.
—— King of Danemark, 62.
—— II., 183.
NIDAROS. *See* Nidrosia.
NIDROSIA, Metropolitan See of Norway, 58.
NORMAN Chronicle, 160, 169.
NORMANDY, 25; duchy of, 128.
NORMAN Kings of Sicily, 186.
NORMANS, the, their conquest of Sicily, 182.
NORTH Italy, formation of Republics, 82; spirit of opposition to Frederic, 215.
NORWAY, 50.

O'ANNOC, 176.
O'CALLAGHAN and the grant of Ireland, 180.

O'CONNOR, Kings of Ireland, 162.
OCTAVIAN, Anti-pope, 95, 247, 248.
O'CHELCHIN, 176.
OFFICERS of monasteries, 39.
O'GLESAIN, 177.
OLAF II., King of Norway, 52.
O'NEAL, Kings of Ireland, 162.
ORKNEYS, 58.
ORLEANS, 26.
ORVIETO, 101, 202, 256.
O'SLUASTI, 177.
OTHO of Wittelsbach attacks Roland, 213, n. 213, 217, 221, 223, 230.
OTRICOLI, 101.
OTTO. *See* Otho.

PADUA, 231, 232.
PALATINE OF THE RHINE, 233.
PALERMO, 193, 196, 199.
PALESTRINA, 87.
PAPAL authority undermined, 30.
—— power as affected by second crusade, 89.
—— troops, disposal of in 1155, 105.
PARACLETE, the, 76, 83.
PARIS, 26, 35, 36, 75.
PARVUS. *See* John of Salisbury.
PASCHAL II., 49.
PATRICIAN of Rome, 88.
PAVIA, Barbarossa crowned at, 101; 230, 231.
PETER. *See* Abbot Peter.
—— Abelard. *See* Abelard.
—— de Blois, 134.
—— de Bruis, 82-83.
—— of Clugny, 81.
—— the Hermit, S. Bernard compared to, 46.
—— Pontiniacus, 255.

PETER's pence in England, 32; in Norway, 59; in Sweden, 61.
PIEDMONT, 104.
PISA, 231.
PISTOJA, 232.
PIT, John, 94; his version of Boso's death, 95.
PIUS VII., 17.
POITOU, 26, 33.
POLYCRATICUS, 139-152.
PONTECORBO, castle of, 187.
PONTE Lugano, 124.
POPE, claims of, 29; relations of, to England, 30; spiritual head of Latin Church; temporal authority of, limitations of temporal power, 30; dignity of the, 112; temporal power of the, 156; in Rome, denied by Barbarossa, 243.
PORTA del Popolo, 107 n.
PORTUGAL, Cardinal Boso sent on a mission to, 95.
PRINCE John, son of Henry II., 167.
PROVENCE, 3, 34, 36.

QUINTUS Severus, 147.

RALPH de Diceto, his copy of the Irish bull, 168; inaccuracy of, 172.
RAMSAY Abbey, 56.
REINOLD, Chancellor of the Empire, 210.
REGULAR canons, description of, 38, 39.
RELIGIOUS adventure, 69.
REPUBLICS of North Italy, formation of, 82, 231, 232.
RHEIMS, council of, 29, 75, 138.
RHINE, river, 115.
RHONE, river, 36.

RICHARD, Abbot. *See* Abbot.
—— Count of Aquila, 189.
—— Count of Fondi, 195.
—— Earl of Striguil (Strongbow), his campaign in Ireland, 163, 164; his marriage, his treatment by Henry II., 164-166; his death, 167.
RICHELIEU, Suger compared to, 27.
RINALDO, Duke of Burgundy, 232.
ROBERT, Abbot. *See* Abbot.
—— Breakspear, funeral of, 7.
—— Brekespere. *See* Robert Breakspear.
—— de Camera, 3.
—— Count de Loritelli, 188.
—— of Gorham. *See* Abbot Robert.
—— Guiscard, Duke of Apulia, 183.
—— de Monte, 160, 172.
—— of Normandy, 33.
—— Prince of Capua, 189.
RODERICK O'Connor, King of Ireland, 162, 167.
ROGER I., Count of Sicily, 182, 183.
—— II., King of Sicily, 125, 183; war with Honorius II., 183; captures Innocent II.; his death, 184; 205.
—— de Wendover, his copy of the Irish bull, 168, 172.
ROHRBACHER, extract from "Histoire Universelle de l'Eglise Catholique," 157.
ROLAND, reads Adrian's letter to Frederic, 210; his behaviour at Besançon, 213, 214; returns to Rome from Besançon, 216; 219, 259.
—— Alexander III., 247-8.
—— Bandinelli. *See* Roland.
—— Chancellor at Besançon, 209.
ROMAN Catholic Church, intolerance of, 107; opportunity lost of leading thought, 81.

ROMAN republic, deputation to Barbarossa, 108.
ROME, republic of, 48, 64; at Breakspear's accession, 68; effects of teaching of Arnold, 86, 87; rioting in, 122; 226, 227, 230; citizens of, disaffection in 1159, 243, 255.
RONCAGLIA, 91.
—— Diet of, 235.

S. ALBANS, 1, 6, 7, 8, 24, 54; and Cardinal Boso, 94.
—— Abbey, 129; privileges granted to by Adrian IV., 133.
S. ALBAN, 252 n.
S. ANGELO, castle of, 95, 105, 122.
S. AUGUSTINE, rule of, 38, 39; 252.
S. BENEDICT, 253.
S. BERNARD and Eugenius III., 41-43; birth, life, and character, 71-72; his character, 74; the hope of the Church, 74, 76; and Abelard, 77; at the Council of Sens, 79, 80; report of Abelard's trial, 81; 85, 88; his opinion of the Romans, 89; his death, 90; compared to Adrian IV., 94; and Innocent II., 184.
S. CASCIANO, monastery of, 202.
S. CUTHBERT, 252 n.
S. DIONYSIUS' day, 130.
S. EDWARD the Confessor, 253 n.
SS. GIOVANNI e Paolo, Church of, 255.
S. GREGORIO, Church of, 255.
S. HENRY of Upsala, 61.
S. HUGH of Lincoln, 253 n.
S. JOHN'S Clerkenwell, Priory of, 15.
S. JOHN, Hospital of, 15.
—— of Jerusalem, Knights of, 201.
S. MARCIAN, Church of at Beneventum, 199.

S. MARY the Virgin, Harefield Parish Church, advowson of, 14.
S. MICHAEL of Pavia, church of, 101.
S. OLAF, 52, 58.
S. OMER, town of, 27.
S. PATRICK, 253 n.
S. PETER, cathedral of, 121, 246.
S. QUIRICO, Barbarossa encamped at, 103.
S. ROMUALDO, 259.
S. RUFUS, Abbey of, 3, 12, 37.
S. SYLVESTER, 145.
S. THOMAS of Canterbury, 177.
S. WULSTAN, 155 n.
SALERNO, 190, 199.
SALZBURG, 114.
SARACENS, the, and South Italy, 182.
SARDINIA granted to Guelph VIII., 230; 231, 242.
SAXON Chronicle, 23.
SAXONY, 228.
SCANDINAVIAN kingdoms, 50; mission to Rome, 53; mythology, 52, 53.
SCOTTICHRONICON, 176 n.
SECOND Crusade, 42, 43, 45-47, 115; effect on the papal power, 89.
SEINE, department of, 26.
—— et Marne, department of, 26.
—— et Oise, 26.
SENATE of Rome, 90.
SENS, 26, 80; council of, 79.
SHETLANDS, 58.
SIC et non, 76.
SICILY, chap. x., 182-192, 199; kingdom of, 230; 248.
SIENA, 45, 232.
SIGURD, Prince of Norway, 57, 58.
SISMONDI, his account of the execution of Arnold of Brescia, 107.

SKARA, 61.
SNORROW, the historian, 59.
SODOR and Man, See of, 58.
SOUTH Italy, 184.
SPAIN, frontier of, 26; 181; envoys from, at Besançon, 209; 248.
SPIRITUAL authority. *See* Pope.
SPOLETO, 125; granted to Guelph VIII., 230; duchy of, 242.
STAVANGER, 58.
STEPHEN, King of England, anarchy of his reign, 23; 48, 56.
STRONGBOW. *See* Richard.
SUGER, Abbot of S. Denys, his life, his character, 27; his life of Louis VI., 28; regent of France, 48; 115.
SUTRI, 108, 111; Frederic's camp at, 116, 119.
SUTRIUM. *See* Sutri.
SWABIA, 110, 233.
SWEDEN, 50.
SWENO III., King of Danemark, 50; quarrel with Swercus, 62; invades Sweden, 63; defeated, his murder, 64.
SWERCUS, King of Sweden, 60, 62, 65.
SWEYN. *See* Sweno.
SWITZERLAND, 86.
SYLVESTER, 240.

TEMPORAL authority. *See* Pope.
—— power, Barbarossa on, 240.
TERRA di Lavoro, 189.
TEUTONIC races and the Popes, 31.
THEURY, 27.
THOMAS à Beket, 163, 168.
—— of Walsingham, his account of the English deputation to the Pope, 129-134, 149.

THURINGIA, 114.
TIBER, river, 106, 121.
TIERNAN O'Rourke, King of Breifny, 162.
TIVOLI, 87, 124.
TORFÆUS, 49.
TORTONA surrenders to Barbarossa, 101.
TOURRAINE, 26.
TRENT, 233.
TROYES, 138.
TRUND, 65.
TUAMOND, 162.
TUSCANY, 103, 104, 215; Countess Matilda's possessions in, 226; granted to Guelph VIII., 230; state of in twelfth century, 231.
TUSCULUM, 87, 174.
TYDD, 55.

UGHELL, quoted by Ciaconius, 94.
ULSTER, 162.
UNTASBURG, 114.
UPSALA, 61.
USSHER on Alexander's bull, 174; and the grant of Ireland, 180.

VALENTIA, 12.
VATICAN Library, 179.
VENETIA, envoys from, at Besançon, 209.
VENICE, 216, 230.
VERCELLI, 235.
VERDUN, 207.
VERONA, 230, 231.
VEZELAI, council of, 46.
VIA Sacra, 96.
VICTOR III., 227.
VITERBO, 45, 47, 88; meeting of Adrian IV. and Envoys from Rome, 100; 101, 105, 202.

WALDEMAR I., King of Danemark, 52.
WALES, 115.
WATERFORD, 164, 166.
WATTERICH, 5.
WESTERN Church, the, 51.
—— islands of Scotland, 58.
WESTMINSTER Abbey, 25.
WILKINS, Concilia, 178.
WILLIAM, Abbot. *See* Abbot.
—— Duke of Apulia, 183.
—— I., King of England, 25, 31; refuses to swear fealty to the Pope, 32; and Ireland, 155; 161.
—— King of Sicily, 125; compared with Roger II., 184, 185; proposals of peace to Adrian IV., 190; relieves Brundisium, 192; besieges Brundisium, 193; his capture and treatment of Brundisium, 193, 194; his campaign against Adrian IV. in 1156, 193-196; negotiation with Adrian IV., 1156, 197; crowned by Adrian IV., 199; 218, 222, 232, 243.

WILLIAM of Newburgh, 4; trustworthiness of his writings, 9; his life of Breakspear, 10; on the state of England in twelfth century, 23; account of Breakspear and Eugenius III., 44-45.
—— Plantagenet, 128.
—— de Swanland, 16.
—— son of Henry I., 20.
—— son of Robert of Normandy, 33.
WINCHESTER, 24, 161, 167.
WINDSOR, 161.
WITTELSBACH. *See* Otho.
WRAJO, favourite of William of Sicily, 185, 186.
WORMS, Diet of, 228; treaty of broken by Barbarossa, 235.
WORMWOOD, 74.

YORK, province of, 58.

ZAHRINGEN, 233.
ZURICH, 86.

www.ingramcontent.com/pod-product-compliance
Lightning Source LLC
Chambersburg PA
CBHW021202230426
43667CB00006B/520